100 BOOKS EVERY BLUES FAN SHOULD OWN

BEST MUSIC BOOKS

Lists abound for the best 100 songs or best 50 albums. But with so much fine writing and scholarship on music, how do we know which are the best books on jazz or rock 'n' roll or classical music? Contributions to **Best Music Books** provide definitive lists of those book-length works that every fan of any major musical genre should consider owning. Written by established experts in the field, each title offers summaries and evaluations of key works and their contribution to our understanding of today's many musical traditions.

100 Books Every Blues Fan Should Own by Edward Komara and Greg Johnson, 2014

100 Books Every Folk Music Fan Should Own by Dick Weissman, 2014

100 BOOKS EVERY BLUES FAN SHOULD OWN

EDWARD KOMARA
AND
GREG JOHNSON

ROWMAN & LITTLEFIELD
Lanham • Boulder • New York • Toronto • Plymouth, UK

Published by Rowman & Littlefield
4501 Forbes Boulevard, Suite 200, Lanham, Maryland 20706
www.rowman.com

10 Thornbury Road, Plymouth PL6 7PP, United Kingdom

British Library Cataloguing in Publication Information Available

Library of Congress Cataloging-in-Publication Data
Komara, Edward M., 1966–
    100 books every blues fan should own / Edward Komara and Greg Johnson.
        pages ; cm. — (Best music books)
    Includes index.
    ISBN 978-0-8108-8921-7 (cloth : alk. paper) — ISBN 978-0-8108-8922-4
(electronic) 1. Blues (Music)—Bibliography. I. Johnson, Greg, 1977– II. Title.
III. Title: One hundred books every blues fan should own.
    ML128.B49K65 2014
    016.781643—dc23

                                                            2013030912

Printed in the United States of America

CONTENTS

FINDING THE BLUES 100

ACKNOWLEDGMENTS

EDWARD KOMARA WISHES TO THANK BENNETT GRAFF, editor at Rowman & Littlefield, for inviting him and Greg Johnson to write this book. His confidence in our writing without editorial assistance, and his advice when we needed it, made for ideal working conditions. He also thanks Jay Sieleman of the Blues Foundation, Memphis, for referring Bennett to us in 2011 when this project was a mere idea. Komara's share of the manuscript preparation was aided greatly by the granting of a sabbatical for spring 2013 by the State University of New York at Potsdam College Libraries. He wishes to thank Libraries Director Jenica P. Rogers and the libraries' Personnel Responsibilities Committee for facilitating and approving his application for sabbatical. He found that most of the Blues 100 books spoke for themselves, but occasionally he discussed a few books with their authors. He thanks Lawrence Cohn, Guido van Rijn, Alex van der Tuuk, Dave Rubin, Daniel Beaumont, and Gayle Wardlow for their comments and, in some instances, copies of revised editions of their classic books, which had appeared during the writing of the manuscript. Also, he thanks Justyna

Zajac of Oxford University Press and Laurie Matheson of the University of Illinois Press for copies of other books selected for the Blues 100. Finally, he thanks Glen Bogardus and Shelly Schmiddy of the SUNY Potsdam College Libraries Interlibrary Loan division for their assistance in arranging use of books from other libraries for this project.

Greg Johnson thanks the faculty and staff in Archives and Special Collections in the University of Mississippi's J. D. Williams Library for allowing him some extra time in preparing this book. He is extremely thankful for all previous blues archivists and staff for creating such a comprehensive collection of blues materials; all of the Blues 100 books and many more were always a few feet away. Finally, he wishes to thank Shaundi Wall and his family for encouraging him through this project.

INTRODUCTION
Nothing but the Books

THE PREMISE FOR THIS BOOK IS SIMPLE ENOUGH: WHICH books should every blues fan own? As former and present blues archivists at the University of Mississippi (Komara, 1993–2001; Johnson, 2002–present), we are asked that question every day. When our Scarecrow Press editor, Bennett Graff, posed it to us two years ago, we were ready to write an answer.

Why We Accepted This Assignment

Why did we agree to do this project? For one obvious reason, we needed an excuse to read blues books. Contrary to what many blues fans may think, we are not given much time during the work-day to read books and listen to CDs. Instead, we have to attend administrative meetings, conduct research appointments, write letters and e-mails, and field telephone calls. During a typical day, we have time to read only as much of a book as necessary to answer a question. Rarely can we read a book from cover to cover. So we couldn't pass up this opportunity to read whole those books that we often use piecemeal. Once the contracts were signed, we arranged relief time from our supervisors to spend on this project, including a sabbatical that Komara obtained from his institution.

For another reason, as research librarians in the field of blues, we welcomed this project to explore various editions of some titles and to exercise our book citation skills. Third, frankly speaking, as librarians working in the "publish or perish" environment of academia, we needed the publication opportunity. Coincidentally, many of the books we selected had been written by college and university professors under similar pressures to publish.

A final reason was that our project was very compelling. Which one hundred books should every blues fan own or at least seek to own? We thought of it as the desert island scenario—which five records would you have if you were living in isolation?—but with many more books allowed than records.

Our Tasks and Criteria for Selection

We began our work by compiling a list of candidates for our "Blues 100." We took suggestions from the following:

1. Paul Garon's "Historiography" entry in the *Encyclopedia of the Blues* (New York: Routledge, 2006)
2. The Blues Foundation Hall of Fame awardees for Classics in Blues Literature
3. The Blues Foundation Hall of Fame unawarded nominees
4. The book collection at the Blues Archive, University of Mississippi
5. Robert Ford, *A Blues Bibliography*, 2nd edition (New York: Routledge, 2006)

We knew that book publishing about the blues has not been as extensive as magazine publishing. Komara remembers that in 1993, the Blues Archive had five or six shelves (or about eighteen linear feet) of books, compared with about seventy-five to eighty shelves of periodicals and newsletters. The book collection doubled in size over the next ten years, but then again, many of the new publications were reprints in response to reader demand during the 1990s blues boom. We had thought about including fiction and plays, but we decided to stick to nonfiction. Eventually, we compiled a list of some three hundred titles to consider.

Our criteria for inclusion in the Blues 100 were:

Substance. Does the author bring new information or a fresh perspective to his or her subject?

Style. Is the content written well? Poetic flair is a plus. Among the academic books, we settled for a readable style.

Discipline. Does the book serve as a fine example of a research approach to the blues, whether it is a work of history, anthropology, journalism, instruction, or transcription (lyrical or musical)?

Influence. Has the work been cited by other books, or does it serve as a building block for later books?

Coverage. Is it a book of quality about a particular historical era or about a geographic area?

Availability. Is it in print or easily available through used book services?

Reasons for noninclusion, on the other hand, comprised:

Research and/or findings were not original to the author.

The writing was unreadable.

The work set a bad example for a discipline (especially true respecting some histories and biographies).

The book has largely been ignored by other writers for understandable reasons.

The work is unfocused with respect to the era or area (a problem from which several folklore titles suffered).

The book is unavailable, out of print, or altogether too scarce.

Some boundaries to the scope of this project were inherent to the topic. For example, there are few books in the Blues 100 published before 1959. Until that year, blues was almost completely within an oral culture. What little that appeared in print through 1958 lived in jazz collector magazines about the "classic" women blues singers on records before 1932. Samuel Charters's *The Country Blues* (1959; no. 63) and Paul Oliver's *Blues Fell This Morning* (1960; no. 64) changed all that. In tandem with the nascent folk music revival, those two titles introduced the topic of blues to white literate culture. That these two authors are still alive at the time of this writing (2013) indicates how young blues literature still is.

Also, all of the books presented here are in English. That does not mean that there is no international research on the blues. But for the most part, foreign-language publications have been periodicals: *Jefferson* in Sweden, *Soul Bag* in France, and *Block* in the

Netherlands are some of the oldest titles. Moreover, since African American blues are in English, international writers have had to learn English to understand them. So when they have written books about the blues, they've tended to write them in English. Guido van Rijn (nos. 42 and 69), Alex van der Tuuk (no. 20), and Gerhard Kubik (no. 7) are recent authors from outside the United States and the United Kingdom who have written in English.

Other scope limits were placed by us. For the most part, the books treat African American blues and its surrounding cultures. That means we made the conscious choice to set aside works on white British and American blues, including blues-rock, and other musicians around the rest of the world who play blues. We had considered including songbooks, instrumental methods, and notated music transcription books, but we decided midway through the project to exclude them from the Blues 100. We also decided to leave out reference works such as *The Penguin Guide to the Blues* and Routledge's *Encyclopedia of the Blues*. Among discographies, only *Blues and Gospel Records 1890–1943* by Robert M. W. Dixon, John Godrich, and Howard Rye (no. 41) falls within the Blues 100. We had considered including some African American fiction and plays, especially Ralph Ellison's novel *Invisible Man* and August Wilson's drama *Seven Guitars*, but at the last minute we decided to not include these works.

Even though we decided not to include all of these books in the Blues 100, nonetheless they have served as books that informed the writing of the Blues 100. Blues fans should be aware that some libraries do have them available for their reference use. To acknowledge and promote these useful and important works, we include a special chapter, "The Books behind the Blues 100."

One admission: we have included some books for which we, as blues archivists, had assisted the authors in researching and a few that we had written ourselves. Familiarity and a little bias were factors in some of our choices. Then again, other works by us or in which we had some role also were subject to the same strictures that eliminated works from inclusion. For those books selected in which one of us had some involvement, the other partner wrote the entries.

After applying these criteria, we had a list of seventy-five books. In order to have a hundred, we relented and relaxed on the criteria of style and availability. That means that some of the books included could prove difficult reading for blues fans. Some of the most important books in the Blues 100 were written by academics for other academics. As such, these works adopt academic, sometimes arcane, terminology (or jargon, depending on how one responds to these things). Our entries here serve as helpful primers to these books.

In their editions of the magisterial discography *Blues and Gospel Records 1890–1943* (no. 41), Dixon, Godrich, and Rye had posed the question: "What is a 'blues' or a 'gospel' record?" Their answer was "the whole listing [the discography] itself is a definition of what we mean by 'blues and gospel'—African American secular and sacred musical styles, exclusive of jazz." Likewise, we pose the question "What is a 'blues' book?" Because our list of one hundred books is selective, we do not claim that it is a definition of what is meant as "blues." Furthermore, since the authors of several of the chosen books incorporate African American secular and sacred musical styles *and* jazz within their definitions of "blues," we recognize that a bibliographic sense of blues may exceed a discographic one. However, blues and jazz both make use of the twelve-measure blues form. A book about the blues, therefore, should present, examine, teach, or anticipate the "what," "how," "where," and "why" that the standard blues form is sung and listened to.

Entry Features

Each entry contains four elements. The first is a short "headline" that states briefly the purpose and appeal of the book. The second is a bibliographic citation for each book. It includes prices for those titles still in print, with the understanding that such pricing is provisional. (To that end, Amazon.com, the bibliographic utility WorldCat, and Robert Ford's *Blues Bibliography* have been invaluable sources of citation data.) Here we add a note about author names: we give the name currently used on an author's current book printing so that readers can quickly identify listings for books in bookstores, websites, and library catalogs. Therefore, Amiri Baraka for Leroi Jones (for *Blues People*, no. 68) and Julio Finn for Jerome Arnold (for *The Bluesman*, no. 94) are used, but Jon Michael Spencer is retained (for *Blues and Evil*, no. 98), even though he goes today by Yahya Jongintaba. The third is the body of the entry, in which we summarize the contents, compare the findings to the opinions of other authors, and give some collector's points if a book has been published in multiple editions. Finally, at the suggestion of our editor, we recommend a blues recording illustrating or pertaining to the book; these songs should be available on CD, licensed downloads, or streaming media via Amazon, Rhapsody, Pandora, or Emusic, among other digital music vendors.

The Order of the Book Entries

Upon making the choices, we read the books. We began first with Lawrence Cohn's *Nothing but the Blues* (no. 1) and Paul Oliver's *The Story of the Blues* (no. 2). From them as beginning bases, each of us picked, read, and drafted entries on the books where our reading and interests took us. Later, when the first draft was 80 percent complete, we made some changes to the Blues 100 list to improve the balance of coverage among the books. When the first drafts of the entries were completed, we then determined the order of their presentation in this book.

We could have run the entries in the order in which the books had been published, or in alphabetical order by author's last name, or by title. But we decided to proceed in the order of historical coverage, starting first with the overviews, then with the books about the 1890s and 1900s, then those about the 1910s, and so forth. This order reveals a number of things. One is that a kind of literate history of the blues begins to emerge, with much concentration on the pre-1942 (prewar) era. The 1930s and the 1940s were so well represented that, at the 80 percent completion mark, for the sake of balance, we sought for inclusion additional books about the blues after 1950. We hope that this resulting book may be read from beginning to end as a history of the blues as depicted through the best books about the blues.

A second element noticeable in our ordering is the emergence of African American commentary amid that of white critics. For many years up to the beginning of the 1980s, the disciplines of folklore and anthropology had prevailed as those academic fields where the blues was researched and studied. Moreover, nearly all folklorists and anthropologists who have written on the blues have been white. Some of them have cited as their forebears Charles Peabody, Howard Odum, John Lomax, and Alan Lomax. Folkloric and anthropological findings have underscored the abiding and present characteristics of the blues, its musicians, and its audience culture. What had changed or fallen into disuse was of lesser concern—yet they were of most interest to blues historians, just about all of whom are also white.

However, many historians of the blues since the 1960s were and still are independent researchers and record collectors with few ties to colleges and universities. As a result, the folklorists and anthropologists on the one hand and the historians and collectors on the other, at the very least, view each other with skepticism and distrust. Only fireworks can produce more sparks than a war of words between these two camps.

Yet African American scholarship in the blues has emerged nearly unnoticed among these white writers, except for scholar/ bookseller Paul Garon in his "Historiography" entry for the Routledge *Encyclopedia of the Blues*. Starting with Amiri Baraka and his seminal text *Blues People* (1963; no. 68), the African Americans publishing research and commentary on the blues have been few, but their collective message of the proper appreciation of blues on their scholarly terms stands in marked contrast to the folklore and history factions: if assimilation is to take place, it is going to have to be white adapting to black, not the other way around as has happened for the past four centuries. If folklorists think of Robert Johnson's crossroads as a sense of place and historians regard it as an intersection, then African Americans (especially Houston Baker, no. 93, Julio Finn, no. 94, and Jon Michael Spencer, no. 98) see it as a place beyond conventional values to turn and return to often for a reaffirmation of their values of pride, power, and magic, which are often in danger of becoming obscured by Western-style civilization.

Third and final, the entry order points to gaps in book coverage of blues history. Much more about the blues can and should be written. What cries out most for coverage is the blues since 1980, especially Southern soul blues. Also, most white musicians in the blues have imitated African American bluesmen too well to become masters themselves, but the few who have found their own artistic ways deserve critical recognition through writing.

Some Final Remarks

Because of the limited number of books—one hundred—readers can regard and use *100 Books Every Blues Fan Should Own* as a prescribed canon of blues research, including blues history.

Rather than avoid the appearance of canonicity—something viewed with disfavor by liberals and conservatives alike, if for different reasons—this 100 Books volume embraces such a role. The editors' responsibility in assigning canonicity to blues books is not so much to set standards—although many of the titles will be appraised for the examples they set—but rather to point out contrasting perspectives on the blues, setting up a virtual conversation among the books.

There were some days while writing the entries when our intent was to make *100 Books That Every Blues Fan Should Own* the 101st that every blues fan should own. But sincerely, we wanted to call attention to significant books about the blues. Many of the authors are still alive and may come to regard such attention as formal recognition of their efforts. Some living authors whose works are not included may well complain. All we can say is that we will be glad to introduce them to those who might feel miffed at having been included in the Blues 100.

We suspect there may be a few.

THE BLUES 100

1. The Grand Debate of the Blues

Nothing but the Blues: The Music and the Musicians. Edited
by Lawrence Cohn. New York: Abbeville Press, 1993. 432
pp. ISBN 1-55859-271-7 (hardcover), ISBN 0-789-20607-2
(paperback)

Lawrence Cohn's *Nothing but the Blues* may be the most visually
attractive book in the Blues 100. It is printed indelibly on heavy
paper stock, bound in signatures (this is as true for the paperbound
version as for the hardbound), and bursting with photographs and
record label reproductions supplied by leading collectors and historians. This is not be mistaken with the anthology of the same title
that was edited by Mike Leadbitter and published in 1971 (see "The
Books Behind the Blues 100" chapter). The Cohn version is bigger,
splashier, and—figuratively as well as literally—weightier. It is an
excellent first book for the fan new to the blues to buy.

The main content is given in the eleven essays by ten expert
writers. Samuel Charters writes on the African antecedents and early
American roots of the blues. David Evans treats rural pre–World
War II blues. Richard "Dick" Spottswood surveys women in the
blues, focusing on the pre-1942 singers in the cities and in the counties. Mark Humphrey contributes two pieces, one on the relation
of blues to black sacred music, the other on blues in the cities from

the 1900s to 1970. Bruce Bastin presents Piedmont blues in the Carolinas. The late country music historian Charles Wolfe provides a detailed history of cross-relations between blues and early country music. John Cowley looks at the field recording trips undertaken by commercial labels and folklorists through 1960. Barry Pearson gives a short history of rhythm and blues through the mid-1950s. Jim O'Neal assesses the blues revival of the 1960s, and for the concluding essay, Mary Katherine Aldin sketches the blues history up to the early 1990s. An extra contributor is Frank Driggs, who provides many of the historical photographs of blues musicians and African American culture to illustrate the essays. Thanks to Driggs, *Nothing but the Blues* is the blues counterpart of his great compendium of jazz images, *Black Beauty, White Heat* (New York: William Morrow, 1982; reprint, New York: Da Capo, 1996).

The individual pieces serve as good introductions to other writings by the authors. The Blues 100 contains selected books by Charters (nos. 29, 63, and 82), Evans (no. 14), Bastin (nos. 27 and 28), Pearson (no. 92), and O'Neal (no. 91). The other writers deserve additional comments here. Spottswood compiled and published the authoritative discography *Ethnic Music on Record* (Urbana: University of Illinois Press, 1990; 7 volumes), and he continues to host a radio show of pre–World War II music. Charles Wolfe's books on classic country music are too important even for a blues lover to ignore, such as his history of the Grand Ole Opry, *A Good-Natured Riot* (Nashville: University of Tennessee Press/ Country Music Foundation, 1999). In addition to blues, John Cowley has undertaken research in Caribbean music, including calypso. Through December 2011, Aldin hosted the radio show "Alive and Picking," and since then she has maintained her music research on her website, http://aliveandpicking.com, which among other offerings provides access to her selective index of blues magazines. Mark Humphrey has been a freelance writer since 1979, and for many enterprises he has often been a most thoughtful contributor; a book collecting his best pieces would be welcome.

To be sure, the essays may not combine to form a complete history of the blues. In his preface, Cohn demurs from claiming completeness, stating he is presenting an expert overview of the major aspects of the blues. When several aspects are presented individually and fully in an anthology, discrepancies are bound to occur, and indeed they do in *Nothing but the Blues*. For example, Charters supposes that the blues came from rural Mississippi.

Evans thinks instead that it came from the rural southeastern United States. In his essay "Bright Lights, Big City: Urban Blues," Humphrey asks that early blues in the cities be given every due consideration, since they appeared at the same time as the kinds of rural blues that Charters and Evans discuss. It would be too easy to criticize Cohn for not editing these and other differences toward achieving a consistent historical narrative like Paul Oliver's *Story of the Blues* (no. 2). On the other hand, though, these same differences may be viewed positively as questions for debate. Over the past twenty years, these questions have still not been answered, and so *Nothing but the Blues* remains as fresh now for comparison and discussion as it was upon its publication.

The hardcover and the paperback editions are the same in size and content. As of this writing, the paperback edition is still available through Abbeville Books and Amazon. Hardcovers may be obtainable from online used-book dealers at prices equal to or slightly higher than new paperback copies. However, many libraries purchased the book in the early 1990s, and so some hardcovers on the used-book market may be worn discards, often lacking the dust jacket. —*EK*

2. A History of the Blues from the Mouths of Many

The Story of the Blues. By Paul Oliver. London: Penguin, 1969. London: Barrie and Rockliff/Cresset Press, 1969. Philadelphia: Chilton Book Company, 1969. Reprint, London: Book Club Associates, 1972; London: Barrie and Jenkins, 1972, 1978; Hammondsworth: Penguin, 1972, 1978; Radnor, PA: Chilton Book Company, 1975. Spanish translation, Madrid: Nostromo Editories, 1976. Japanese translation, Tokyo: Shobunsha, 1978. German translation by Walter Hartmann published as *Die Story des Blues.* Reinbek bei Hamburg: Rowohlt, 1978. Second edition, London: Northeastern University Press, 1997. ISBN 1-55553-355-8 (hardcover), $50.00, ISBN 1-55553-354-X (paperback), $22.95

First published in 1969, *The Story of the Blues* was the first in-depth history of blues from its origins to the first decades after World War II. Indeed, all subsequent blues histories owe a huge debt of gratitude to Paul Oliver's seminal work. While works such as Lawrence

Cohn's edited *Nothing but the Blues* (no. 1) might be easier reads for an introduction to the blues, *The Story of the Blues* still remains the most important solo-authored history of the blues. Anyone interested in a general history of the blues through the first half of the twentieth century should read this book.

As Oliver notes in the introduction, blues has had a profound impact on the development of modern popular music, particularly on rock and roll. As such, people often talk about blues as an influence on other types of music. Oliver determines to examine blues for its own sake and finds it "necessary to place blues in its cultural context" (vii). Oliver seems driven by the need to get to the old-timers before their memories have faded: "Today it's no longer possible to hear the history of the blues from the mouths of many of those who shaped it" (2). [A 1960 expedition across the southern United States with his wife and Arhoolie Records founder Chris Strachwitz formed the basis for many of the interviews for this book but receives fuller treatment in *Conversation with the Blues* (1965).]

The Story of the Blues comes out of an exhibition Oliver curated for the United States Information Service at the American Embassy in London in 1964. The more than five hundred photographs used in the exhibition form the basis for the book. The book draws on government data, the emerging body of blues scholarship of others, interviews with blues musicians, and Oliver's already extensive publication record: *Bessie Smith* (1959), *Blues Fell This Morning: Meaning in the Blues* (1960), *Conversation with the Blues* (1965), and *Screening the Blues: Aspects of the Blues Tradition* (1968).

Oliver begins his blues narrative with an examination of the slave trade and its legacy, looking at African antecedents to the blues as well as how the institution of slavery and its aftermath influenced the development of the blues through field hollers, work songs, and the blending of diverse musical cultures. In chapter 3, Oliver examines the development of the blues techniques in the Mississippi Delta, and, in chapter 4, he looks at guitar and piano music developments in Alabama, Georgia, and Texas. The next two chapters address jug and string bands, as well as the rise of the "classic blues" female singers through vaudeville, tent shows, and minstrel shows. Oliver next examines the migration of southern piano blues styles northward into Chicago and Detroit and then looks at boogie-woogie developments in the midwestern cities. "Hard Time Everywhere" studies the record industry, paying most attention to the post-Depression era. Oliver once again takes us back to Chicago and the major developments of blues there in the 1930s and 1940s. We travel back south in the next chapter to look at rural blues music in Mississippi up to World War II. The Piedmont styles of blues, particularly in Tennessee and the Carolinas, are examined in the following chapter. Oliver then turns to the barrelhouse piano sounds of Kansas City and the migration of blues to California. In "King Biscuit Time," Oliver explains the role of radio in the dissemination and influence of blues in the post–World War II era. The final chapter, "Blues and Trouble," traces the rise of rhythm and blues and other early post–World War II blues sounds and examines the emerging international audience for blues sounds.

If any sections of this blues history seem lacking, gaps get filled in when *The Story of the Blues* is seen as one part of a much larger work, that of Oliver's entire output. African influences are examined in much more depth in *Savannah Syncopators* (no. 6), the meaning behind blues lyrics in *Blues Fell This Morning* (no. 64), or sacred/secular issues surrounding blues and gospel music in *Songsters and Saints* (no. 19).

Despite his primary education and profession as an architecture historian, Oliver does write quite well about music and has established himself as one of the world's top experts on blues. While most of Oliver's scholarship is extremely good, the descriptions of the musical aspects of the blues occasionally miss the mark. When describing the piano, for instance, Oliver writes that it is "tuned to a European diatonic scale and with a purity which is alien to blues" (94). While he was attempting to show that the piano's fixed pitches don't allow for microtones and bending of notes, Oliver should have substituted "chromatic scale" for diatonic, as this is technically accurate. In describing washboard playing, he writes, "The player often wore metal thimbles on his fingers to obtain a crisp, rattling sound, more satisfying to the blues ear than the drums" (52, first edition). What exactly is the blues ear? While he drops the subjective comparison in the second edition, he still makes reference to a seemingly unified blues ear (57). He also uses language that sounds poetic but isn't musically clear: "tweed-textured holler" (44) or "rough complaining voice" (49).

The "thrust" of the 1997 edition is "as it was originally conceived," though it does have a few "minor adjustments," which Oliver says are "mainly biographical, reflecting the emphasis of research in the past quarter-century." There are also some corrected transcriptions, and the newer edition includes fewer photographs than the original and groups them all together in photo sections in the center of the book, unlike the first edition, which interspersed the photos throughout the text. The original book was published as a quarto (12" × 9"), allowing for larger images than the newer 9¼" × 6" edition.

A companion double LP was released on Columbia in 1970 and rereleased by Sony as a two-CD set in 2003. The CD release left off the last three songs from the original recording but includes thirteen additional tracks. —*GJ*

3. A Hands-On Definition of the Blues

12-Bar Blues: The Complete Guide for Guitar. By Dave Rubin. Milwaukee: Hal Leonard, 1999. ISBN 0-7935-8181-8, $19.00

Every blues fan should seek a definition of the blues, and whenever one thinks one has found it, one should continue seeking. Some of the dopey definitions are one-word ones: blues is "life," blues is "truth," blues is "nourishing." Thankfully, the definitions offered by many authors of the one hundred books we present are much better, yet they reflect the educations of those authors. For example, an African Americanist may say the blues is "celebration," an anthropologist may say it is "ritual" and "culture," a folklorist may state that blues is a "folk art" or "folk music," a literary critic may call it "poetry," and a musicologist may describe it as an American combination of African music and European music. Cohn's *Nothing but the Blues* (no. 1) and Oliver's *Story of the Blues* (no. 2) contain some definitions of relevance for most readers. But it is good if one can learn a few musical rudiments toward identifying blues forms during a performance. Dave Rubin's *12-Bar Blues* is a basic primer for many styles of blues, along with the use of the blues form in jazz and rock.

Since 1993, Rubin has supervised the Inside the Blues series for the publisher Hal Leonard. After publishing some volumes, he realized that a basic presentation of the twelve-measure blues form was needed to give a comprehensive technical ground to the series. Of less concern to Rubin were the various lyric schemes to the twelve-measure form, such as the AAB (four-plus-four-plus-four) scheme, and the two verse-and-refrain schemes (whether four-plus-eight or eight-plus-four), as they were well documented and discussed as definitions in other blues books. Rather, he wanted to present the most common styles of guitar blues and some examples of blues for other instruments such as the piano. Moreover, he envisioned an interactive "hands-on" manual, which he expected his readers to try to play on guitars and thus produce the sounds for themselves.

All together, Rubin offers nineteen styles, ten of them relevant to blues. He starts with two types of slow blues, in 12/8 meter with its latent extension of the basic 4/4 beat (that latency becomes important in the boogie examples later in the book). Both of these slow 12/8 examples use seventh and ninth chords, which Rubin says may be heard in many postwar blues records. For the Mississippi blues of Robert Johnson, Muddy Waters, and Jimmy Reed, there is a "Moderate Boogie Shuffle (no. 1)," and also a "Riff Blues (no. 3)." For the Chicago blues styles of the 1950s and 1960s, there are two "Chicago Riff Blues," a "Moderate Boogie Shuffle (no. 2)" that may be played with trumpet and harmonica players, and a "Riff Blues (no. 2)." For the 1960s and early 1970s approaches of Albert King, Willie Cobbs, and B. B. King, a "slow minor blues" is given. For blues-rock, the remaining "Riff Blues" (numbered one in the book) is offered.

The remaining ten style examples come from boogie-woogie piano and jazz. Although the two "Boogie Woogie Blues" are notated in 4/4 meter, they should be played in the 12/8 lope (the book's attached CD of performed examples should demonstrate the similarity of "feel" in playing blues in these two meters). Rubin explained to me that the reason why he notated the 12/8 swing rhythms in 4/4 time with the eighth-note/quarter-note swing symbol and triplets is that, in his teaching, his students have an easier time reading in 4/4 than in 12/8. The two "swinging shuffles" introduce the styles of 1930s Kansas City jazz and Western swing; Rubin further explores shuffles in blues and jazz in *The Art of the Shuffle*. Later jazz styles are demonstrated in "Bebop Blues" for mid- to late 1940s jazz, "Jazzy Minor Blues" (such as Kenny Burrell's 1963 "Chitlins Con Carne"), advanced "Jazzy Blues" and "Jazzier Blues" exercises using thirteenth and diminished chords, and the "Jazziest Blues" in the chromatic manner of jazz guitar masters Wes Montgomery and Joe Pass.

To help readers get closer to the performance of blues, Rubin adds lessons on providing accompanying chords to piano soloists, performing introductions at the start of a blues number, inserting "turnaround" licks during the last two measures of each blues chorus, and keeping one's cool while playing a featured blues solo. Readers who have never taken a music lesson should understand at least the blues and boogie exercises, but they may find the definitions for terms and notation at the end of the book to be very helpful for the rest of the book.

As an introduction, Rubin provides an account of the origin of the twelve-measure blues form; it was cowritten by this book's coauthor, Edward Komara. They present twelve-measure song antecedents in British music, Irish ditties, and mid- to late-nineteenth-century American song, ending with W. C. Handy's sheet music blues of the 1910s. The authors emphasize twelve-measure song as the structural basis of imitation and adaptation. (Later, in his definition of "blues" for the Routledge *Encyclopedia of the Blues* [2006], Komara would go on to state that the first twelve-measure blues [whatever it was] was likely an adaptation of a twelve-measure song and not a tailoring of a blues in eight measures or sixteen measures, as previous blues writers have suggested.)

12-Bar Blues has been published only in paperback. If one has to buy a used copy, one should make sure the CD of performed examples is included. —*EK*

4. Where the Blues Is a Feeling

The Devil's Music: A History of the Blues. By Giles Oakley. London: BBC, 1976. ISBN 0-563-16012-8. New York: Taplinger, 1977. ISBN 0-8008-2189-0. As *La Musica del Diavolo: Storia del Blues*, Milan: Mazzotta Editore, 1978. ISBN 88-202-0236-0. New York: Harcourt Brace Jovanovich, 1978. ISBN 0-15-625586-3. As *Blues: Die Schwarze Musik*, Bergisch-Gladbach: Bastei Lübbe, 1981. ISBN 3-404-60054-1. London: Ariel, 1983. ISBN 0-563-21014-1. As *Devil's Music: Une Histoire du Blues*, Paris: Denoël, 1985. ISBN 2-207-23120-8. As *Blues Tarihi*, Istanbul: Ayrinti, 2004. ISBN 975-539-388-9. Second edition, New York: Da Capo, 1997. ISBN 0-306-80743-2, $16.95

In November and December 1976, BBC Television aired in England *The Devil's Music*, a five-part series about American blues produced by Giles Oakley. As anyone who has attempted to produce even a short film about the blues knows, there is a very small amount of surviving footage before 1960 of blues musicians and their cultures. This paucity of early film may explain why the 2003 American Public Broadcasting System series *Martin Scorsese Presents the Blues* took a thematic approach, each episode treating one specific topic, instead of a historical narrative spanning the whole series. As part of his preparations for the BBC series, Oakley undertook a trip in the United States to film interviews and performances of African American blues musicians who had been active since the 1920s and 1930s. He returned with enough material to produce five television episodes, a companion book, and three LPs of music.

The book is worth attention, even though its coverage of pre–World War II blues overlaps with Paul Oliver's *Story of the Blues* (no. 2). Oakley intended to explore the social and psychological "impulses" for the blues. How to explore them is not well formulated by Oakley in the book's introduction. He states matters better in his liner notes to the first LP companion (Red Lightnin' RL 0033): "We wanted to piece together a picture of how the music fits into the way of life that produced it, reasoning that any activity that supposedly inflames the wrath of the Lord and risks Hell Fire and Damnation, must be pretty important to people. What does the blues mean to its performers and how do they feel about its being condemned as sinful? Why, in the first place, is blues called the Devil's Music?"

Toward answering the question of the blues as "the Devil's Music," Oakley explains the purpose of blues as a feeling. Today, the phrase "the blues is a feeling" is probably the most hackneyed description of the genre, suggesting that since blues is equal parts inspired and inspirational, everyone can share in it. Historically speaking, the blues as feeling was probably formulated to serve as a secular counterpart to sacred teachings. As Oakley writes (50, first edition), "Despite the conflicts between them, the two worlds frequently overlapped, with many a singer 'getting religion,' or a preacher turning to the blues. The blues singer was able to articulate feelings and attitudes less frequently touched on by the Church. The global view provided by religion was complemented by the interior world of personal feeling, of emotions experienced by individuals but shared by the group. When asked to define the blues, most blues singers reply that 'the blues is a feeling.'" The devil's music is the personal emotional counterpart to the Lord's communal, sometimes ecstatic music. The devil's nature, however, is not described by Oakley; that matter would be explained by Jon Michael Spencer in *Blues and Evil* (no. 98).

For the book, Oakley takes slavery as his starting point, at which he notes the kinds of music sung and played by African Americans before the blues. But the recurring topic that drives the narrative is the migration of black labor from the southern farms to the northern cities. He introduces it in the context of the 1910s, when many older ex-slaves were seeing their children and grand-children beginning to head north. Oakley quotes (84, first edition) a middle-aged son of an ex-slave about raising his own son: "Yet in bringing up my own son, I let some more of the old customs slip by. . . . He says, 'When a young white talks rough to me, I can't talk rough to him. You can stand that; I can't. I have some education, and inside I has the feelings of a white man. I'm going.'"

When the blues matured as music in the 1920s, it became a means of reflecting the work of day as well as the pleasures of night. In the longest chapter of the book, Oakley shows how musical craft and human needs came together in the blues of the 1930s. He explains very carefully the economics of cotton farming, including the margins of profit for the landowner and the earnings to sharecropping farmers, black and white alike. At the same time, he shows the downside along with the upside of working in the cities, whether Atlanta in the South, or Chicago or Detroit in the North. Despite the risks, many African Americans made the urban move, and others heard of the cities as "the Promised Land." With such biblical references infused into the promotion of migrating, the secular function of blues seems to be a contrast to such sacred purpose, even though the blues sup-plied many musical expressions of the wish to earn more money and live more prosperously. For a standard history of the black migration, many readers should look into Nicholas Lemann's *The Promised Land: The Great Migration and How It Changed America* (New York: Vintage, 1992) or Isabel Wilkerson's *The Warmth of Other Suns: The Story of America's Great Migration* (New York: Random House, 2010). But in 1976, Oakley told the migration story remarkably enough to stand well today for blues readers.

The Devil's Music, for the most part, covers blues through the 1940s, giving only a short chapter for the music from the 1950s to the 1970s. Also, it doesn't give as much attention to the black sacred opposition to blues, although some comments are made in the section about Mississippi blues of the 1930s. Yet this book was read and quoted in the books by Julio Finn (no. 94), Jon Michael Spencer (no. 98), and Angela Y. Davis (no. 22), so it should be acknowledged for paving a contextual way for these African Americans' writings in the 1980s and 1990s.

The book version of *The Devil's Music* is currently available as a second edition in paperback from Da Capo Press. Blues book collectors should also seek a used copy of the early editions published in London by the BBC and in New York by Taplinger, for the crisp reproductions of photographs; some of its cultural and contextual images are not in any other blues book.

Oakley's 1976 BBC series has not been made available either on DVD or by licensed media stream. In July 1979, BBC Television aired a second series in four parts hosted by British blues mentor Alexis Korner; it is this series that is offered for viewing through the BBC's website, http://www.bbc.co.uk/programmes/p00lfs2m.

Oakley issued through the Red Lightnin' label two volumes of music from his 1976 filming trip to the United States, *The Devil's Music* (Red Lightnin' RL 0033, two-LP set, 1976) and *More Devil's Music* (Red Lightnin' RL 0038, 1983). Broadly speaking, the material is divided between Memphis and Mississippi styles, featuring Big Joe Williams, Houston Stackhouse, Sam Chatmon, and Laura Dukes, and Chicago styles from Little Brother Montgomery, the Aces, and James DeShay. The contents of these two Red Lightnin' issues were reissued on a three-CD set (*The Devil's Music*, Indigo Records IGTOCD 2537) with recordings of the 1963 American Folk Blues Festival tour. —*EK*

5. The Blues as Oral History

Nobody Knows Where the Blues Come From: Lyrics and History. Edited by Robert Springer. Jackson: University Press of Mississippi, 2006. ISBN 1-57806-797-9 (hardcover), ISBN 1-93411-029-9 (paperback), $25.00

Nobody Knows Where the Blues Come From is a selection of papers originally presented during a conference. For that reason, this volume may not make for the kind of unified reading experience that many blues readers expect of books. But it was chosen because some of its contents cover historical subjects otherwise not presented in the Blues 100 books and because a few others are supplements to those on our list.

In September 2002, Dr. Robert Springer of the University of Metz, France, hosted the second conference on "The Lyrics in African American Popular Music." The previous one had been held in 2000, from which some of the lectures were published as the book *The Lyrics in African American Popular Music* (Bern: Peter Lang, 2001). Likewise, at the sequel conference there were several presentations that merited publication, and it is fortunate that the University Press of Mississippi has made them available in an affordable edition in paperback (the hardcover edition has long been sold out).

In his preface (vii), Springer states that the main purpose of the conference was to focus "on the historical dimensions of the lyrics with the intention of setting the record straight or creating a record where none existed." One outcome of this event, he reports, was the establishment of "the significance of African American popular song as a neglected form of oral history." A chief speaker was Paul Oliver, whose writings since *Blues Fell This Morning* (1960, no. 64) have influenced many blues researchers, including "almost without exception" (as Springer says) the other conference participants. Oliver spoke on the concept of the city bully in blues lyrics from "Bully of the Town" (circa 1890s) to "Wang Dang Doodle" (1960).

However, Guido van Rijn may be said to have set the current standard for presenting the blues as oral history. His method of examining historical events and then the blues commemorating them was developed through writing his book series on blues about the American presidents (see nos. 42 and 69). The conference papers by David Evans, Luigi Monge, and Thomas Freeland and Chris Smith acknowledge and follow his method. Van Rijn's contribution, "Coolidge's Blues," looks at some topical blues on general issues that President Calvin Coolidge faced in 1923–1928. While it is a supplement to *Roosevelt's Blues* (no. 42), this piece on the Coolidge era shows a broadening of the scope of song selection for study to include some blues indirectly about the president along with the direct ones. Van Rijn would adopt this strategy for the last of his "White House blues" books, *The Carter, Reagan, Bush Sr., Clinton, Bush Jr., and Obama Blues* (Overveen, Netherlands: Agram Blues Books, 2012).

David Evans's "High Water Everywhere" treats the recorded blues about the spring 1927 Mississippi River flood. The natural disaster had inundated farmlands and villages in Mississippi and

Louisiana within several hundred miles of the breached riverbanks. Every blues fan should know of the event because it inspired the creation of many excellent recorded blues, chief among them Bessie Smith's "Backwater Blues" and Charlie Patton's "High Water Everywhere." Evans's extended study is a critical appraisal of these and other performances as lyric histories, and it serves as an introduction to the general books about the flood and its impact on American life and politics.

Two additional historical events are discussed in the papers by Luigi Monge and the team of Thomas Freeland and Chris Smith. Monge evaluates the recorded memorials for the victims of the 1940 Rhythm Club fire in Natchez, Mississippi. While Preston Lauterbach (in no. 52) presents the circumstances of that horrifying evening, Monge proceeds a little later in time to show its remembrance through memory and song. Freeland and Smith wonder about a ballad recorded by a black musician, Roger Garrett, about the murder of a white law enforcement officer committed by another black, Ruell Eaton. The two writers find that the song has more traits in common with white ballad repertory, and they conclude that Garrett had played it because he thought perhaps that was what the visiting white ballad hunters John A. Lomax and Ruby Terrill wanted to hear.

John Cowley's "West Indies Blues" is a pathbreaking history of the mutual presences of West Indian music and American blues from the early 1920s through the early 1950s. Cowley sets the context with a description of the migration of African West Indians from the Caribbean to the American East Coast, especially to New York City. He then develops the history with capsule biographies of Marcus Garvey, Louis Belasco, and Sam Manning. The lyrical and musical examinations range from the song "West Indies Blues," composed by Edgar Dowell, Clarence Williams, and Spencer Williams in 1922, to the post–World War II recordings of calypso music through the early 1950s.

Two short pieces round out the collection. Robert Springer's "On the Electronic Trail of Blues Formulas" follows the uses of common blues phrases like "will a matchbox hold my clothes." As he admits in his conclusion (183), "It was not always the earliest recorded example(s) of a formula which acquired popularity and led to imitation." In the case of the "matchbox" phrase, its appearance in Blind Lemon Jefferson's famous "Match Box Blues" (1927) may be a garbled version of a lyric from Ma Rainey's "Lost

Wandering Blues" (1924). But the Jefferson rendering has been appropriated more times than Rainey's. Randall Cherry's profile on Ethel Waters reminds us of her early career as a blues singer and dancer. I wonder, though, how the blues Waters sang would fit in Houston Baker's blues ideology (no. 93) and Angela Davis's black feminism (no. 22). —*EK*

6. What Should "Africa" Mean to the Blues?

Savannah Syncopators: African Retentions in the Blues. By Paul Oliver. New York: Stein and Day, 1970. ISBN 0-8128-1315-4 (hardcover), ISBN 0-8128-1319-7 (paperback). Tokyo: Shobunsha, 1981. Reprinted with an afterword in *Yonder Come the Blues: The Evolution of a Genre.* Cambridge: Cambridge University Press, 2001. ISBN 0-521-78259-7 (hardcover), $113.00, ISBN 0-521-78777-7 (paperback), $46.00

Savannah Syncopators contains Paul Oliver's research and thoughts about African antecedents in the blues. He did not include them in his narrative history *The Story of the Blues* (no. 2). *Savannah Syncopators* is important for identifying specific regions of West Africa, not the whole continent, as relevant to the history of blues and jazz. It has also raised many critical responses.

Through the 1960s, Africa was regarded as relevant by writers as a geographic and cultural source for jazz and blues antecedents. Exactly which parts of Africa, and which kinds of African music, were left vague by early historians of jazz, including Rudi Blesh, Marshall Stearns, and Gunther Schuller. Oliver was bothered by the fact that their published histories lacked indications of where in Africa musicians were singing with lyrics and performing with stringed instruments. Furthermore, while teaching in West African universities during the 1960s, Oliver listened firsthand to music in the rainforest areas for what historians posited as African antecedents of jazz, but he was hearing none of the characteristics he was seeking. However, he found many of them in the music of the savannah regions north of the rainforest, especially in that performed by griots in the Arab African cultures.

Oliver's resulting study is organized in six chapters. Readers may find some of the text to be very detailed, perhaps dense, so in order to follow the author's arguments, they should write down the seven questions he poses at the end of the first chapter. Answers to some questions are presented clearly, and those to the others have to be inferred from his discussions. For example, for the first of these questions, "What is meant by 'Africa'?" Oliver does not provide a direct answer, but the reader can quickly realize from the first chapter that his references to Africa are focusing on northwestern Africa, specifically the rainforest and the savannah north and northeast of it. Answers to the second question, "Where in Africa can musical forms related to the blues be found?" may be found in chapters 3, 4, and 6: the sub-Saharan savannah region, for the qualities of vocal singing, rhythm, "swing," string instruments, and wind instruments; for the performing griots' reuse of melodies to new words; for collective singing; and for call-and-response processes in singing.

In like manner, answers for the other five questions may be found or at least inferred. Take, for example, the third question, "Is there any justification for assuming that slaves came from these regions, if they exist?" For my part, I had to infer that Oliver's justification is in the fact that the culture of the south coast of West Africa lacks those aspects of savannah culture noted for question 2. Question 4 is: "Can African peoples be considered as homogenous, or do they divide into specific groups?" In his fifth and sixth chapters, Oliver says that there were two divisions of the West African peoples: one was that the Muslim Arab Africans coming to the savannah from northern Africa were distinguished from and by the western coastal inhabitants; the other division occurred by slave traders in the West Indies who determined on the basis of physical type and health who among the captive Africans were to be sent for sale in the United States. Question 5 asks, "Can African music be considered as homogenous, or does its character vary over the territories which supplied the slaves?" This answer has to be inferred, but it seems that Oliver thinks no, it is not homogenous, and its character does vary between the rainforest and the savannah, such as the different types of instruments played. Question 6 asks, "Are there any characteristics of music and instrumentation that do, or do not, accord with those in North America?" Again, answers to this question may have to be inferred from chapter 6, where Oliver draws parallels between the savannah griot and the African American bluesman while acknowledging differences, too. Finally comes the seventh question, "Were there circumstances in North America that would inhibit African retentions and were there any that would promote them?" Oliver gives two answers. One is the commonly given observation that Protestant slave owners had prohibited their slaves from singing and drumming, while some places like New Orleans touted as local attractions the displays of African American dancing and drumming. But he also says that one circumstance that may have promoted African retentions was white communities who performed and danced to music descended from Scotch and English forms, which could have been congenial to the kinds of music that savannah Africans and Arab Africans had enjoyed before captivity.

Because answers to four of the seven questions have to be inferred, Oliver's points should best be read as theses to be researched, not as assertions to be accepted or disproven. Because of the critics' tendency to read this book as assertions, an odd critical history has developed over the years (which Oliver relates in the afterword to the 2001 reprint): odd because the critics have not attacked the book in its seeming inability to answer its own questions except through inference. Forty-four years after its first publication, the book still needs to be addressed fully, whether by its critics or by its students. Whether for or against Oliver, each respondent will have to give one's own answer to the third question, "Is there any justification for assuming that slaves came from these regions, if [musical forms relevant to the blues] exist?"

The preferred edition of *Savannah Syncopators* is the 2001 reprint (Cambridge University Press) with its newly written afterword as part of the volume *Yonder Come the Blues*, which also presents two other texts originally published in the 1970–1971 Blues Series, Tony Russell's *Blacks, Whites and Blues*, and Robert M. W. Dixon and John Godrich's *Recording the Blues*. Older readers who have the original Studio Vista/Stein and Day publication should keep it for the photos not reproduced in the reprint.

Those who purchase *Yonder Come the Blues* should acquire the companion CD of the same title (Document DOCD 32-20-1), which provides three performances from Oliver's African field tapes. Often pricey but worth seeking is the 1970 British LP companion, *Savannah Syncopators* (CBS [UK] 52799), which contains ten tracks that were not reissued on the *Yonder* CD. This thought-provoking record alternates performances by West African musicians with those by African American bluesmen, suggesting some blues characteristics as retentions from West African practice. —*EK*

7. Leaving and Returning to Africa

Africa and the Blues. By Gerhard Kubik. Jackson: University Press of Mississippi, 1999. ISBN 1-57806-145-8 (hardcover), ISBN 1-57806-146-6 (paperback), $25.00. Italian translation by Giorgio Adamo as *L'Africa e il Blues,* Subiaco: Fogli Volanti, 2007, ISBN 8-89548-200-X

Most studies of African music in the blues and jazz fields have been undertaken by writers with little field experience in Africa. For the blues, Paul Oliver has spent some years there in the 1960s, but he recognized in his book *Savannah Syncopators* (no. 6) that he could carry his inquiry into African retentions in the blues only so far. It was remarkable that David Evans invited Gerhard Kubik to write on the blues, because Kubik had been studying music in Africa since 1959, undertaking many field recording trips throughout the continent. *Africa and the Blues* was Kubik's resulting book.

Kubik agrees with Oliver that the area of Africa in which to seek antecedents for the blues is the savannah, but he recommends extending the geographic scope east toward Sudan. In his book's sixth chapter, Kubik says the blues, especially southern rural blues, has had in common with savannah-Sudan music the following traits:

1. A solo singing tradition, whether as field hollers or (in Africa) hunting shouts.
2. "Wavy intonation" using vocal melisma, tonal slurs, gliss tones, and "timbre-melodic sequences."
3. Slow and medium tempi.
4. A relationship between the voice and the melodies played on instruments that is guided by the "principle of unison" (or "heterophony") or a simple background drone/ostinato played on the instrument.
5. Instruments suitable for individual or small-group music.
6. Some Western factory-made instruments may serve for African instruments known in the past, such as the mouth harmonica for the panpipes.

Kubik also notes what is lacking in both the blues and the savannah-Sudan music. Polymeters and complex polyrhythms, whether of drumming or of melodic layering, are absent in both kinds of music, although these characteristics are to be heard in music of the African Guinea coast, the Caribbean, and South America. Another lack is what Kubik calls an "asymmetric time-line pattern" in drumming and percussion: if a drumming pattern calls for twenty-four beats, "asymmetric" means that the perform-ers may split those twenty-four beats not as twelve-plus-twelve subgroups, but, for example, as eleven-plus-thirteen subgroups. His thorough presentation of asymmetries in the third chapter prepares the reader to notice their absence in Kubik's side-by-side examinations of savannah-Sudan music and blues in the follow-ing two chapters. In these two findings, Kubik confirms deeply Oliver's position that the African savannah is the region to seek characteristics shared with the blues.

As a third chief finding in his book, Kubik explains the seem-ing "blue notes," which in a Western diatonic scale would be the flatted tones found between the second and third scale tones and the sixth and seventh scale tones. For many years, Western writers and musicians have described these "blue notes" as the result of the clash of African scales with Western harmonic chords. From his perspective acquired from many years in Africa, Kubik states that it isn't the African scales that are clashing, it is the Western chords. In his explanation, Kubik shows how African harmonies are derived from "natural" derivations from African instruments and speech and that the "blue notes" are compatible with such harmonies. But to Western tempered tunings that have prevailed in Europe and the United States for the past three hundred years, those same "blue notes" will clash, and Kubik shows the quantitative difference of that clash. This chapter is required reading not only for blues readers but also for jazz fans.

There is one claim in the book for which Kubik devotes much discussion: the presence of a three-line AAB lyric scheme in savannah-Sudan music. According to Kubik (42), he recorded in 1960 such an example, and it is the only example known to him. Titled "Baba ol'odo," it was an "alo" chantefable sung in the Oyo/Yoruba culture, whose members were "free of both Arabic/Islamic influences that had been absorbed in the nineteenth century from Hausa music, and European influences." Careful transcriptions of lyrics and pitches are provided for the readers' considerations. Avowedly, Kubik backs off from claiming that "Baba ol'odo" is in twelve measures, for he quickly adds that "if the alo piece were actually written in twelve bars, each bar would contain six pulses, which is something not found in the blues" (in the blues style, each bar would have four beats). Furthermore, he explicitly states (45) that "I do not suggest that blues is a derivative of Yoruba chantefables." His reticence, if not his dubiousness, about the relevance of this alo to the blues is also shown by the absence of its recording from the CD companion to the book. My own opinion is based on Kubik's statement (26) that the blues is a literary and musical genre with its words and tones intertwined and that "devoid of words, the sound patterns lose much of their original meaning." The three-line AAB lyric scheme of "Baba ol'odo" may be the result of the singer's tailoring of an existing four-line song (or of a two-line song) in order to fully retain in the music the original meaning or purpose of the lyrics. I do not read anything in Kubik's account of this peculiar chantefable to suggest that the singer had selected the form from a previously existing piece of music. Since Kubik admits that this alo is unique to his knowledge, I doubt it is enough to qualify as a characteristic of savannah-Sudan music. For this reason, I think the three-line AAB lyric form should not have been included in Kubik's list of characteristics shared between the blues and savannah-Sudan music in chapter 6.

Nonetheless, Kubik seems to argue later in his book how a three-line AAB alo could have evolved in the New World to become, eventually, the blues. To follow his argument, one will have to concede that "Baba ol'odo" is not unique, that there are other pieces like it but that have not yet been found in northwest and north-central Africa, and therefore its lyric scheme is a characteristic of the region's music. On page 46, immediately following the presentation of this alo, Kubik states that the idea of a three-line AAB lyric scheme would have been remembered by African Americans in the United States during the eighteenth and nineteenth centuries. He writes: "The question is, of course, how such a 'memory' could have survived until the *end* of the nineteenth century. Here, my theory of 'unconscious transmission of culture traits' . . . might give an answer." He adds (47): "Cultural reinforcement of any of these songs traditions by newcomers cannot therefore be excluded, until at least the mid-nineteenth century. These latest cultural imports may have come from odd places in Africa." If I may break from quoting Kubik momentarily, I ask: Is Yoruba one such odd place? On page 97, "unconscious transmission of culture traits" seems to be reworded as "cultural underground currents." If today's prevailing twelve-measure AAB blues lyric form had originated in Yoruba, how could have it have grown from such obscure beginnings, even for Africa? Kubik offers a theory of a "dominating minority" (98): "What probably happened in this process was that early in the nineteenth century one or another minority group among the African descendants in the Deep South gained prominence culturally over the others." This minority can consist of just one person (as Kubik says earlier on p. 13). If that theory is granted credence, what then of the artist? Is he an innovator or merely an unwitting keeper of a cultural underground current?

The last section of the book is a "Return to Africa." Kubik reports where recordings of African American blues have been brought to Africa and the influence of that music. He states that only two regions may be said to have experienced such a blues impact. One is South Africa, where after World War II American big-band recordings of instrumental blues pieces were brought, purchased, and played. Eventually, black South Africans developed a blues-derived style of jazz called *kwela*, using as instruments a string bass and a pennywhistle. *Kwela* was an active style from 1950 to 1964, but it was supplanted by the new styles, *mbaqanga* and *chimrurenga*. The other region is west savannah and central Sudan, where a musical return of blues to its ancestral region has been undertaken, especially by the guitarist Ali Farka Touré. The result is an African market label of "blues" for any music recorded in the savannah and the adjacent areas of Sudan, which Kubik admits would be beyond musically what Oliver had sought for as African retentions for the blues.

Kubik's *Africa and the Blues* confirms from the African music side what Oliver posited in *Savannah Syncopators*, and its best-demonstrated findings deepen our knowledge of African antecedents for the blues. An Italian translation was published in 2007 by the firm Fogli Volanti. The English-language edition from the University Press of Mississippi remains in print, although in paperback with fuzzy photograph reproductions. Serious blues book collectors should seek used copies of the out-of-print hardcover edition for its crisp-appearing illustrations. A companion CD titled *Africa and the Blues* was issued in 2001 in Austria on the Neatwork label, providing much music from Kubik's field tapes (but not that alo "Baba ol'odo"). That CD has been long out of print and is now quite expensive on the used CD markets. For that reason, the Italian translation may be worth finding, as it includes the CD with the book. —*EK*

8. The Blues Fan's Introduction to the Spirituals

The Spirituals and the Blues. By James H. Cone. New York: Seabury Press, 1972. ISBN 0-8164-0236-1 (hardcover), ISBN 0-8164-2073-4 (paperback). Reprint, Maryknoll, NY: Orbis Press, 1991, ISBN 978-0-88344-747-5 (hardcover); 1992, ISBN 978-0-88344-843-4 (paperback), $16.00

Spirituals are to American popular music what Gregorian chant is to Western art music: the sacred melodic basis for many later kinds of music. The spirituals should be recognized in themselves and in the derived songs, and they should be respected. There are important collections in notated music form: *Slave Songs of the United States* (1867, currently available in a Dover Books reprint); I. B. T. Marsh's *The Jubilee Singers and Their Songs* (1877, also available from Dover); and *The Book of American Negro Spirituals* by James Weldon Johnson, J. Rosamund Johnson, and Lawrence Brown (1925, 1926, currently available in a Da Capo Press reprint). There are also several historical narratives, such as Dena Epstein's *Sinful Tunes and Spirituals* (Urbana: University of Illinois Press, 1977) and John Lovell Jr.'s *Black Song: The Forge and the Flame: The Story of How the Afro-American Spiritual Was Hammered Out* (New York: Macmillan, 1972). The blues fan may ask, "That is all well and good, but why should I care whether or how spirituals relate to the blues?"

Dr. James H. Cone is an influential theologian, based at the Union Theological Seminary in New York City since 1970. As suggested by the titles of his first two books, *Black Theology and Black Power* (1969) and *A Black Theology of Liberation* (1970), he developed a theology of African American "self-determination" in the face of systematic racial oppression and exploitation in the United States. His tenets for African Americans are based on the Bible, especially on its portions written during the Roman occupation of the Jewish homeland, but informed with culture familiar to blacks. *The Spirituals and the Blues* was his effort to deepen his theology with black music past and present. His main challenge in this project, though, was reconciling black sacred music with the blues, each of whose listeners have little to do with each other (as Bruce Cook learned while writing the gospel music chapter for *Listen to the Blues*, no. 86). The blues reader has to be patient, as the first five of the six chapters are solely about spirituals, but the final chapter will deepen one's appreciation for the blues.

Cone begins with a brief survey of critical opinions about spirituals, finding them lacking the "thought underlying the slave songs that has so far escaped analysis." Reviewing the history of slavery in the United States, Cone describes "a people in the land of bondage, and what they did to hold themselves together and to fight back," and that the spirituals' dual meanings within and outside the singing culture are reflections of such holding together and fighting back—and of liberation, which Cone says is the "central theological concept" of the spirituals. The slaves affirmed themselves as the children of God who should not be oppressed by white owners. By arguing that nineteenth-century spirituals should be still functional as 1970s freedom songs, Cone shows their timely past-to-present side.

Yet spirituals also have a timeless past-and-present-to-future side as well, and Cone points to Jesus as the abiding agent toward that future. He shows how some spirituals told of Jesus returning in a second coming at the end of time for the last judgment of oppressors and oppressed. This leads to an African American–oriented discussion of eschatology, or "the last things." Cone interprets "eschatology" in four ways. One is as historical, as slaves escaping to the northern United States and Canada. The second is affirmational, for slaves in the South as children of God. The third is apocalyptic, when the last judgment occurs. The fourth is ethical, as "heaven on earth" shared among the slaves, at the very least. The notion of ethical eschatology is ever new, as affirmed for African Americans by Cone here, and yet very old, as recorded by the New Testament writers as the "good news" shared among the Jews in the Rome-dominated Israel (for a short account of Jesus and Jewish ethical eschatology, see John Dominic Crossan, *Jesus: A Revolutionary Biography* [New York: HarperCollins, 1997]).

It is with the notion of ethical eschatology that Cone ties spirituals with blues. The times from 1865 to 1970 had changed somewhat, in that systematic economic exploitation had replaced legal slavery, and racial segregation was only very slowly being removed. Spirituals as sacred music were replaced in some sections of the South with sanctified music, then across the country with gospel music. At the same time, the blues emerged as secular ethical expression. In one section in the last chapter, Cone celebrates blues as a sexual ethical expression, which I find remarkable since most writers about blues shy away from sexual topics. In hindsight, it is interesting to see that Cone is discussing blues at a time when young African Americans were listening to soul and then, developing later in the decade, funk and rap. Nonetheless, Cone strives to maintain a sense of sacred community with the blues culture if not the church congregation. A recent sequel may be Ralph Basui Watkins's *Hip-Hop Redemption* (Grand Rapids, MI: Baker Academic, 2011), which tries to restore that sense of sacred community in the contemporary urban culture left behind when many African American churches moved to the suburbs. But even today in the 2010s, whenever a listener discerns a sacred melody in a blues— whether spiritual, sanctified, or gospel—he or she had better recognize the song as a call to social duty to the next person. *—EK*

9. Paving a Highway for the Blues

Out of Sight: The Rise of African American Popular Music 1889–1895. By Lynn Abbott and Doug Seroff. Jackson: University Press of Mississippi, 2002. ISBN 1-57806-499-6 (hardcover), ISBN 1-60473-244-3 (paperback), $40.00

After emancipation and before the blues, the spectrum of African American music was impressively wide. There were jubilee singing of sacred music, concert performances of art songs and arias, brass bands, minstrelsy, domestic and "barbershop" music making, and ragtime. While it is convenient for blues readers to speak of music before the blues as "pre-blues," it is also wrong, because not all African American music of the late nineteenth century evolved into the blues. Every blues reader should have some basic knowledge of African American music before the blues. For secular and sacred types of music during slavery times, there is Dena Epstein's classic survey *Sinful Tunes and Spirituals* (Urbana: University of Chicago Press, 1977). Any one of the recent—or older—histories of Fisk University and its original Fisk Jubilee Singers will tell of the earliest international interest in African American music through the 1870s. But as a starting context, Lynn Abbott and Doug Seroff's *Out of Sight* is most pertinent for blues readers.

Abbott is the associate curator for recorded sound at Tulane University's Hogan Jazz Archive. For many years, Seroff has held auctions of rare records of jazz, blues, gospel, and other American music. The authors' research interests have encompassed more than the blues. As a matter of fact, the work on *Out of Sight* was begun in order to take a survey of black music and entertainment before ragtime. The result is a remarkable compilation of written reportage published in African American newspapers from 1889 through 1895, especially from the *Indianapolis Freeman* newspaper. The compilers do give some guiding remarks before presenting some articles, but for the most part they let the texts speak for themselves. My appraisal will try to present some basic trends and innovations that blues readers should notice in this book.

In the mid-1880s to late 1880s, a number of African Americans were performing on concert stages. To be sure, the jubilee singers authorized by Fisk University had not toured since 1878 (one such group did travel in 1890). But their successors and imitators were on the road, especially Frederick Loudin, who led a "Fisk Jubilee Singers" group on a three-year lucrative stay in Australia. Notable at this time was the Hampton Institute Quartet, whom Abbott and Seroff pointed out as changing the format of jubilee singing from groups to quartets. Some women singers opted to present themselves not in groups or ensembles but as solo classical artists. As a result, an African American version of the diva emerged in 1889–1895, embodied perhaps best by Matilda Sissieretta Jones, who was billed as the "Black Patti," in reference to the internationally famous soprano Adelina Patti. On the lowbrow side of the music spectrum, there were the minstrel troupes that since antebellum times were offering broad comedy and imitations of black music. After the Civil War, African Americans toured nationally and even internationally in their own minstrel shows, even though they may have seemed to reinforce some stereotypes about themselves to the public. By 1891, these troupes spiffed themselves up with updated material and music, improved actors, and new kinds of music; as Handy remembered in his *Father of the Blues* (no. 12), "the composers, the singers, the musicians, the speakers, the stage performers—the minstrel shows got them all" (including Handy himself for some time).

Was African American music meant to be uplifting, or was it meant to be merely entertaining? The year 1893 brought two answers to that question. One was provided by the Czech composer Antonín Dvořák, remarking to the *New York Herald* newspaper (May 21, 1893) what "a splendid treasury of melody which you have" in African American music: "In the Negro melodies of America I discover all that is needed for a great and noble school of music." This so-called Dvořák Statement remains a key moment in the development of American classical music from the prevailing European styles. On the other hand, for Abbott and Seroff, the 1893 Columbian Exposition in Chicago gave little acknowledgment to blacks and offered little employment for willing black workers. Furthermore, the circumstances behind Theodore Thomas's resignation as the exposition's musical director signified to the compilers "the popular rejection of *all* music seen as projecting 'aspirations' rather than entertainment." Everything that Abbott and Seroff write as their conclusion to the exposition section (294–296) bears the most careful reading because they set forth their view that if new African American styles like ragtime (and, if I may add, the blues) were to emerge, such styles would have to be nurtured within and by commercial entertainment, even if they are uplifting and worthy enough to be called art.

The remaining years in the survey, 1894–1895, seem to support the compilers' conclusion. Divas like "Black Patti" Jones and her rival Marie Selika increasingly add minstrel-type acts to their bills to attract general audiences. If the persistence and flourishing of black and white minstrel shows were not demeaning enough to some African American audiences, there was the "Black America" reenactment in 1895 in Brooklyn, New York, of a southern plantation. Yet the early surviving printed mentions of ragtime may be read in some of the last news items in the book, especially with some established artists crossing over from minstrelsy and quartet singing, such as Ernest Hogan and the Whitman Sisters.

While there are virtually no direct references to blues, this book provides much about how the means and ways that the first traveling blues performers would follow were established. After all, the routes that W. C. Handy and Ma Rainey would later take had existed before them. The few printed mentions of blues through 1895 (see 186, 302–303) give some food for thought. Was the blues already heard in the mid-1890s but absent from printed notice because it was ingrained in the oral cultures? Or did it not yet exist in 1895, so when it emerged in the late 1890s and early 1900s, it was a fresh novelty, even to African American ears? —*EK*

10. Until There Were Enough Blues Songs for a Whole Evening

Ragged but Right: Black Traveling Shows, "Coon Songs," and the Dark Pathway to Blues and Jazz. By Lynn Abbott and Doug Seroff. Jackson: University Press of Mississippi,

2007. ISBN 1-57806-901-9 (hardcover), $75.00, ISBN
1-61703-645-5 (paperback), $40.00

Ragged but Right is the sequel to the authors' previous book, *Out of Sight* (no. 9). That predecessor closed its history at 1895. The following year, the popular song "All Coons Look Alike to Me" became a national hit through performances and sheet music, and it ushered in the ragtime era, which lasted for about twenty years. For a focused account of ragtime, the classic history *They All Played Ragtime* by Rudi Blesh and Harriet Janis (New York: Knopf, 1950) is still recommended. But blues readers need a broader account of ragtime that will show how that music was succeeded by the blues in the music marketplace. Abbott and Seroff take us from 1895 through 1920, a time when many of the earliest blues singers on records learned their first blues songs.

In their introduction, Abbott and Seroff assert that ragtime provided the "first real professional opportunities for a wide range of black performers." However, by the term "ragtime," they mean not just the piano rags composed by Scott Joplin and other composers in St. Louis and Indianapolis but also the "coon songs" that appealed broadly to the masses, white audiences at that. Today, writing and singing "coon songs" may seem demeaning to African American musicians, but around 1900 their popularity gave many people their start in show business. What they made of that start depended on how they and their audiences grew beyond this "coon" repertory. A thesis of this book is that "every branch of the black stage profession included artists who saw race elevation as a part of their professional responsibility" (3). Abbott and Seroff call such branches the "avenues of professional opportunity," namely the stage and sheet music, the "Smart Set" tours, the circus side-shows, and the traveling tent shows.

What the authors call the first ragtime hit, "All Coons Look Alike to Me," was popularized by the African American entertainer Ernest Hogan in 1896. Within five years there were white female singers specializing in "coon songs" and a few white males, too. In their chapters on ragtime and the stage, including the tours by several African American companies known as "the Smart Set," Abbott and Seroff examine the careers of Ernest Hogan, George Walker and Bert Williams, and Bob Cole with J. Rosamund Johnson. The "coon song" fad was fading by 1910, but by then the successes of Hogan, Walker, Williams, and Cole helped to gain footholds in city show business for other African Americans. Furthermore, the national spread of ragtime songs filtered down into the pre-1942 blues repertory. The authors show which "coon song" lyrics turned up in the folklore fieldwork of Howard Odum and Alan Lomax and in the "prewar" commercial recordings by John Hurt, Gus Cannon, and Son House.

One valuable service by the authors is their affirmation of the black brass bands for circuses and Wild West shows as musical attractions unto themselves. They present the careers of P. G. Lowery (for the Sells Brothers Circus and other circuses), Roy Pope (Ringling Brothers Circus), James Wolfscale (Barnum and Bailey Circus), A. A. Wright (Sparks Brothers Circus), John Eason (Yankee Robinson Circus), J. C. Miles and his singer wife, Lizzie, and L. K. Baker. Through the 1900s these bands played a variety of music, from marches and concert numbers to ragtime and "coon songs," but in the early 1910s they began playing blues, often from arrangements purchased from W. C. Handy's Pace-Handy firm. As Abbott and Seroff conclude (207), much of white America heard the blues for the first time as played by the African American bands in circus promotional parades and sideshows.

The longest chapter is devoted to the minstrel "tent shows" that flourished before World War II. The tents were not little canvas backdrops for medicine shows but really "big tops" whose sizes rivaled those of the bigger circuses. These traveling shows made their ways into villages and hamlets that did not have theaters and stages, such as Drew and other sites in the Mississippi Delta, where the shows made much money in the 1910s and 1920s. They offered a variety of entertainment: comedy, singers, contortionists, dancers, and (around 1914, as near as the authors can determine) the blues. The histories of four tent shows are presented. Allen's New Orleans Minstrels (1899–late 1920s) set the pattern, including travel by its own train cars. The Rabbit's Foot company (1900–late 1950s) featured much blues in its shows, which in the 1910s was sung by Lillian Lockhart, who unfortunately did not make records. The Florida Blossoms (1906–c. 1934) had several blues singers early in their careers, most notably Bessie Smith. Silas Green from New Orleans (c. 1910–1958) was in its heyday a wildly popular show. Seroff and Abbott reprint glowing accounts of two of the show's better-remembered singers, Princess White and Evelyn White, who did not make records of their blues singing.

Ragged but Right may not have the answer to how or where the blues began, but it does present the venues where many people black as well as white had heard the blues for the first time. For that matter, it also presents where many singers celebrated later for blues happened to be in the 1900s and 1910s: Clara Smith was in a "Smart Set" troupe; Charles Elgar, Viola McCoy, Cleo Poteet, and Lizzie Miles were sideshow musicians; and Ma Rainey, Ida Cox, Bessie Smith, and Mary Johnson were in tent shows. Also, the book suggests very strongly that when each of these singers took up the blues, he or she sang them as part of a great variety of repertory, including ragtime songs, "coon songs," and other popular songs. Why not sing blues all of the time? I suggest that in the 1910s there may not yet have been enough blues to fill a whole evening's time. Abbott and Seroff remind us that the African American audience's demands before 1920 were much wider than the blues, anyway. —*EK*

11. The Blues on Paper

Long Lost Blues: Popular Blues in America, 1850–1920. By Peter Muir. Urbana-Champaign: University of Illinois Press, 2010. ISBN 978-0-252-03487-9 (hardcover), $85.00, ISBN 978-0-252-07676-3 (paperback), $35.00

In 1920, Okeh Records released the first blues record for African American customers, Mamie Smith's "Crazy Blues." However, the song on that record is not the earliest datable blues. Indeed, through the early 1930s, other African American musicians recorded some blues whose words or melodies may be traced to the 1910s, the 1900s, and even to the late 1890s. People who are fascinated with the earliest blues seek them in books and music scores printed before 1920. For the 1910s, the sheet music publications offer the best nonrecorded evidence of the blues, not only for how the blues was written in music notation, but also for how the earliest blues was witnessed firsthand by some composers. Some of these printed blues, in turn, were taken up by songsters and bluesmen for their busking.

Peter Muir's *Long Lost Blues* rescues from silence a decade for people now used to hearing blues on records. He begins with an overview of how sheet music dominated the popular music market one hundred years ago. He also presents the 1910s trend of "curing the blues with the blues," using appropriately quaint period words such as "homeopathic" and "allopathic." It seems back then that many people—and not just African Americans—wanted to hear the blues in order to lighten their depressions and moods, as we do today.

At the heart of the book are the appraisals of the 1910s blues publications by several African American composers. Chief among them is W. C. Handy, nine of whose blues are examined here, most of them best-selling titles like "Memphis Blues," "Hesitation Blues," and "St. Louis Blues." Other featured composers are those published by southern sheet music firms, namely Euday Bowman, Perry Bradford, and George W. Thomas, in whose music Muir discerns some then-contemporary southern street-performer practices. Handy and Bradford are highly regarded historical figures who later wrote autobiographies (see Handy, no. 12, and Bradford, no. 13), but here they are treated as musical craftsmen nearing the primes of their careers, when the blues was a novelty.

After completing his appraisal of the surviving printed blues of the 1910s, Muir spends the remainder of the book developing a highly informed opinion of how the earliest blues may have emerged and been shared among musicians during the 1900s and what he calls the "proto-blues" of the 1890s. This is very risky as there are very few reliable recordings of African American music of the 1900s. But Muir makes a worthwhile attempt by exploring the life of composer Hughie Cannon and by taking a survey of various twelve-measure songs that share the same tune as "Frankie and Johnny" (or "Frankie and Albert"). Does Muir help us find the first blues? Probably not, but his book and those by Seroff and Abbott (*Out of Sight*, no. 9, and *Ragged but Right*, no. 10), narrow the gap of likely styles and songs much closer than historians of early blues had thought twenty years ago.

To many blues fans today, the idea of white people trying to play sheet-music blues on their parlor pianos may seem "inauthentic," to use a term often used today to describe blues performers coming from outside African American cultures. But with a little sympathy, Muir affirms the home players' contribution to the spread of early blues in American popular music. "There were hundreds of thousands, even millions, of amateur singers, pianists, and other instrumentalists eager to try the latest musical novelties flowing from the printing presses of New York and Chicago," he writes. "While the result may have often been readings that were more enthusiastic than stylistically empathetic, the fact remains that domestic performance of blues was a crucial means of dissemination in the mainstream" (23).

The proportion of sales of sheet music to records has reversed over the past one hundred years since the earliest published sheet-music blues, with records now outselling printed music. The irony is that the blues has had a significant impact and influence on the record industry's effort to shift the customers' attentions from the composers to the performers. Muir helps us to appreciate again the composers. He even uses recording technology to draw attention not to himself as author and performer but to the composers. For the notated songs presented as illustrations in the book, Muir recorded his piano renditions, many of them in complete performances. The resulting recordings may be found for free on the companion website to the book, http://longlostblues.com/audio-examples-cover (accessed May 30, 2013). —*EK*

12. Blues to Be Heard and Seized

Father of the Blues: An Autobiography. By W. C. Handy. Edited by Arna Bontemps. Foreword by Abbe Niles. New York: Macmillan, 1941. London: Sidgwick and Jackson, 1957. London: Jazz Book Club, 1961. New York: Collier, 1970. New York: Da Capo, 1985, 1991. ISBN 0-306-80421-2 (paperback), $16.95

It is all too easy today—too fashionable, perhaps—to fault W. C. Handy for what he was not. He was not the "father of the blues," he was not a blues singer or improviser, and he didn't make records that appeal to us today. But in truth, our values for bluesmen have changed since Handy's 1958 death. We now prize improvisers over composers, hence we collect records as primary sources instead of sheet music. We mistrust notators of music more so than performers. Folklorists and the politically correct often emphasize equally the also-rans with the trendsetters. As a result, a great musician, like Handy, who had a widespread influence on the blues of the 1910s and 1920s, is now ignored, or worse, damned with faint praise.

His autobiography *Father of the Blues* appeared in 1941, at a time when the blues was beginning its transition to big-beat rhythm and blues and when the Great Migration of black labor was making one of its largest pushes to northern cities. Also, jazz was gaining some respectability among white listeners, with important books and magazine coverage being printed. Handy himself was recognized as "father of the blues" in a 1938 radio broadcast of "Ripley's Believe It or Not," which senior jazzman Jelly Roll Morton used to touch off a war of written words regarding Handy in the pages of *Downbeat* magazine. To some extent then, *Father of the Blues* may be read as Handy's most lengthy reply to Morton (Handy's recent biographer, David Robertson [*W. C. Handy: The Life and Times of the Man Who Made the Blues* (New York, Knopf, 2009), pp. 215–218], suggests reading it as such). But Handy always presented himself as a tall man who took the high road whenever possible, and his autobiography should be read whole as a journey on that high road.

William Christopher Handy was born in 1873 in Florence, Alabama, in an African American family that today we would call upper middle class and that, in their time, were called "respected." Handy's parents insisted to their children that they have an education and professional aspirations, regardless of the systematic limits being placed on blacks in the 1880s. Understandably, they were cross when the twelve-year-old Handy brought a guitar home, sending him back out to trade it for a dictionary. But there was no deterring him from music. In 1893 he made an extended sojourn to Chicago's World Fair and to St. Louis. From then to 1900, he toured as a trumpet player with Mahara's Minstrel Men. For two years, he took up a stable, nontouring job as an instructor at the Agricultural and Mechanical College in Normal, Alabama, although it meant taking an 87.5 percent pay cut from music. Returning to music and its higher wages was an easy decision for him to make, despite the uncertainty of the touring life.

Almost immediately, Handy received two offers to lead bands, one for a white band in Michigan, the other for an African American band in Clarksdale, Mississippi. Here we arrive at the most cited chapter in the book—the only chapter most people cite, it seems. One passage, undated by Handy, records the first time he heard a blues slide guitarist, at a train station in Tutwiler, Mississippi. The other, likewise undated, is when he allowed a few musicians—probably of the first generation of bluesmen in Mississippi—to play blues during a break in a concert in Cleveland, Mississippi, and thereby saw for himself that the blues could be profitable. Both incidents likely happened in 1903. Both passages are important to today's historians for documenting two of the earliest memories of blues in Mississippi. But for Handy, what they meant to him was crossing over from his middle-class standing to the poor class and its "low folk forms," as he put it. Up until then, music was a force of nature for him to hear, to seize by understanding, and to notate on paper. Likewise for the blues, although its difference was that it was not necessarily natural to Handy but rather artificial, and it was played by an economic class of people that he didn't interact with very often. The smart thing that Handy did— and he did do this, if nothing else—was recognizing in the novelty of the blues a potentially enduring appeal as a national music. In those days, sound recording had not yet replaced sheet music as the means of introducing new music. So Handy had to write down some blues songs, of his own composition if need be, to help the nascent blues endure.

Writing the music was the easy task. Marketing it was more difficult, and the remainder of *Father of the Blues* deals with the lessons learned in the business of music. Due to naivete, Handy let himself be cheated out of the copyrights for his first published blues, "The Memphis Blues," which turned out to be a big hit. Having learned his lesson, Handy protected himself with his firms Pace and Handy and Handy Brothers for his massive seller, "St. Louis Blues," and the follow-ups "Yellow Dog Blues" and "A Good Man Is Hard to Find." However, the success meant heightened expectations and more hard work, the increasing pressures of which Handy thought had led to his temporary spell of blindness in the early 1920s. The founding of the Negro Actors Guild of America and Handy's admittance into the performing rights organization ASCAP, both organizations he discusses later his book, helped to ease his worries for the long-term effects of his ongoing success.

Through it all, Handy lived in an economic class more prosperous than the bluesmen whom he encountered in Mississippi. When the city of Memphis dedicated Handy Park to him in 1931, the local blues musicians like Memphis Minnie, Frank Stokes, Furry Lewis, Gus Cannon, and the Memphis Jug Band were scuffling and hustling, as were Charlie Patton, Son House, and the young Robert Johnson across the state line in Mississippi. Yet racism and the threat of racial violence were factors in why he left the South around 1918. His success as a composer and sheet music publisher in New York pushed back the racial worries but never eliminated them. The last six chapters seem to lull the reader into a false sense of security with their recitations of honors and concerts. But then he relates a few incidents of discrimination occurring during his travels in 1939 and 1940, and his penultimate chapter, "Black and White," brings out in full the theme of race, in counterpoint to the prevailing theme of economic class. What he learned bitterly all his life was that class didn't matter. At the end of *Father of the Blues*, written when the United States was on the brink of entering World War II, Handy hopes—and sees through the ASCAP organization—a glimpse of a time when race no longer matters. —*EK*

13. Blues to Be Hustled

Born with the Blues: Perry Bradford's Own Story; The True Story of the Pioneering Blues Singers and Musicians in the Early Days of Jazz. By Perry Bradford. New York: Oak Publications, 1965

This short autobiography was published only in 1965, in hardcover and paperback editions. With over 340 copies reported in libraries, readers should easily be able to borrow a copy. Book collectors may find used copies with prices ranging from $25 to $55. Whether one wants to pay that much depends on how much patience one has in reading it.

A pioneering composer of blues, Perry Bradford (1895–1970) wrote a curious book: some boasting, some autobiography, and a lot of invective. Furthermore, he does not tell his life story in chronological order, but rather, he scrambles the order of events toward making an argumentative claim for himself in blues history. In some of his fourteen chapters, he seems to become "unstuck in time" (to borrow a phrase from Kurt Vonnegut's novel *Slaughterhouse-Five*). For example, in chapter 2, he starts in the 1960s present, then goes to 1920, then nearly back to the 1950s and 1960s, and then to his 1895–1907 childhood. In the fourth chapter, he rails against some music publishers in 1932, then criticizes sharply some jazz publications from 1938 and 1948, and then goes backward in time to his minstrel troupe experiences in 1907 and 1908. The fourteenth and final chapter begins in 1910, steps backward a bit to 1909, then back to 1910, peeks forward into 1921, shifts back to 1910, and ends with a conversation he had in 1946 about 1910. I can sympathize with those who have quit trying to read what can be a very confusing book.

Using the page numbers in the 1965 Oak edition, I suggest the following order of pages that can be used to read Bradford's life events in the order in which they happened. 1895–1907: pages 17–24; 1907–1908: 32–35; 1909–1910: 161–172; 1913: 94–95; 1917: 46–47, 158; 1918–1920: 13–14, 97–129; 1921: 153–155, 168, 130, 138–40, 150–52, 155–60; 1923: 130–135; 1925: 135–138; 1932: 25; 1939: 28–32, 88–92; 1939–1940: 93, 95–96; 1941: 48–49; 1945: 50–55; 1946: 172; 1948: 26–27; 1951: 15–16; 1950s–1965: 12–13.

The account that emerges from this reading emphasizes Bradford's prime years (1918–1921) in New York as a mover and shaker in early jazz and blues. He was born in 1895 in Alabama and raised in Georgia. In 1907 he joined a minstrel troupe, spent a little time in Chicago as a pianist, and arrived in New York in 1910. It seems he was active mostly in vaudeville during the 1910s. In 1918, he and singer Mamie Smith achieved some local stage success with his song "Harlem Blues." He spent 1919 and most of 1920 trying to get a record label to record Smith performing blues with a black band. In 1920, Okeh Records took a chance on Bradford, recording and issuing two records with him and Smith, the second of which had "Harlem Blues" retitled "Crazy Blues." The commercial success of "Crazy Blues" demonstrated that African Americans were willing to buy records by artists of their race. Through the mid-1920s, Bradford enjoyed additional success and profits from records and theater shows. However, his earnings dropped off sharply during the Depression, but he remained in New York. His personal drama of the 1930s and 1940s came not from lack of money but from the lack of acknowledgment of him in the early histories of jazz, especially in *Jazzmen* by Frederic Ramsey and Charles Edward Smith (1939) and *New Hot Discography* by Charles Delaunay (1948). Bradford's stated reason for writing *Born with the Blues* was to correct what he thought these writers had gotten wrong and in doing so had misguided local jazz fans. He was concerned about posterity, not prosperity.

Bradford didn't so much write as he asserted, bragged, reclaimed for himself what others took credit for, and claimed what others forgot. What he said most forcefully was that, yes, blues by African American singers were available on records for several years before Bessie Smith's first 78s in 1923 and that he should know because he was the one who made the first blues record in 1920. To give rhetorical impact, he rearranged his life's events so that the 1920 Okeh recording sessions with Mamie Smith are recounted as the late climax of the book, not midway, where it would have been told if he had proceeded in chronological order. Therefore, in chapter 2 he asserts that he was the one who was responsible for the first blues records. Two chapters later, he rails against the books by Ramsey and Smith and by Delaunay. In chapter 10, he gives his account of the 1920 Okeh sessions, and in the following chapter, he says that Delaunay had been misled by what he had been told in Paris by cornetist Johnny Dunn, whom Bradford had introduced only in the previous chapter about Smith's "Crazy Blues" session.

For me, there is an odd omission: Bradford does not mention pianist Willie "The Lion" Smith. The Lion is included visually in the book, in the 1920 publicity photo of Mamie Smith with the Jazz Hounds. A year before Bradford's book appeared, the Lion published *Music on My Mind: The Memoirs of an American Pianist* (New York: Doubleday), in which he claimed that he, not Bradford, had played piano at the 1920 "Crazy Blues" session for Okeh and, furthermore, that he didn't recall Bradford even being present. I wonder whether Bradford knew of the Lion's memoirs before *Born with the Blues* went to press, or at all. If he did, his fury would have been greater surely than what he felt about Ramsey, Smith, and Delaunay. —*EK*

14. The Two Ends of the Blues Spectrum

Big Road Blues: Tradition and Creativity in the Folk Blues. By David Evans. Berkeley: University of California Press, 1982. Reprint, New York: Da Capo, 1988. ISBN 0-306-80300-3, $18.00

Big Road Blues is the chief manual for applying folklore methods to the study of blues. As folklore has been one of the chief approaches to blues research, *Big Road Blues* may well be one of the most important books about blues. It is certainly one of the most ambitious in scope. As its author, David Evans, wrote in his introduction (7), "The folk processes that I shall discuss in this study are mainly those of transmission, learning, composition, recomposition, and handling of repertoire by blues singers." In other words, Evans aims to recast the researching of blues as a discipline of folklore, in contrast to the historical and discographical approaches to blues that other writers practiced at least since the first books by Samuel Charters and Paul Oliver appeared in the late 1950s (see nos. 63 and 64).

For such a radical work, *Big Road Blues* is not an easy book to read. It was originally a thick academic dissertation (*Tradition and Creativity in the Folk Blues*) submitted in 1976 toward a doctoral degree in folklore and mythology at the University of California at Los Angeles. The University of California Press published the manuscript mostly as it stood in its dissertation form, deleting some passages and adding subheadings to break up visually the lengthy text. Furthermore, Evans switches between present tense as appropriate for folklore writing style and past tense as appropriate for historical writing style, which often confuses my understanding. That most, if not all, of Evans's 1960s and 1970s field musicians have since died and hence are now historical would confuse the book's new readers in the 2010s as to what is living folk and what is completed past. Finally, as the book was a dissertation that was subject to approval by academic folklorists, it has an "underdog" tone affirming folklore as a viable approach to analyzing blues, which may be read as polemical by many readers with historical minds. Regardless, the serious reader about the blues is not excused from reading this influential text.

The key toward understanding this work may be found on page 3, where Evans admits, "Not all blues are purely folk blues, by which we mean traditional blues. Or rather, we should say that the 'folk' element is stronger in some blues than some others." Toward assessing a blues song, Evans recommends that "folk [blues] and popular blues should be viewed as two ends of the blues spectrum. The blues at one end are related to and affect those at the other end, and many blues would fall somewhere in between." To explain, on one hand, there are the "traditional blues" shared orally among common folk that have mostly gone unrecorded except for those "field recordings" made by Evans, John Lomax, Alan Lomax, Harry Oster, William Ferris, and other folklorists and anthropologists. Such recordings are made by these men for academic study, and therefore few have been released to the public, and they have ample documentation such as interviews with the musicians, photographs, and the researcher's supplementary notes. On the other hand, there are the "popular blues" composed or transcribed for publication as sheet music or recorded by musicians for commercial sale to blues fans and record collectors. As such, most commercial recordings are released to the public shortly after being made, with only so much text and photos as are necessary to promote the sale of the recording. There is a chance that a musician may record for a CD label a song he heard as a child among his uncles, and the resulting CD or download may become a new favorite among blues record collectors—in which case, the commercial end of Evans's blues spectrum is affecting a song shared at the traditional end, pulling it toward the middle of the spectrum. Yet also, there is the chance that a hit blues record may be shared among a group of listeners—its melody and best lyrics be sung aloud on some occasions—long after that record has gone out of print. In that case, the traditional end of the blues spectrum is affecting a song sold at the popular end, pulling it toward the middle of the spectrum. Therefore, it is not surprising that, as Evans says, most songs are somewhere in the middle. The task of the blues researcher while assessing a blues song is to determine from which direction it was pulled to its current location in the middle of the spectrum: from the traditional end, or from the popular end? For example, what would it mean for Tommy Johnson's commercial recording of "Big Road Blues," released in 1928 by the Victor Record Company?

To begin answering that question for himself, Evans has to unravel what was meant by "folk blues" and "popular blues" in a massive first chapter titled "Folk and Popular Blues." It may help some readers to know that this book chapter was originally three chapters in the 1976 dissertation. The description of blues (book pp. 16–32) was dissertation chapter 2, "The Blues" (pp. 45–75), the expository contrast of traditional/folk to popular (book pp. 32–87) was dissertation chapter 3, "The Development of Folk and Popular Blues" (pp. 76–182), and the history of folklore approaches in blues research (book pp. 87–105) was dissertation chapter 4, "Blues Scholarship" (pp. 183–225). First-time readers of *Big Road Blues* should read carefully that central section (pp. 32–87), but they may skim the remainder of that lengthy chapter. In the next book chapter, "The Blues Singer," Evans distills some techniques of lyric improvisation and word play that he discerned during many performances in the 1960s and 1970s of Mississippi bluesmen whom he had met and identified as being from the culture engendering "traditional" or "folk" blues. Also, he relays some observations on how the same singers adapted songs from commercial records, no matter how old or new are those records.

What Evans has to do next toward developing fully the "folk blues" end of the spectrum is to group together some "traditional" or "folk" blues singers into a regional or "local tradition." The third book chapter, "The Local Tradition," presents the blues from the 1920s through the 1970s associated with the town of

Drew, Mississippi. Presenting a local tradition is difficult because of the harnessing of several distinctive blues musicians to that tradition, and it is more difficult if the tradition is less noticeable to the musicians than to the researcher. Every word that Evans writes about "The Local Tradition" must be considered in light of the first two chapters. His sections on the characteristics of blues by musicians then still living in and around Drew bear the most careful attention. As for those sections examining commercial recordings, an impatient reader may criticize them and similar passages in the following chapter, "The Traditional Blues Song," especially if those records are by dead bluesmen and have been described previously and only by historians. But readers should focus less on the book's opinions on historical matters as dogmatic ends but rather concentrate more on its methods in folklore as dynamic means. More important, they should not lose the goal of being able to place any blues song within the spectrum between folk and popular. Therefore, every reader should proceed to the subsequent "Traditional Blues Song" chapter examining Tommy Johnson's "Big Road Blues" in order to see where Evans places the song within the spectrum and why. Previous writers had put the record toward the end of popular and commercial blues. Certainly Evans succeeds in pulling the song at least to the center, achieving an even balance between folk culture and commercial popular acclaim. Whether he has pulled it beyond the center to the folk end of the spectrum depends on how well the "Local Tradition" chapter has convinced the reader.

The only hardcover edition of *Big Road Blues* was the 1982 printing by the University of California Press. The Da Capo reprint available for the past twenty-five years has been only in paperback. Collectors should look into acquiring a copy of the 1976 dissertation (see appendix section about dissertations), as it has many passages later deleted from the book, including discussions of several songs and musicians not mentioned otherwise in the book version and additional critical assessments of previous research from the 1920s through the 1960s in folklore and blues. —*EK*

15. The Sexual Intensity of Ma Rainey

Mother of the Blues: A Study of Ma Rainey. By Sandra Lieb. Amherst: University of Massachusetts Press, 1981. ISBN 0-87023-394-7 (paperback), $24.95

Often referred to as the mother of the blues, Gertrude "Ma" Rainey (1886–1939) bridged the end of the minstrel show era and the early development of the blues. She fused elements of minstrel shows, vaudeville, and country blues into her music and performances. Her three-decade performing career at the beginning of the twentieth century, influence on the other classic blues singers of the 1920s (particularly Bessie Smith), and almost one hundred recordings solidify her place as one of the most important figures in early blues history.

Born in Columbus, Georgia, Gertrude Pridgett began performing as early as 1902, first with the Bunch of Blackberries and then with the Rabbit Foot Minstrels, which she joined after marrying Will "Pa" Rainey. She would later lead her own Georgia Smart Set group. She recorded exclusively for Paramount and toured for them on the TOBA (Theater Owners Booking Association) circuit.

Most of the biographies of Ma Rainey, Lieb's included, place her in comparison to Bessie Smith. They often point out that while Bessie learned from and perhaps got help getting her start from Ma, had the better voice, and was better looking, Ma Rainey often put on the better show. Unlike Bessie Smith, who often performed in New York and captured the attention of more urban jazz artists and critics, Rainey stayed mostly in the South and in Chicago and retained much more of a "down-home" sound. Bessie Smith received significant publicity in the more mainstream press, partly from critic Carl van Vechten's infatuation with her. Ma Rainey, on the other hand, was publicized quite well by the black press; the *Chicago Defender* ran many Paramount ads for her recordings. Lieb covers Ma Rainey's bisexuality, probable relationship with Bessie Smith, and sexual attraction to younger men but doesn't venture into sensationalism or tabloid-style writing.

While the first blues artists to be commercially recorded on a large scale were female, serious scholarship of these classic blues singers came rather late. Of course they were written about in the general histories (Oliver, Charters, etc.); Paul Oliver and Chris Albertson had written books on Bessie Smith, and Derrick Stewart-Baxter wrote the short *Ma Rainey and the Classic Blues Singers* (Stein and Day, 1970), but it wasn't until Sandra Lieb's *Mother of the Blues* was published in 1981 that a work significantly examined the music of Ma Rainey.

Mother of the Blues is the product of Sandra Lieb's 1975 Stanford dissertation, "The Message of Ma Rainey's Blues: A

Biographical and Critical Study of America's First Woman Blues Singer." Lieb's research draws upon existing published biographical information about Ma Rainey, advertisements for Rainey's records in the *Chicago Defender*, interviews with musicians who knew and worked with Rainey (Thomas Dorsey, Sam Chatmon, Clyde Bernhardt, Sunnyland Slim, and Willie Humphries), her own lyric transcriptions, and examination of lead sheets deposited at the Library of Congress for copyright purposes. The book is well documented with extensive endnotes, bibliography, and general and song title indexes. Lieb also includes a very useful classification guide for all of Ma Rainey's recordings, indicating song titles, matrix numbers, issue numbers, and song form (i.e.—twelve-bar blues, eight-bar blues, popular forms, etc.). Another appendix gives the author, publisher, and date for every song recorded by Ma Rainey. The book includes twenty-two illustrations.

Despite all the documentation and analysis provided by Lieb, there are still areas of Ma Rainey's biography that need fleshing out. Since most people who would have known her have passed away, much of this information is unfortunately probably lost to history. The section on Ma Rainey's life is the thinnest part of the book. Most of the biographical information here is a retelling of what is already published in other sources. Lieb makes it very clear, however, that this book "does not intend to be . . . the final biography of Ma Rainey." She states that the purpose of this book is "to explore her life and performance style and to analyze the themes of her recorded song lyrics." The second chapter of the book is an examination of Ma Rainey's style. The last two chapters are analyses of themes within Ma Rainey's songs and a critical examination of the lyrics.

The analysis of thematic concepts in Ma Rainey's songs is the strongest part of the book. Lieb took great care in creating the most authentic transcriptions of Rainey's work to date. It is easy to fall into the trap of assuming all blues lyrics are autobiographical, though Lieb is careful to note authorship of all works analyzed. While Ma Rainey did personally write one-third of the songs she recorded, the majority were written by others and often contain lyric fragments from earlier sources. Lieb points out that the songs Ma Rainey did write don't show any major thematic differences from those written by others. Even many of the songs about love (three-quarters of her total output) and ill treatment by cheating men were penned by male songwriters. But this is often the nature of the blues: performers can sing the words and stories of others and make them their own and, in so doing, publicly share in common experiences felt by many. Lieb writes, "Her great theme is the intense sexual love between men and women, and her secondary themes concern the sensual, earthy, and often rough side of life: music and dancing, drunkenness and superstition, lesbianism and homosexuality, women in prison, jealousy and murder."

Ma Rainey was truly one of the most significant figures in early blues history. Sandra Lieb's work helped draw attention to that importance, and *Mother of the Blues* has been influential on later examinations of female blues artists and feminist studies of blues women, including Daphne Duval Harrison's *Black Pearls: Blues Queens of the 1920s* (no. 17) and Angela Davis's *Blues Legacies and Black Feminism: Gertrude "Ma" Rainey, Bessie Smith, and Billie Holiday* (no. 22). —*GJ*

16. The Empress of the Blues

Bessie. By Chris Albertson. New York: Stein and Day, 1972. Revised and expanded edition, New Haven, CT: Yale University Press, 2003. 314 pp. ISBN 0-300-09902-9 (hardcover), $29.95

Known as "the Empress of the Blues," Bessie Smith was the most powerful singer of the classic blues era, influencing singers such as Victoria Spivey, Billie Holiday, Mahalia Jackson, Janis Joplin, Queen Latifah, and many others. Though she recorded over 150 songs with musicians like Louis Armstrong, James P. Johnson, and Fletcher Henderson, many biographies devote most attention to her death in a 1937 automobile accident. Columbia talent scout John Hammond helped perpetuate a rumor that Smith's death was partly the result of her being refused treatment at a whites-only hospital. This falsehood was so much a part of public consciousness that Edward Albee penned the play *The Death of Bessie Smith* in 1959.

Born in Chattanooga, Tennessee, in 1894, Bessie Smith would soon go on to busk with her brother Andrew to help raise money for the family. Around 1912, with the help of her older brother Clarence, she joined a traveling show as a dancer and began learning from Ma Rainey, improving her skills as a singer and entertainer. Bessie Smith's recording career began in 1923 for Columbia with "Gulf Coast Blues"/"Downhearted Blues." The record quickly became a hit, helping launch her popularity as one of the top entertainers of the decade. She was even featured in the 1929 film *St. Louis Blues*, singing W. C. Handy's titular song, for which she was known from her 1925 recording.

Bessie Smith has had more books written about her life than just about any other blues artist, with the exception of Robert Johnson. In 1959, Paul Oliver penned the first substantial work on her life, *Bessie Smith*, as part of Cassell and Company's Kings of Jazz series. Edward Brooks wrote *The Bessie Smith Companion: A Critical and Detailed Appreciation of the Recordings* for Cavendish Publishing in 1982. Angela Y. Davis's 1999 book *Blues Legacies and Black Feminism: Gertrude "Ma" Rainey, Bessie Smith, and Billie Holiday* (no. 22) looks at Smith and other classic blues/jazz singers through a feminist lens, showing how these singers empowered black women. In *Blues Empress in Black Chattanooga: Bessie Smith and the Emerging Urban South* (University of Illinois, 2008), Michelle R. Scott uses Bessie Smith's biography as a framework to examine African American history and sociological struggles in the postslavery South. Bessie's bisexuality is the major focus of Jackie Kay's *Bessie Smith* (Absolute Press, 1997). There have even been children's books written about the Empress of the Blues, such as Sue Stauffacher and John Holyfield's *Bessie Smith and the Night Riders* (Putnam, 2006).

Chris Albertson's *Bessie*, though, is the best single source on Bessie Smith. Albertson has established himself as the top Bessie Smith scholar. He won a Grammy for the liner notes he wrote for Bessie Smith's 1970 Columbia album *The World's Greatest Blues Singer* and also wrote extensive notes for Columbia/Legacy's *Bessie Smith: The Complete Recordings* (1991). Like many biographers who are great fans of their subjects, Albertson is not without bias; he often rationalizes Bessie's bad behavior while demonizing it in others, particularly in her estranged husband, Jack Gee.

Albertson's interviews with Bessie's niece Ruby Walker Smith and others help provide an intimate look at the various spheres of Smith's life: public entertainer, friend, family member, and lover. More than most authors, Albertson shows more of Bessie Smith's personal life, with all of its complexities, without falling into sensationalism.

Bessie gives an excellent overview of the TOBA (Theater Owners Booking Association) touring circuit and the classic blues period in general. Albertson also does a good job of showing inequality and the often unethical practices of the recording industry. Bessie Smith received more money than any other African American performer of the 1920s, but she received no royalties, just a small amount for the actual recording session—and then only for those sides that were actually pressed.

The 2003 revised and expanded edition of *Bessie* is a significant expansion from the first edition of 1972, adding over sixty pages with a smaller font size. In the thirty years since the book was first published, Albertson was able to interview more people who knew Bessie Smith and shed more light on her youth. The most significant addition is an epilogue discussing new findings after the initial publication and various movie proposals based on the life of Bessie Smith. Albertson also updates the discography to include newer reissues of her works. One issue with the 2003 version is that the images are generally smaller than those in the 1972 edition, making it harder to see some details.

Anyone wanting to learn about Bessie Smith should turn first to *Bessie*, revised and expanded edition. —*GJ*

17. Going Public through the Blues

Black Pearls: Blues Queens of the 1920s. By Daphne Duval Harrison. New Brunswick, NJ: Rutgers University Press, 1987. 285 pp. ISBN 978-0-8135-1279-2. Reprint, 1990. 299 pp. ISBN 978-0-8135-1280-8 (paperback), $25.00

In *Black Pearls*, Daphne Harrison asks why and to what effect did African American women singers record the blues during the 1920s. This overall question had not been considered previously by Derrick Stewart-Baxter in his overview book, *Ma Rainey and the Classic Blues Singers* (London: Studio Vista, 1970), and only in part by Chris Albertson and Sandra Lieb in their respective books on Bessie Smith (no. 16) and Ma Rainey (no. 15). As an African American professor at the University of Maryland, Baltimore County, Harrison was well situated to evaluate as a collected group the "classic blues" women of the 1920s through history, culture, women's studies, and music. In so doing, she found some answers about the need and purpose for women to have sung the blues in the ways they did during the 1920s.

In the first three chapters, Harrison shows that during the 1910s, southern singers of the blues performed in traveling "tent" shows and northern singers in the cabarets. But after World War

I and during the 1920s, the Theater Owners Booking Association (TOBA) established a national circuit for African American entertainers, including the most popular blues singers. While there were male performers on the TOBA circuit, the African American women singers and dancers are remembered more. Why were there so many women? For a start, young women who were born after 1900 were part of the first generation of African Americans who had some secondary education, including geography (201). At the same time, the railroad networks were developed fully, offering cheap travel from farms to faraway American cities. As part of the early waves of the Great Migration, black women flocked to the cities where there were prospects of good jobs, performance theaters, and, after 1920, recording firms that were interested in recording women blues singers.

The high sales of Mamie Smith's first blues release, "Crazy Blues," on its appearance in 1920 indicated a high consumer interest among African Americans for blues on records. From then through 1926, the vast majority of blues on records were sung by city women. To be sure, recording industry executives didn't think of male blues singers (and wouldn't think of them until Blind Blake and Blind Lemon Jefferson made their first 78s in 1926). In the critical third chapter, "Wild Women Don't Have the Blues," Harrison gives many reasons why the women singers were willing to record as many blues as they did. There was good money to be made as a recording artist, especially if one had a hit record, and there was much publicity to be had through record advertisements. There was and still is a catharsis of emotion through blues singing, yet Harrison singles out and values the aspects of articulateness and toughness, which are hallmarks of today's African American oral arts, including rap. Most important—a chief finding of *Black Pearls*—is the purpose of blues singing as "retaliation" or "going public." As Harrison explains (89): "This tactic derives from a practice employed by African and Afro-Caribbean women to embarrass men who either neglected or abused their women. Usually when black women 'go public,' it is to negotiate respect, asserts anthropologist Roger Abrahams." During the 1920s, there was much for African American women to "go public" about: inadequate housing, crummy food, little pay, men leaving to find better work elsewhere, the same men finding new women where they had found better work. As Harrison summarizes (89), "Blues of this nature communicated to women listeners that they were members of a sisterhood that did not have to tolerate mistreatment."

Harrison then presents the life stories of four women singers and how each of them "went public." She had met each of them, and she asked them questions about matters that the records and documents hint at or fail to explain. Sippie Wallace was known as the "Texas Nightingale" for her earthy shouts and moaning wails, and in the 1920s she performed to African American audiences on the TOBA circuit. Harrison notes that many of Wallace's blues lyrics dealt with themes of abandonment, yet through singing them Wallace resolves such hurts by asserting a sexual prowess (119). Victoria Spivey moaned with a dry-sounding, nasal tone, which on records makes her seem like a second-tier singer compared to the greats (but not second rate). Nonetheless, Spivey was a "queen of the blues," promoting the music for over sixty years and helping friends and younger musicians with opportunities in performing and recording. Edith Wilson sang on the TOBA circuit, but she also took bookings on the Keith and Orpheum circuits for white audiences. Her performance style of her low-down blues was somewhat cool and restrained in a manner befitting a "class act." Alberta Hunter likewise was a city singer, but one who sang more in cabarets than in theaters. Harrison describes her style as swinging, with an assertiveness of a liberated city woman (200). Moreover, Harrison discerns from Hunter's performances a woman's sense of when to persist in a tough situation and when to leave it (207–208).

How much of what Harrison learned from the still-living singers may be applied to those who died a long time ago? In an appendix, the author herself seeks what is valid by looking at eight singers, especially at length for Lizzie Miles, Clara Smith, and Trixie Smith, but also at Ida Cox (a great singer for Paramount Records in the 1920s), Lucille Hegamin, Rose Henderson, Chippie Hill, and Sara Martin. As one reads through the book, three names recur often: Florence Mills, Sophie Tucker, and Ada "Bricktop" Smith. Florence Mills was a top African American entertainer on New York stages who was too versatile to be classed as a blues singer; no sound recordings of her singing survive. Sophie Tucker was white, her singing style on records a bit too sultry and hammish for today's tastes, but according to Harrison, in the 1920s she had as much influence on African American singers as they had on her in the 1910s. Bricktop Smith was as versatile a singer and dancer as Mills, but her legend rests chiefly in being a cosmopolitan operator of nightclubs in Paris and Mexico City. These three women may seem phantomlike, but perhaps Mills and Smith, at least, had shared in the same "going public" ethos that their blues counterparts enacted.

Black Pearls is currently available in paperback; the hardcover edition has been long unavailable, but affordable copies may be found on used-book websites. The important chapter "Wild Women Don't Have The Blues" was serialized in 1988 in three parts in *Living Blues* magazine no. 79 (March/April 1988), 25–30; no. 80 (May/June 1988), 28–30; and no. 81 (July/August 1988), 27–31. —*EK*

18. Nostalgia in Memphis for the Days When Jug Bands Were King

Memphis Blues and Jug Bands. By Bengt Olsson. London: Studio Vista, 1970. ISBN 0-289-70033-7 (out of print)

Memphis has long been a center for the blues. Musicians from the Mississippi and Arkansas Deltas gravitated to the streets of Memphis, hoping to escape sharecropping and make a living doing what they loved. For most of the twentieth century, towns in the Delta lacked any real recording studios. Memphis provided the closest outlet for talented performers to try to cut a hit record or simply to make it performing in the many clubs on Beale Street.

Much has been written of W. C. Handy and other important figures of the Memphis music scene. Swedish author Bengt Olsson chose to focus *Memphis Blues* on the lesser-documented figures of this area. He leaves out people like Memphis Minnie and Rev. Robert Wilkins, feeling they have been covered well by *Blues Unlimited* magazine. Since Olsson's publication, more research has been done on artists such as Gus Cannon, the Memphis Jug Band, Furry Lewis, and others, but when *Memphis Blues* came out, little had been written on many of these artists. Even more than forty years after *Memphis Blues*, there has been little documentation of people like Jim Jackson, Robert Burse, Milton Roby, Dewey Corley, Jed Davenport, and others examined by Olsson.

Much of Olsson's book comes from a trip he took with fellow Swede and music enthusiast Peter Måhlin to Memphis in 1969. Like many other European blues enthusiasts of the time, Olsson's first exposure to the blues was through records. Olsson would make several more trips to the United States, where he would record a number of lesser-known artists for Flyright. Some of these were reissued, along with previously unreleased tracks, by Birdman Records in 2005–2006 and Sutro Park in 2010.

Memphis Blues documents the world of late-1960s house parties and picnics, street musicians around W. C. Handy Park and Beale Street, and jug bands and medicine shows. While the book centers on musicians living in and around Memphis in 1969, through their stories, Olsson presents an abbreviated history of jug bands and raw blues players of this area.

Jug bands had their heyday in the early decades of the twentieth century, with the Memphis Jug Band most active in the late 1920s through the 1930s, roughly contemporary with Cannon's Jug Stompers. Some of the jug bands would reform for various occasions up through the 1960s. These bands featured washtub or oil-can bass (sometimes called a bull fiddle), banjo, guitar, fiddle, kazoo, ukulele, and the jug. The backbone of the jug band is, of course, the jug. Players blow across an empty jug to produce a variety of low-pitched tones to serve the role of a bass, trombone, or tuba within the ensemble.

Memphis Blues provides some of the earliest research into the world of Memphis blues and jug bands. It helped set the stage for much subsequent research in this area. There are, however, some problems with the book. Some of the language is a bit sensationalist and often waxes nostalgic for the days when jug bands were king. Sections of the book awkwardly shift to the next topic with little or no transition. Within a section, Olsson may give a few brief words about an artist and then present quotes about that musician from those who knew him or her. These quotes are often awkwardly juxtaposed and sometimes read like a list of randomly assembled facts and opinions. At times it is unclear whose voice we are reading; is it Olsson's, or is he still quoting? The photo quality is quite poor for most images in the book. Facial features can barely be made out in a number of shots. Despite their artistic flaws, it is great that Olsson was able to photographically document some of these little-known figures.

Plans were in the works for Taylor and Francis to publish a major expanded (256 pages) edition of *Memphis Blues* in 2008, but Bengt Olsson passed away on January 19 of that year. It is unknown what plans are in place to see this updated manuscript published.

Other books have documented the Memphis blues scene but have overlooked many of the artists covered by Olsson. The Ernest Withers and Daniel Wolff photo book, *The Memphis Blues Again: Six Decades of Memphis Music Photographs* (no. 66), features blues and soul heavyweights like B. B. King, W. C. Handy, Isaac Hayes, and others. In 175 pages, the only photo of any of the musicians covered in Olsson's book has a caption simply reading "Opening of the Al Jackson, Sr., Esso Servicenter, 1963." The musicians in the photo, Laura Dukes, Milton Roby, and others, aren't even acknowledged. William Bearden's *Memphis Blues: Birthplace of a Musical Tradition* (Arcadia, 2006) focuses mostly on later blues developments in the city. Despite the advertising quote by R. J. Smith on Robert Gordon's *It Came from Memphis* (Faber and Faber, 1995) that "this is a book where Gus Cannon is more important than Elvis," Cannon receives only passing mention.

There are some works that have gone into more detail of the musicians included in Olsson's book. Fred Hay's *Goin' Back to Sweet Memphis: Conversations with the Blues* (University of Georgia, 2001) includes an extensive interview with Laura Dukes, who performed with the Memphis Jug Band. Dave Harris's self-published *Head, Hands, & Feet: A Book of One Man Bands* (2012) has an excellent section on one-man bands in the Memphis area, focusing particularly on Joe Hill Louis. Paul Oliver's *The Story of the Blues* (no. 2) includes a chapter on jug bands and medicine shows in Memphis. *Living Blues* magazine has included a number of more extensive interviews with musicians covered by Olsson.

Memphis Blues includes an appendix of 1929 and 1930 Brunswick recordings in Memphis, a short sampling of lyrics (transcribed by Tony Russell) recorded by Memphis artists, a bibliography of Memphis blues (compiled by Tony Russell), and a discography of Memphis musicians' recordings.

Despite its flaws and brevity, *Memphis Blues* gives a good look at the changing world of music in Memphis in the late 1960s, where many of the old jug-band players were dwindling and new sounds were emerging. —*GJ*

19. Blues Was Only Half of Black Music during the 1920s

Songsters and Saints: Vocal Traditions on Race Records. By Paul Oliver. Cambridge: Cambridge University Press,

1984. ISBN 0-521-24827-2 (hardcover), ISBN 0-521-26942-3 (paperback), $43.00

"The Half Ain't Never Been Told" was a 1928 sermon record by Rev. F. W. McGee, which Paul Oliver takes as his point of departure for *Songsters and Saints.* As Oliver explains in his introduction, if the history of blues was the half about African American music that was told previously, the other half was the African American street songs and sacred music recorded through 1932. Since Oliver had told very well *The Story of the Blues* (no. 2) in 1968, he knew he had to present a study of the rest of what was listed in Dixon and Godrich's prewar discography *Blues and Gospel Records 1902–1943* (no. 41), whose third edition was published in 1982. Therefore, *Songsters and Saints* is the companion to *The Story of the Blues*; blues readers who have one need to acquire the other.

The keystone of the work is the fourth chapter, titled "Fantasy, Reality, and Parody," placed between the three chapters about secular music and the four others about sacred music. The chapter's title words seem random, perhaps arbitrary, but in Oliver's context, they form his overall message. "Fantasy" refers to the surface impressions of African American life as happy and carefree as they seem to people observing from outside the culture. It would also refer to an ideal utopia where its people would indeed be happy and carefree; it would not necessarily be the "the land of milk and honey," but it could be the attainment of "American Dream"—new house, new car, faithful spouse, and healthy kids. "Reality" would be the conditions of living of those who fail to attain the American Dream or, worse yet, fail to "keep up with the Joneses." "Parody" would thus be the ridicule of that communal fantasy by using the hard lessons learned personally from "reality." I presume, then, that the laughter resulting from such parody would be the kind of "laughing to keep from crying." It is interesting to note that this chapter leads immediately to the part about preachers, about whom the songsters sang of leading profane lives under sacred pretenses, such as Charlie Patton's "Elder Greene."

As Oliver explains in the opening chapter, the term "songster" is a borrowing from the little books of song lyrics that were sold during the nineteenth century. Likewise, a singer as a songster would know hundreds of lyrics and their related melodies. As examples who recorded before 1932, Oliver names Peg Leg Howell, Sam Jones, a.k.a. Stovepipe Papa no. 1, Gus Cannon, Blind

Blake, Harvey Hull, Jim Jackson, Frank Stokes, Willie Newburn, and Henry Thomas. There are many other such musicians whom Oliver mentions briefly, but his comments and asides on each are worth looking up (the general index is invaluable for such use). Initially, Oliver discusses the dance songs and show routines, many of which he says are helpful to suggesting likely dates of origin, regardless of when a musician recorded his or her rendition in the 1920s or 1930s. Then he studies the "songs of the ragtime era"—territory later to be explored in greater detail by Abbott and Seroff in *Ragged but Right* (no. 10)—but he discusses the songs less for the musicians who recorded them later in their careers and more for the composers. While he mentions the song composers Chris Smith, Elmer Bowman, and Cecil Mark, he singles out Irving Jones as one whose material was widely performed by the songsters. He adds a chapter about the "road shows"—the tent shows and the circuses, and also the smaller-scale medicine shows where some musicians like Pink Anderson were most likely going to be heard by white audiences.

As for the "saints," Oliver provides valuable comments about the Baptist preachers sermonizing, the Sanctified sect's singers hollering, and the independent "jack-leg" preachers singing. Many listeners of reissues tend to skip over the recorded spoken Baptist sermons, but Oliver reminds us that in their time, these records sold very well, pointing out several features that made the discs worth buying and playing often. He affirms the spoken performances by J. C. Burnett and A. W. Nix, and he presents at length the long career of Rev. J. M. Gates. In accordance with their musical policy, singers of the Sanctified sect and the Holiness denomination performed with guitars and brass instruments and often sang loudly, assertively, and ecstatically. Oliver encourages the reader to explore the records made by Rev. D. C. Rice and by pianist Arizona Dranes, both of whose legacies are reissued on Document Records. He also does well to point out women in sacred music, including my favorites, Bessie Jackson, Mother McCollum, and Sister Callie Fancy. If one wishes to hear instead ethereal singing, one should listen to Washington Phillips, whom Oliver selects to open the chapter about the independent "jack-leg" preachers on records; some of them are also known as "guitar evangelists." Some of these musicians were as active in blues as in religious music, especially Blind Lemon Jefferson of Texas and Charlie Patton and Roosevelt Graves of Mississippi. But others seemed to have performed only sacred material, like the superb Blind Willie Johnson, on whose records Oliver dwells at length. The "jack-leg" chapter closes with an examination of topical songs about the *Titanic* and other contemporary disasters. In such preaching context, these topical songs seem not as oral news or commemorations but rather as righteous admonishments on the folly of man. Likewise for the "survivors of the ballad tradition" like John Henry, Frankie of "Frankie and Albert," Stagger Lee, Railroad Bill, the boll weevil, and the racehorse Ten Broeck. The air of righteousness from the "jack-leg" chapter is sustained into the discussion of these turn-of-the-century narrative ballads, however epic and often celebratory they are.

Songsters and Saints remains in print in paperback. Its 1984 hardcover edition has no differences from the paperback version. Book collectors seeking a hardcover copy should expect to spend through the used-book market double or triple the price of a new paperback copy, especially if they wish to acquire one with its dust jacket. Also, as companions to the book, there were two double-LP record sets, *Songsters and Saints: Vocal Traditions on Race Records,* volumes 1 and 2, on Matchbox Records in England (Matchbox MSEX 2001–2002 and MSEX 2003–2004). To my knowledge, neither set has been reissued on CD. However, the book's appendix, "A Guide to Reissued Recordings," lists the contents of the two sets so that the readers can find each track on the various Document CD reissues or through Document's authorized mp3 web sources. —*EK*

20. Music More Durable Than Furniture

Paramount's Rise and Fall. By Alex van der Tuuk. Denver, CO: Mainspring Press, 2003. ISBN 0-9671819-4-1 (hardcover). Revised and expanded edition, 2012. ISBN 0-98520-042-8 (paperback), $39.00

For about ten years until 1932, Paramount Records recorded and issued many classic performances of blues, from the city vaudeville singing of Lucille Hegamin and Alberta Hunter to the rural string-band playing of the Mississippi Sheiks. Every blues lover has at least three or four CDs of Paramount-made music. For the many great performances it recorded, one would think that Paramount was all about the music. But as one reads about the label, one realizes that Paramount was all about making money for the Wisconsin Chair Company and that the records

Paramount made were all about selling phonographs in cabinets made by that company. Older blues fans who still have their issues of *78 Quarterly* will remember the remarkable five-part series about Paramount written by Stephen Calt and Gayle Dean Wardlow (issue nos. 3–7 [1988–1992]). But Alex van der Tuuk succeeded in telling the history of Paramount not from the perspective of Paramount, but from that of Wisconsin Chair.

The Wisconsin Chair Company lasted from 1888 to 1954. As van der Tuuk points out in his introduction, the firm not only made furniture for homes and schools, but it also made money from real estate, mining, and leasing for oil and gas. In 1917, it entered the recorded music business as a "loss-leader" accessory to the phonograph cabinets it manufactured; in fact, the original logo on Paramount disc labels was of an eagle holding a phonograph cabinet. Not long after replacing the cabinet with planet Earth on the logo, Paramount began recording blues and black sacred music, whose sales eventually led to the label yielding more profit for Wisconsin Chair than the phonograph cabinet venture.

What made Paramount attractive to record buyers were its blues and sacred artists. Through the mid-1920s, in studios in Chicago and New York, it recorded music by the leading African American acts in jazz and blues, including King Joe Oliver with young Louis Armstrong, Alberta Hunter, and Ma Rainey. Then, in 1926, it presented Texas singer/guitarist Blind Lemon Jefferson, whose commercial success led Paramount to find and record guitar blues talent across the South, including Blind Blake and Charlie Patton. In 1929, at Wisconsin Chair's Grafton, Wisconsin, campus, Paramount set up its own recording studio. In its desire—soon to become desperation—to have one more hit record, Paramount executives recorded anyone whom its retail salesmen recommended, including those artists whose performances now sound exotic to our ears, like Son House, Skip James, Geechie Wiley, and King Solomon Hill.

To the Wisconsin Chair executives, success with their Paramount Records subsidiary meant squeezing every last penny of profit. One example was the composition of the 78 rpm discs. Thirty percent of a typical record released by Victor and Columbia was shellac. Paramount's records were 20 percent shellac, the remainder consisting of mineral black, lampblack, cotton flock, and "rotten stone," which was limestone mixed with silica. In later years, abrasives were added as ingredients, which van der Tuuk describes as resulting in an asphalt-like base. It is no wonder that even freshly pressed Paramount 78s on their first playing sounded rough, as if already worn. But in the early years of Paramount as a "loss leader" for Wisconsin Chair, this and other cost-cutting measures meant that much money was saved from loss and, at the height of Paramount's distribution, that much money was saved as precious profit. The life of Paramount was a crass existence at best. Several assistants and scouts worked without set salaries and fees, instead earning their money through song copyrights (as did African American executive and producer Mayo Williams) and retail sales (as did Henry C. Speir, a scout who ran a record store in Jackson, Mississippi). If later Paramount executives like Art Laibley seem now to cast long historical shadows, it is because the sun was setting on their days. The last Paramount discs were released in 1932. A year later at a Christmas party, in an action worthy of the movie villain Henry F. Potter (of *It's a Wonderful Life*), the management fired the remaining Paramount employees.

Van der Tuuk relates the whole Paramount history from the overall perspective of Wisconsin Chair, not from the ground view of the artists, scouts, and label executives as had Calt and Wardlow in their articles. In taking that perspective, van der Tuuk succeeded in locating descendants of Wisconsin Chair, who helped him tell the rest of the story of the company. After closing Paramount, Wisconsin Chair endured the Depression by regaining a share of the furniture market and earned additional profits through munitions contracts during World War II. The end came quickly: the leading salesman left and took several accounts with him, and the company found it could not compete with the southern furniture firms who paid lower wages to their nonunionized employees. The remaining Wisconsin Chair plant in Port Washington, Wisconsin, was closed in 1954 and was eventually demolished. Although considered disposable in their time, the Paramount 78s and the music they contain abide more in our culture than does Wisconsin Chair furniture.

Paramount's Rise and Fall has appeared in two editions. The first was published in 2003 in hardcover, and it was subtitled *A History of the Wisconsin Chair Company and Its Recording Activities*. The second, in 2012 in paperback only, is a revised version with two new chapters, and it is subtitled *The Roots and History of Paramount Records*. Since copies of the 2002 hardcover publication fetch a minimum of $50 and considerably more on used-book websites, blues newcomers should not hesitate in purchasing the updated and expanded paperback edition. In recent years, Van der Tuuk has published more about Paramount that lovers of that old label may want to look into purchasing. To date, he has published with Guido van Rijn three volumes of Paramount discographies (*The L Matrix Series, The 20000 & Gennett Matrix Series,* and *Roseheaver, Marsh and 2000 Series,* all Overveen, Netherlands: Agram Books, 2011, 2012, and 2013, respectively; they may be ordered through van Rijn's Agram website, http://home.tiscali.nl/guido/index.htm., accessed June 19, 2013). For lovers of the music, he has edited two deluxe volumes of Paramount recordings for Revenant Records, whose ample documentation contains much previously unpublished information. —*EK*

21. The Shellac Broadside

78 Blues: Folksongs and Phonographs in the American South. By John Minton. Jackson: University Press of Mississippi, 2008. ISBN 978-1-934110-19-5 (hardcover), $50.00, ISBN 1-61703-042-2 (paperback), $30.00

One feature of some blues records made before World War II are the bits spoken by the performer at the beginning of and during the performance. Country "hillbilly" records of the same period have them, too. In what way are we to hear them? It is too easy to dismiss them, concentrating instead on the musical performance, including the sung lyrics. But many singers spoke on their records, so they must have intended some kind of communication through the shellac. John Minton explored possible answers to this question in his 1990 doctoral dissertation "Phonograph Blues: Folksong and Media in the Southern United States before the Second World War" (University of Texas at Austin), which he later published under the title *78 Blues.*

How did the people who purchased blues and hillbilly records before 1942 listen to them upon getting home? While there are no interviews or written studies from that time about this topic, Minton says clues toward some answers are provided on and in the records themselves. The clues become noticeable when the 78 rpm records are thought of as successors to the printed broadsides. Broadsides were sheets printed with lyrics to individual songs, and they were posted, sold, and shared in England

and the United States during the eighteenth and nineteenth centuries. As his thesis for the book, Minton says that Americans, especially southern Americans, between the two world wars carried their habits and ways of reading and singing from broadsides over to listening to records. Such carrying over, Minton argues, required the listeners to adjust mentally—to reimagine—to the sounds they were hearing on the records from how they were hearing music performed live. Such reimagining could lead to thinking of records not merely as audio documents but as vessels of unfolding musical events that invite some active participation from the listeners. Therefore, the spoken utterances from the performers are not mere asides but a way to draw listeners into the record's playback event despite the distances from and time since the location and circumstances of the recording.

Minton thinks there were at least four such means, each of which he demonstrates in individual chapters. The first he treats (chapter 3) is the imitation by the performers of a public event where music is played, such as a dance or a party. As blues examples, Minton cites rent parties (Bill Broonzy's "House Rent Stomp"), dance venues (Henry Brown's "Stomp 'Em Down to the Bricks"), church services from river baptisms to funerals, and neighborhoods (Gus Cannon's "Madison Street Rag"). "This real-life play-acting," asserts Minton (61), "seems a natural response by community-based musicians to a novel medium," that is, records for southern Americans. The second means (chapter 4) includes the record's listeners with its performers in a joint imitation of the sharing of folk music. How is such folk-music sharing achieved when the performers' role in shellac is unchangeable? Most likely by the recording musician encouraging the listener to sing along. Minton suggests that those musicians who on early records encouraged sing-alongs did so because they were more used to making music for participating listeners and dancers than for immobile microphones.

The remaining two means have the performers accept and refer to 78 rpm record releases during the performance. The third of the four means entails the record serving as its own context for the performance. In other words, recording musicians would refer to fellow recording artists whom the purchasers would have known through other records, even if the purchasers may never have heard those artists in person. The best example that Minton uses is the memorial song, especially the kind written and recorded in

1930 in memory of Blind Lemon Jefferson, the popular bluesman known throughout the South for his Paramount Records releases. The fourth means goes a step further than the third, where the physical record affirms its own existence and—most important to this means—commissions new music created solely for the recording studio and not for rent parties and dances. Since 1950, some blues and much jazz, rock, and country music are studio creations which have yet to be tested by being performed live in front of audiences. This is far different from the simulations of live performance conditions that early southern artists recorded.

To illustrate his presentation, Minton drew from many recordings of southern music, including blues, black sacred, and early country music. From the many photographs of white musicians and the transcriptions of their sung and spoken materials, *78 Blues* may seem to some blues readers to be mostly about "old-time" music and hence of little blues interest. In truth, this book is essential toward an appropriate appreciation of early recorded blues and toward a better understanding of why Robert Johnson mumbled "Can't you hear the wind howl?" on "Come on in My Kitchen." —*EK*

22. The Blues Sisterhood

Blues Legacies and Black Feminism: Gertrude "Ma" Rainey, Bessie Smith, and Billie Holiday. By Angela Y. Davis. New York: Pantheon, 1998. ISBN 0-679-45005-X (hardcover), ISBN 0-679-77126-3 (paperback), $17.00

What makes Angela Davis's *Blues Legacies and Black Feminism* essential are her lyric transcriptions of the songs recorded by Gertrude "Ma" Rainey and Bessie Smith. If not every song they recorded is included, then nearly every one is. To my knowledge, the only competing sets of transcriptions are for the Smith songs only, one by Edward Brooks for *The Bessie Smith Companion* (New York: Da Capo, 1982), which has been long out of print, the other prepared for the Sony/Columbia reissue in five boxed sets. R. R. Macleod included few, if any, of their songs in his self-published lyric transcription series based on the Yazoo and Document reissues, because Yazoo and Document left the task of reissuing Smith to Sony/Columbia, and Macleod did not live long enough to transcribe Document's Rainey volumes. With Davis's meticulously prepared transcripts, composer credits are given for each song.

The value of the rest of the book may vary according to the reader. Its appearance in 1998 was an event for the admirers of Dr. Davis's feminism and activism. College professors often assign the book to their students. Readers who have admired Daphne Harrison's *Black Pearls* (no. 17) will find *Blues Legacies* to be a worthy sequel (and Davis does hope that her book serves as such). However, those who have read several times Sandra Lieb's *Mother of the Blues* (no. 15) and Chris Albertson's *Bessie* (no. 16) may scratch their heads over Davis's fuss. The typical white male listener who listens to Charlie Patton and Robert Johnson won't bother with this book.

Nonetheless, the main body of *Blues Legacies* deserves one fair reading. Even though the book was published as a trade edition by Pantheon Books, its written style has the common academic characteristic of using nouns as verbs. In that regard, it can be as challenging to read as Houston Baker (no. 93), Paul Garon's *Blues and the Poetic Spirit* (no. 87), and Evans (no. 14). Its theme is how the "blues legacies" of Rainey, Smith, and Holiday have preserved what was then unacknowledged "black feminism" consciousness. Whether these singers anticipate, herald, or implement assertions of African American woman pride is the overall question.

Davis finds what assertions she can in the blues recorded by Ma Rainey and Bessie Smith. At the very least, the songs they sang reflected the circumstances of black relationships and the attitudes about love and sex among their female listeners. While many of the lyrics were and still are brutal, the manners in which they were sung cut to the core truths about women and men—"going public," as Harrison says in *Black Pearls*. In many blues, Rainey and Smith assert themselves to be as sexually independent, mean, restless, and grouchy as any no-good man. For that reason, their performances live and recorded were more appealing to lower-class working women than to the emerging black "bourgeoisie" middle class, and it is in the lower-class "sisterhood" that Davis will seek elements of feminism. It was at the blues shows featuring women singers, and not at the churches led by male preachers, Davis argues, where the black working women congregated for sister bonding. For Davis, Rainey is a figure signifying the origins of the blues, but Smith is the one who led many women to make the transition from postslavery times to city life and, in so doing, brought to the blues what I see Charles Keil calling later (no. 76) a "city" attitude in which the southern wisdom was retained within the ghettos.

Lady Sings the Blues was the title of jazz singer Billie Holiday's autobiography. Just how many blues she sang still hasn't been counted. For Davis, there is one song in Holiday's repertory that matters more than any blues, and that is the antilynching song "Strange Fruit." Nonetheless, her portrait of Holiday is painted along the lines of Houston Baker's ideology of buying one's freedom with the riches gathered and sold from one's African American blues background. Readers who haven't read Baker's *Blues, Ideology and Afro-American Literature* (no. 93) should do so in order to appreciate what Davis achieves with Holiday. Many jazz fans favor Holiday's early recordings, often dismissing her gritty post–World War II performances as the efforts of a strung-out junkie. But viewed from Baker's ideology, the sales of those later records were sufficient to help her maintain a respectable (if not triumphal) independence within modern jazz trends instead of confining her to pop music.

Readers familiar with Dr. Davis's previous books listed on the frontispiece will recognize aspects of her activism and academic agendas in *Blues Legacies*. She remains today a polarizing public figure, especially among men of the cloth, whether an academic gown or a church vestment. There is one statement about the blues that Dr. Davis is uniquely qualified by her activities to make (42): "It is important, I think, to understand women's blues as a working-class form that anticipates the politicization of the 'personal' through the dynamic of 'consciousness-raising,' a phenomenon associated with the women's movement of the last three decades" (presumably of the 1960s, 1970s, and 1980s). Blues writers have written of blues singers as secular preachers and of preachers as sacred bluesmen. But what of the possibility of blues singers as feminist activists? If Davis doesn't succeed in making as strong a case for Smith and Rainey as activists as she does for Holiday, she is unswervable in her faith that they are. And for the possibility of activists as blues feminists? I am not sure very many activists would understand as well as Davis what blues feminism would demand of them. —*EK*

23. Get on Your Feet!

Stomping the Blues. By Albert Murray. New York: McGraw-Hill, 1976. Reprint, New York: Vintage Books, 1982. Revised edition, New York: Da Capo Press, 1989. ISBN 978-0-306-80362-8 (paperback), $16.95

Ask any group of ten strangers about the blues and you are bound to hear sadness as a prominent theme. So many stereotypes and jokes of blues as a sad music have existed for so long, it is no wonder jazz critic, author, and cofounder of Jazz at Lincoln Center Albert Murray felt the need to write *Stomping the Blues*. Indeed, this refutation of blues as being a music of sadness is the central theme of the book.

Murray's exploration of the blues aesthetic was the first major work to break out of the formal academic tones describing blues in a narrative historical fashion, by bringing a poet's touch. The introduction reads as an incantation or a riddle, describing everyone's eventual affliction with the blues at some point, through some means. Murray acknowledges the suffering of existence and, like the Buddha's Four Noble Truths, says there is a way out of this suffering; for Murray, it is music and dance. Murray eloquently describes blues music as a means of stomping down the "blue devils" (a term existing at least since the sixteenth century to describe depression or sadness and the source of the word "blues"). Murray certainly isn't the first to make the point that blues music is actually an antidote to sadness, but he is arguably the first to do so with poetic eloquence.

While it may seem blatantly obvious that blues is not about wallowing in sorrow, apparently the idea of blues as a sad music has long been held up through standard definitions of the term in most of the typical dictionaries and encyclopedias. In chapter 5, Murray examines the definitions in the then-latest editions of reference books from Webster, Funk and Wagnalls, American Heritage, and even the *Grove Dictionary of Music and Musicians*, finding they all upheld this misconception.

Murray gives good explanations of blues structure and form, but the book is really about the blues aesthetic more than what most people would consider blues music itself. In fact, the framework for the entire book's discussion of blues is jazz. Murray devotes more time to Duke Ellington than to all musicians from the Mississippi Delta combined. Readers will not find Son House, Charlie Patton, Muddy Waters, or B. B. King in this book. There is only cursory mention of figures like Robert Johnson or Blind Lemon Jefferson. Of the figures lumped into the traditional blues category, only Bessie Smith and Big Joe Turner receive more than passing mention. But this book isn't really about strict definitions of blues, it is about the blues aesthetic, particularly as it shapes jazz. It is in many ways a celebration of the dance hall and music's ability to get people on their feet and literally stomp away the blues. Murray sees this best through the lens of jazz. While Murray acknowledges the importance of Leadbelly and Blind Lemon Jefferson to American music, he feels "there is a good deal more to be said for the no less authentic extensions and refinements that have resulted from the playful options taken by such consecrated professionals as Jelly Roll Morton, Louis Armstrong, Bessie Smith, Lester Young, Charlie Parker, and Duke Ellington." He adds that "unless the idiom is not only robust and carthy enough but also refined enough . . . it is not likely to be a very effective counter-agent of the blues."

As anyone who has attended a goat roast picnic and shuffled feet to the sounds of African American fife and drum music or danced the night away to the "hypnotic boogie" of North Mississippi hill country blues knows, you don't need a sixteen-piece band, matching uniforms, and augmented ninth chords to drive down the blues. The idea that only the most "refined" music is the most effective at "stomping the blues" is perhaps the weakest argument of the book.

Despite Murray's obvious bias for jazz over more folk forms of blues, this book is worthy of a read. Indeed, music critic and author Stanley Crouch wrote that it is "the most eloquent book ever written about African-American music." *Stomping the Blues* ultimately recognizes the transformative power of music to bring us out of the doldrums.

Murray's points are brought to life with over 250 black-and-white photographs, though the image clarity is superior in the first edition (hardback and paperback). —*GJ*

24. A Railroader for Me

Long Steel Rail: The Railroad in American Folksong. By Norm Cohen. Music edited by David Cohen. Urbana: University of Illinois Press, 1981. ISBN 0-252-00343-8 (hardcover). Second edition, 2000. ISBN 978-0-252-06881-2 (paper-back), $34.00

This magisterial compendium of American railroad folk songs is required reading for every lover of American music, not just of the blues. For those who were too young when the book first appeared in 1981 in hardcover, a paperback reprint with a new introduction came out in 2000. It was clearly a labor of love for Norm Cohen. At the time of his research, he was a physical chemist by day, but in his spare time he was the executive secretary of the John Edwards Memorial Foundation research archive of folk music then housed at UCLA. While the scope of the book covers comprehensively through song the history of American railroads from the 1840s through the 1960s, it succeeds in bringing forth through lyrics and lore the attitudes of common people about the railroads that, were it not for Cohen, would have been little noticed today.

The first three chapters are introductory in character: a brief history of American railroads; an overview of how music was sold, sung, and heard through broadsides, sheet music, and sound recordings; and a broad initial sample of railroad-inspired popular music from 1828 through the next 140 years. The remaining nine chapters present short histories behind eighty-five songs, each of them with melodies and lyrics prepared by Norm Cohen with David Cohen. We first hear about the "Heroes and Badmen," a few of them historical figures who were celebrated in song for being both good and bad in a glamorous, outlaw way. "The Fatal Run" may be the most spectacular chapter, dealing with railroad wrecks, with special attention accorded to "The Wreck on the C & O (Engine 143)" and "The Wreck of the Old 97," the latter being a case study of the business of music in the mid-1920s. The next two chapters treat parlor songs that were lighthearted or sentimental. The eighth chapter treats songs about hoboes, taken from performances by white musicians; for a study of hobo songs sung by black musicians, see Paul Garon and Gene Tomko's *What's the Use of Walking If There's a Freight Train Going Your Way? Black Hoboes and Their Songs* (Chicago: Charles H. Kerr, 2006). The following two chapters on railroad blues and songs will be examined below, and another on hammer-song themes as well as a concluding section on hell-bound and heaven-sent trains round out the volume.

The blues reader will find plenty of interest. For a start, the "Heroes and Badmen" chapter begins with "John Henry," the African American steel-drivin' man who remains shadowy after years of historical research. There is also "Railroad Bill," another African American who led a "desperado" life until he was killed in 1897; the song bearing his name may be classified as a protoblues or, as Cohen terms it, a blues ballad. The historical Casey Jones was white, but for the song about his 1900 wreck, Cohen selects for examination Furry Lewis's 1928 Victor recording "Kassie [*sic*] Jones." A much lesser-known blues, "J. C. Holmes Blues," is featured through Bessie Smith's recording.

The chapter "I've Got the Railroad Blues" contains discussions of nine African American blues, the first two of which are lesser-known 78s by Charlie Patton, "Pea Vine Blues" and "Green River Blues." The other selections were taken from various substyles of the blues, whether rural (Charlie McCoy's "That Lonesome Train Took My Baby Away" and Sleepy John Estes's "Special Agent/Railroad Police Blues"), city (Leroy Carr's "How Long How Long Blues"), or in between (Big Bill Broonzy's "The Southern Blues"). The chapter concludes with three blues from women singers, namely Clara Smith ("Freight Train Blues"), Trixie Smith ("Railroad Blues"), and the superb Lucille Bogan ("I Hate That Train Called the M & O"). Cohen admits that the next chapter, "A Railroader for Me," lacks an organizing theme, but even so, here are found some of the best-known folk songs recorded by black musicians. One was made famous by Leadbelly, "Rock Island Line," which would be often copied, including the influential skiffle version by Lonnie Donegan. "The Midnight Special" is given by Cohen from a recording by Dave Cutrell, but among African American singer/guitarists who recorded it were Leadbelly and "Salty Dog" Sam Collins. There is also presented Elizabeth Cotten's "Freight Train," which became a folk-revival favorite on her Folkways recording in 1958. Finally there is John Hurt's "Spike Driver Blues," transcribed not from a performance from his 1960s rediscovery career, but from his youthful prime in 1928.

What does all this singing about railroads come to for singer and listener? An answer relevant to the afterlife is conveyed in the final chapter, "Life's Railway to Heaven." That trains could take our souls to hell was one answer given by white and black recording artists alike; an ad for Reverend A. W. Nix's 1927 Vocalion release "The Black Diamond Express to Hell" is reproduced. But the words and music to the affirmative "The Gospel Train Is Coming" by Reverend Edward Clayborn are also given. When a song like "When the Train Comes Along" is recorded by singers of both races—Uncle Dave Macon in 1934 as transcribed in the book by the Cohens, and Henry Thomas in 1927—it points to a utopia for which everyone waits at the same station. —*EK*

25. Songster of the Swamplands

The Life and Legend of Leadbelly. By Charles Wolfe and Kip Lornell. New York: HarperCollins, 1992. ISBN 0-06-01682-5 (hardcover), ISBN 978-0-306-80896-8 (paperback), $16.95

Genre classification is a tricky thing. While he was known as a country musician, Jimmie Rodgers wrote many songs in a twelve-bar blues structure, AAB lyric construction, and even had the word "blues" or "blue" in the title of almost a third of his recorded works. Blind Willie Johnson's lyrics were religious, but he is very often classified solely as a blues singer. Often categorized by the music industry as blues, musicians like Charlie Patton, Odetta, and Josh White certainly performed blues, but their recorded and live performing repertoires included large numbers of Anglo-Celtic folk songs, "hillbilly" songs, gospel, and other nonblues songs. Thus is the case with Huddie Ledbetter, popularly known as Leadbelly (though he spelled it as Lead Belly, much popular convention combined it into one word). Leadbelly is probably better described as a songster, a musician in the late nineteenth and early twentieth century who performed a diverse array of folk songs from black and white traditions, ballads, blues, and songs from popular entertainments such as minstrel or medicine shows.

Huddie Ledbetter is most well known for playing the twelve-string guitar, but he also played accordion and piano. He was born in northwest Louisiana near the town of Mooringsport in 1888 and began performing at square dances and other events locally and in nearby Shreveport as a young teenager. At around the age of twenty-two, Leadbelly moved to Dallas, where he would meet and perform with Blind Lemon Jefferson, a huge influence on Leadbelly. From Blind Lemon, Leadbelly learned many new songs and how to play slide guitar. Though he failed to financially benefit from his music, Leadbelly would go on to influence Woody Guthrie, Pete Seeger, Sonny Terry, Brownie McGhee, and countless other folk and blues performers. His songs "Goodnight, Irene" and "Midnight Special" would be recorded by numerous musicians.

In an ideal world, Leadbelly would have become famous on the merits of his music alone. As with many performers today, sensationalism is often what catches the public's attention. Leadbelly served time in a Texas prison for murder and later Angola Prison in Louisiana for assault. John and Alan Lomax, working for the Library of Congress, found and recorded Leadbelly at Angola in 1933 and 1934. One side they recorded on the 1934 trip, "Governor O. K. Allen," was delivered by the Lomaxes to the governor's office. A month later, Leadbelly was freed. Though a letter from the warden states that the release was due to good behavior, these events contributed to many stories about this golden-throated singer who was able to sing his way out of jail. John Lomax went on to tour Leadbelly around the country. On a 1935 trip to New York, papers ran headlines such as "Sweet Singer of the Swamplands Here to Do a Few Tunes between Homicides." Tabloid sensationalism like this fueled rumors and myths about Leadbelly and helped him become a household name.

Separating the man from the legend is a large part of *The Life and Legend of Leadbelly*, by Charles Wolfe and Kip Lornell. Wolfe (1943–2006, country music scholar and professor of English at Middle Tennessee State University) and Lornell (adjunct professor of music at George Washington University and former Smithsonian fellow) sift through the myths, often presented as gospel in earlier works, to produce the most definitive work on Leadbelly yet. Other interesting research traces the origins of "Goodnight, Irene" to a minstrel song published in 1886. Leadbelly's complex relationship with the Lomaxes is described in detail in this book. John Lomax publicly fought for acceptance of African American artists like Leadbelly but still harbored paternalistic attitudes. Wolfe and Lornell blend history with music analysis to create a rich biography of one of the United States' most famous folksingers. Their original research sheds light on previously unknown and/or confusing parts of Leadbelly's life.

Leadbelly has been the subject of a number of other books. John and Alan Lomax's book *Negro Folk Songs as Sung by Lead Belly* (Macmillan, 1936) was the earliest full-length book to look at the music of Leadbelly. The first part tells Leadbelly's story, mostly in his own words. The remainder of the book contains musical and lyric transcriptions of his songs along with commentary by the Lomaxes. The serial *Jazz Music* published a special edition, *A Tribute to Huddie Ledbetter*, in April 1946, which includes several short essays, a discography, and reviews of his records. Julius Lester and Pete Seeger's *The 12-String Guitar as Played by Leadbelly* (New York: Oak Publications, 1965) is an instruction manual on playing the twelve-string guitar, using Leadbelly's songs as a guide. Science-fiction authors Richard Garvin and Edmond Addeo's novel *The Midnight Special: The Legend of Leadbelly* (New York: B. Geis, 1971) is based on Leadbelly's life. While it provides the most entertaining read, note that the authors state that it "contains imagined scenes and reconstructed events." Ledbetter even features at the core of a National Poetry Series collection by Tyehimba Jess titled simply *Leadbelly* (Amherst: Verse Press, 2005).

The Life and Legend of Leadbelly contains twenty pages of end-notes, a thirty-three-page discography, and an index. Twenty-three black-and-white photos and images are printed in the center of the book. The discography is much more extensive than those published in any other works on Leadbelly. There are some abbreviations that don't appear in the discography key, and a few entries list the wrong label number.

Though Leadbelly isn't solely confined to the blues, this book is included in this volume because he did have a significant output of blues songs and the stories and myths surrounding his life exemplify the bad man figure so often associated with blues. Sensationalistic "news" stories of Leadbelly helped define the idea of the "bluesman" to a large number of people; whether blues or not, the figure of Leadbelly symbolizes the iconic bluesman. —*GJ*

26. From Ragtime to Rhythm and Blues

Kansas City Jazz: From Ragtime to Bebop. By Frank Driggs and Chuck Haddix. New York: Oxford University Press, 2005. ISBN 0-19-504767-2 (hardcover), ISBN 0-19-530712-7 (paperback), $20.00

Many blues readers often shy away from any book or CD with "jazz" in the title. But they would be foolish to ignore Frank Driggs and Chuck Haddix's history of Kansas City "jazz" before World War II. Yes, eminent jazz figures like Count Basie, Mary Lou Williams, Lester Young, Jay McShann, and Charlie Parker developed their individual styles in Kansas City. But so did blues musicians like Jimmy Rushing, Big Joe Turner, Pete Johnson, Julia Lee, and Walter Brown. They, too, deserve attention. So does Kansas City as a whole.

For many years through 1938, the nightlife of Kansas City was unregulated, with flowing booze, nonstop gambling, and women for rent by the hour. To read the accounts presented by Driggs and Haddix, the nightlife continued into the daytime: no one in the vice culture seemed to distinguish night from day. The main streets for these activities were Twelfth Street, Fourteenth Street (where most of the prostitutes worked), and Eighteenth Street. Who brought this about was the political boss Thomas Pendergast, who had a weakness for horse racing. Eventually, he was brought down by federal authorities for tax evasion. Until then, Kansas City was wide open.

The one good thing about the times was that the clubs and ballrooms needed live music, for which musicians were hired. During the depths of the Great Depression, touring bands made more money in Kansas City than in the cities along the East Coast. The local musicians competed fiercely through jam sessions for seats in the best bands and for bragging rights; as a result, a distinctive Kansas City style emerged, and it was based on the blues. The innovations of the new local style that were sustained in the blues were the band rhythm section of bass, drums, guitar, and piano, and the practice of "blues shouting" as done by Jimmy Rushing and Big Joe Turner. Rhythm and blues and early rock and roll would be unimaginable without these innovations.

Frank Driggs was the leading collector of pre-1942 photographs of jazz and blues and the main source of images to book publishers. Many of the jazz photos appeared in Driggs's magisterial volume *Black Beauty, White Heat* (with Harris Lewine; Morrow, 1982), and the blues ones in Lawrence Cohn's *Nothing but the Blues* (no. 1). He was also the leading researcher of Kansas City Pendergast-era music. He cowrote this history with Chuck Haddix, director of the Marr Sound Archives at the University of Missouri at Kansas City. Together, they used contemporary news stories about Kansas City vice and music, and they quoted from oral interviews from elder musicians. And they infuse their narrative with much local knowledge.

The resulting book bridges the gap from the 1910s African American ragtime to the 1940s rhythm and blues. It takes up where Abbott and Seroff had ended *Ragged but Right* (no. 10), especially from their presentation of the brass bands that played marches and blues. One linking person is N. Clark Smith, the Kansas City bandmaster during the 1910s and 1920s at Western University and Lincoln High School. Through his teaching, drilling, programs, and influence, Smith trained several generations of future jazz and blues musicians on brass and wind instruments. Another link is Eddie Durham, a jazz brass player and arranger who had early experience in the circus bands.

According to the authors, jazz itself did not arrive in the city until 1917. By then, the African American entertainment district was established at the intersection of Eighteenth Street and Vine Street. Although there were white jazz bands, the most prominent of the early African American ones were those led by George Lee and Bennie Moten, and to a lesser extent Winston Holmes. Through 1932, Moten was the one who undertook a great deal of recording with the national labels and touring to New York and other East Coast cities. To tour the "territories" to the west and south, Kansas City bands had to check first with the "territory bands" like Walter Page's Blue Devils before traveling there. The tables turned, so to speak, when the Depression made touring less profitable: the territory bands came more often than previously to Kansas City, where they often lost their best players to the city's bands. To accommodate so many great musicians, arrangers had to find new ways to make sure the bigger egos among them could be heard. For example, when Oran "Hot Lips" Page joined the Moten band in 1931, Eddie Durham introduced sixth and ninth chords to the arrangements to achieve a five-part brass harmony. (Today these chords are considered basic to the blues, as seen in the initial exercises in Rubin's *12-Bar Blues* [no. 3].)

In 1936–1938, the best local groups attained national stardom, especially the Count Basie band with singer Jimmy Rushing, pianist Pete Johnson with shouter Big Joe Turner, and Andy Kirk's Clouds of Joy with singer Pha Terrell. The 1938–1939 "From Spirituals to Swing" concerts at Carnegie Hall placed in historical and geographic contexts the music of Basie and Turner and Johnson; the live recordings made on location are essential for blues listeners. The departure of these performers from the local scene, the 1938–1939 downfall of Pendergast, and the ensuing crackdown on the nightspots spelled doom for Kansas City music. The last great group to come from the city was the band led by Jay McShann, with alto saxophonist Charlie Parker and vocalist Walter Brown. Today the group is renowned for its recordings with Parker, but in its time it was more famous for its hit record "Confessin' the Blues," which in the 1960s would be covered by B. B. King and the Rolling Stones.

The Driggs and Haddix book is the chief history to buy for Kansas City jazz. Used bookstores often have Ross Russell's history

Jazz Style in Kansas City and the Southwest (Los Angeles: University of California Press, 1971), but Russell relies less on local sources, and he tells his story with Charlie Parker and bebop jazz as his narrative goal. *Kansas City Jazz* is still in print in paperback. —*EK*

27. Tobacco Country Blues

Red River Blues: The Blues Tradition in the Southeast. By Bruce Bastin. Urbana: University of Illinois Press, 1986. ISBN 978-0-252-01213-6 (hardcover), ISBN 978 0-252-06521-7 (paperback), $21.95. London: Macmillan, 1986

Piedmont blues is one of the most accomplished styles in the genre. Its melodies and lyrics are distinctive from the blues of Memphis and Mississippi, its guitar styles are very intricate, and its top musicians are versatile, indeed encyclopedic in their musical knowledge. Oddly, Piedmont blues has never been adopted much by the rock crowd: the Allman Brothers Band's version of Blind Willie McTell's "Statesboro Blues" is a rare example heard on rock radio. So this regional style hasn't been explored much by the white fans who have come to blues by way of rock (not even by the fans of Pink Floyd, who named itself after Piedmont musicians Pink Anderson and Floyd Council). Despite this lack of reader attention, Piedmont blues is the subject of one undisputed blues literature classic, Bastin's magisterial guide *Red River Blues*.

Born in England, Bastin came to the United States in the 1960s, studying folklore at the University of North Carolina. By 1969, he and Peter Lowry were undertaking field interviews with Piedmont blues musicians, among them Buddy Moss, who had recorded commercially thirty-five years previously. Bastin's early writings based on this research were *Crying for the Carolines* (no. 28; London: Studio Vista, 1970) and the Master of Arts thesis "The Emergence of the Blues Tradition in the Southeastern States" (University of North Carolina, 1973). Still, there were many more musicians to find and much music to hear before Bastin and Lowry could complete a comprehensive picture of the Piedmont style and its musical migration to the northeastern United States. Once they did, Bastin had the basis for his narrative *Red River Blues*.

The first five chapters provide the history, the culture, the geography, and the recording contexts. Writing on the earliest blues is very difficult due to the lack of contemporary sound recordings and the few surviving oral testimonies. How Bastin dealt with this difficulty was to take a survey of the historical circumstances and cultures across the South from the Atlantic coast to the Mississippi River before 1910 and then match those generalities to particular traits of the earliest known Piedmont blues. For a starting point to his history, Bastin posits the arrival of the blues in the Southeast sometime between 1900 and 1910, a decade later than the earliest datable blues and blues ballads from Mississippi River towns and cities. He then describes the culture shared among African Americans, including guitars, pawnshops, regional politics, and the impact of segregation laws. He proceeds to examine the recordings of Blind Blake, the first recording star from the region, and the programs of the Fort Valley festivals from 1937 through 1953 (selected artists of the 1940s events were recorded on the premises).

Bastin then reviews the blues activity in a northward state-by-state sweep. He begins with pianists in Georgia of the 1910s and 1920s. Four chapters on Atlanta trace its local blues history from the arrival of displaced country folk to that city, the pre-World War II music of Peg Leg Howell, Barbecue Bob, Curley Weaver, Buddy Moss, Willie McTell, and Frank Edwards, and the postwar musicians like Moss and Roy Dunn (who were acknowledged by Bastin and Lowry as their most helpful sources of oral information). Two chapters on South Carolina follow, the first on Greenville, focusing on the prewar career of Josh White and the initial looks at Gary Davis and Baby Tate, the second on Spartanburg (more about Tate, Pink Anderson), Union County (Gussie Nesbitt, Peg Leg Sam), and Charlotte.

The section on Durham, North Carolina (chapters 12–16), is the heart of the study, and its chapter on Blind Boy Fuller may well be the summation of the whole book. In Bastin's previous volume, *Crying for the Carolines,* he admitted to changing his view of Fuller from an innovator to a gatherer or synthesizer of current styles. It is as synthesizer that Fuller is presented in *Red River Blues,* as someone who took all that he was hearing in the Piedmont and on records as the bases for his own popular blues records in the 1930s. In that chapter devoted to Fuller, his fellow musician Floyd Council and his label scout J. B. Long are depicted at long lengths as Fuller's career associates and as his posthumous informants. The Gary Davis story is continued in a separate chapter, and the individual early careers of Brownie McGhee and Sonny Terry before their famous teaming are reviewed. The last chapter in the North Carolina section covers the preblues styles and the blues traditions persisting in the state in the 1980s; the portion about the North Carolina Folklife Festivals gives the book a symmetry with the earlier chapter about the Fort Valley festivals.

The final chapters cover the states where Piedmont musicians migrated. The first stop was Virginia, where Bastin describes John Jackson, William Moore, Carl Martin, and Frank Hovington. The next ones were Washington, DC, Pennsylvania, and New York, including New York City, where Gary Davis spent the remainder of his life.

Throughout the chapters, Bastin admits that he and Lowry missed out on meeting many lesser-known musicians, and so wherever appropriate he gives their names and known locations of activities. With regard to the Piedmont "lost," a kind of historiography emerges, acknowledging the recovery efforts of the researchers of the 1960s, 1970s, and 1980s. To be sure, Bastin and Lowry loom large, but in the opening chapters, Bastin writes of Kip Lornell for Virginia and Durham, North Carolina, Dena Epstein for Virginia, George Mitchell for Georgia, and Glenn Hinson for North Carolina. One should also remember to include the talent scout J. B. Long, who brought much talent to the recording companies in the 1930s and then lived long enough to talk about the musicians to Bastin and Lowry.

The main publisher of *Red River Blues* is the University of Illinois Press, although Macmillan printed a London edition in 1986. If a preference is to be made among editions, it would be for the University of Illinois Press paperback edition, because only in its preface is the book title explained. "Red River Blues" was performed and recorded by many Piedmont musicians, but no Red River is to be found in the Piedmont region. Bastin reports two Red Rivers in the United States, the more likely one running from New Mexico to Louisiana. Quite how that blues came east to the Piedmont remains a mystery, but implicitly it is relevant to the earliest chapters of the book. —*EK*

28. A Piedmont Blues Odyssey

Crying for the Carolines. By Bruce Bastin. London: Studio Vista, 1971. SBN 289-70210-0 (hardcover), SBN 289-70209-7 (paperback)

It is tempting to think of *Crying for the Carolines* as a dry run for *Red River Blues* (no. 27). After all, both books were written by Bruce Bastin with the research of Peter Lowry, and both deal with the rich past and the diminishing present of Piedmont blues. *Red River Blues* is and will remain the standard history of Piedmont blues, with each artist and each recording set in the narrative within a time-less order. *Crying for the Carolines*, in contrast, is an ongoing account from 1969–1970 of Bastin and Lowry's discovery of places, people, records, music, and lyrics.

This short book begins with a lengthy presentation of Blind Boy Fuller of the central North Carolina area of Winston-Salem. Fuller embodied the pre–World War II peak of Piedmont blues, so in a sense, *Crying for the Carolines* begins with the middle of this region's musical history. Because of Fuller's fame through records and his travels, this chapter serves to introduce several figures who reappear later: J. B. Long, who facilitated Fuller's introduction to the recording industry; the Trice brothers, Willie and Richard; Reverend Gary Davis; and Buddy Moss.

The remainder of the book is a geographical odyssey through the Piedmont. The path along which Bastin leads his readers is a long loop, starting southwest from Durham, North Carolina, to Atlanta, Georgia, and then returning northeast through Greenville and Spartanburg, South Carolina, to Charlotte. The final chapter is a survey of musicians who migrated northward during the 1940s and 1950s. For each location, there is a short profile of population, labor, and culture and then a focused look at the leading musicians. Among those featured are Sonny Terry and Brownie McGhee (the Durham chapter), Buddy Moss (Atlanta), Reverend Gary Davis (Greenville, South Carolina, and the migration chapter), Pink Anderson and Arthur Johnson (Peg Pete) (Spartanburg, South Carolina), and Julius Daniels (Charlotte, North Carolina). For the past musicians by then dead or unrecovered, Bastin writes of them not in a historical sense (as he would in *Red River Blues*), but as though they were abiding and "yet to be rediscovered." Maintaining such a fresh approach to the Atlanta chapter may have been a challenge, as at the time of writing Buddy Moss was the only bluesman alive, with the great Willie McTell, Peg Leg Howell, Curly Weaver, and the Hicks Brothers, "Barbecue" Bob and Charlie, by then dead.

What Bastin does in *Crying for the Carolines* that he does not do in his later book is discuss the music and lyrics of the 78 rpm recordings he and Lowry located of the regional blues musicians. Throughout the short book are lyric transcriptions of several dozen blues, with additional remarks on musical characteristics, whether original to the recording musician or borrowed (stolen) from other musicians on or off records. Bastin maintains an open mind, allowing the historical possibility that a musician who first recorded a song, a lyric, or a musical lick may not necessarily be its creator or originator. By allowing that possibility, Bastin and Lowry would seek and appreciate any qualities in a musician they would meet for the first time, even if those qualities may seem trite or derivative to another researcher.

The title words, by the way, are to be found only on the cover and the title page of the book, but not in the text. "Cryin' for the Carolines" is not a blues but a 1930 popular song by Sam H. Lewis, Joe Young, and Harry Warren that was made famous by Guy Lombardo and Fred Waring. Obviously, its use here is a humorous borrowing from popular culture outside the blues canon.

To those lovers of Piedmont blues, *Crying for the Carolines* is their "you are there" document of the rediscovery of their favorite musicians and their culture. For that reason, and for the kind of discussion of records that won't be found in *Red River Blues*, this early Bastin book is worth seeking. This was among the later volumes of the Blues Series issues that Studio Vista published in hardcover and paperback in the early 1970s, but it has not been reprinted since. So finding an affordable copy may not be easy; typical prices for the paperback copies range between twenty and forty dollars. However, many libraries still have theirs available for borrowing. —*EK*

29. Fighting Racism with the Blues

The Bluesmen. By Samuel Charters. New York: Oak Publications, 1967. ISBN 0-8256-0069-3 (hardcover), ISBN 0-8256-0096-4 (paperback)

The Bluesmen was published eight years after Samuel Charters's pioneering work *The Country Blues* (no. 63). It is billed as "the story and the music of the men who made the blues." In the introduction, Charters states that *The Bluesmen* is just the first part of a trilogy. The second book in this series, *Sweet as the Showers of Rain* (no. 82) was published in 1977. The initially intended third volume would examine postwar blues in Chicago, Detroit, California, and Texas, as well as looking at female country blues artists. Charters abandoned writing a third volume because works like Mike Rowe's *Chicago Breakdown* (no. 47) covered much of this area so thoroughly.

In *The Bluesmen,* after a very brief introduction Charters gives an "African background" of the blues. This short chapter seems to rely mostly on older studies; Charters fails to acknowledge any of the then more recent research Paul Oliver, Harold Courlander, and others conducted in this area. The bulk of the book is a series of short biographical sketches of the lives of those Charters deems to be the most important country blues musicians prior to 1942, along with an explanation of their musical characteristics.

He divides the book into three sections, placing these bluesmen into three geographic areas: Mississippi, Alabama, and Texas. While dividing the book geographically is fine, Charters's choice of division could be misleading. Dividing musicians into states makes sense superficially, but it implies that regional styles begin and end at artificially constructed borders. The major figures covered in their own chapters are Charlie Patton, Son House, Skip James, Robert Johnson, "Bukka" White, Blind Lemon Jefferson, Henry Thomas, and "Texas" Alexander. Other figures are grouped together into single chapters.

Ishman Bracey, Tommy Johnson, the Mississippi Sheiks, Mississippi Jook Band, Big Joe Williams, Tommy McClennan, and others are combined into a chapter shorter than the one for Skip James alone. This unbalanced coverage can give readers inaccurate impressions of how influential various musicians were. Charters's bias seems to be toward those musicians made popular during the folk revival.

Charters's musical descriptions are one of the weaker parts of this book. The musical transcriptions give general contours of a basic version of melodies. Melodic patterns are quantized to the nearest eighth or sixteenth note. It would be fine if Charters intended to do this as a means of simplifying his musical explanations for a general audience, but he never states this. There are a few small errors in lyric transcriptions as well.

The Bluesmen is filled with other errors. H. C. Speir is routinely written out as H. C. Spears. W. C. Handy first heard something like blues most likely in 1903, not 1895 as Charters writes. There are also a number of typographical errors throughout the text. Even the title of the book is spelled inconsistently; the author page spells it as *The Blues Men*.

After being out of print for several years, both *The Bluesmen* and *Sweet as the Showers of Rain* were grouped into one book called *The Blues Makers* (New York: Da Capo, 1991). The two original books are presented as they were originally printed, mistakes and all.

The only new inclusions are a new preface, new illustrations, and an additional chapter on Robert Johnson. Though the new chapter, "Robert Johnson—A New Consideration," provides more information on Johnson than the original chapter, there are still odd errors. Charters writes that much of what he wrote about Johnson in *The Country Blues* was wrong "except that he was from northern Mississippi." Charters contradicts this two pages later when he accurately describes Hazlehurst as being "south of Jackson."

To compound this, Charters spells Johnson's birthplace as "Hazelhurst" instead of "Hazlehurst" (to be fair, it is incorrectly spelled on Johnson's death certificate as well). These inconsistencies and inaccuracies make this a confusing work. In the preface there are additional errors. Charters states that William Ferris worked at the Institute of Southern Culture in Jackson instead of the Center for the Study of Southern Culture in Oxford, Mississippi. Both the original edition and revisited printing in *The Blues Makers* could have greatly benefited from an editor.

Despite the many errors in *The Bluesmen*, Samuel Charters presents some beautiful sketches of pioneering figures in the blues. His style is poetic and more flowing than some of the more scholarly works on the blues, making this book more accessible to a general audience. Charters had nonacademic reasons for writing about the blues. In an interview with Matthew Ismail, Charters states, "For me, the writing about black music was my way of fighting racism. That's why my work is not academic, that is why it is absolutely nothing but popularization" (*Blues Discovery*, 2011, 251). It helps to keep this in mind when reading Charters. Charters's romanticism helped spur many young blues enthusiasts into action, searching for undocumented performers and unheard recordings. Peter Guralnick writes, "Samuel Charters's writing awakened me to a world whose existence and possibilities I had never previously imagined. It was a world of mystery and romance for which Charters served as virtually the only guide." By the time *The Bluesmen* was published, though, much of its information had already been covered in *Blues Unlimited* and other publications.

The original version and reprinting in *The Blues Makers* contain many excellent illustrations. There is no bibliography and only a meager section of notes. The "Records Cited" section of the original book is absent in *The Blues Makers*. Though out of print, copies of the original book can be found through used-book stores and run from eleven to fifty-one dollars.

As of this writing, *The Blues Makers* is also out of print, though used copies can be found for an average price of twelve dollars. —GJ

30. Is There Harm in Singing the Blues?

Early Downhome Blues: A Musical and Cultural Analysis. By Jeff Todd Titon. Urbana: University of Illinois Press, 1977. ISBN 0-252-00187-7 (hardcover). Second edition, Chapel Hill: University of North Carolina Press, 1994. ISBN 0-8078-2170-5 (hardcover), ISBN 978-0-8078-4482-3 (paperback), $33.95

Most writings on the blues approach the subject matter through only one academic lens—historical, sociological, anthropological, and so on. The actual music is often the least successfully studied aspect of blues. All writers on the blues certainly write about music, but most don't have formal training in this area. Many valiant attempts to describe music talk in flowing but confused language (e.g.—"sweet, sinuous, minimalist keytone-pop slides into meadows of folkie fingerpicking," "There is a high, motionless motion," etc.) or confuse lyrics with music. Of course the blues are more than just music; they are poetry, a feeling, an expression of shared cultural experience, and more. *Early Downhome Blues* utilizes a more multidisciplinary approach to understanding blues, fusing Jeff Todd Titon's two graduate disciplines: American studies (itself an interdisciplinary field) and ethnomusicology. Titon played guitar with Lazy Bill Lucas in the late 1960s and early 1970s, putting him in the position of participant-observer for part of this study (something Titon didn't realize at the time). The end result is a well-rounded study of the blues.

Early Downhome Blues came out of Jeff Todd Titon's 1971 dissertation in American studies at the University of Minnesota. The first edition was published in 1977 and remained in print until 1990. The second edition was published in 1994.

Since the 1959 publication of Samuel Charters's *The Country Blues* (no. 63), most scholars tended to refer to the opposite of urban blues as country blues. Titon prefers the term "downhome," saying that it "refers not to a place but to a spirit, a sense of place evoked in singer and listener by a style of music." He sees "country" as problematic, since "downhome blues songs were performed regularly in towns and cities and by people who grew up there."

In part I, "The Music in the Culture" (chapters 1–2), Titon defines the title of his book and then uses sociological and anthropological studies written in the first third of the twentieth century to give a historical context to the life conditions of those musicians who helped create and define the sound of the blues.

Titon's training in ethnomusicology informs part II, "The Songs" (chapters 3–5) as well as much of the second chapter. Chapter 3 provides excellent melodic transcriptions of the vocal lines for forty-eight representative songs as well as transcriptions for the lyrics. Titon points out that transcription is not "an exact science," but these are quite well done. The notation indicates whether pitches are slightly higher or lower than Western notation typically allows. He also indicates slurs to both definite and indefinite pitches. Each transcription is accompanied by brief biographical information about the singer, discographical information about the recording, and suggested readings to learn more. In chapter 4, "Musical Analysis: Toward a Song-Producing System," Titon analyzes blues music, using examples from the previous chapter, in order to create a "performance model, a set of instructions for producing early downhome blues songs." He is clear that this model is "suggestive, not exhaustive," but the "melodic grammar" or "tonal lexicon" his analysis derived is quite good. This and the previous chapter provided some of the most unique contributions to blues scholarship. In the second edition's afterword, Titon says that chapter 5, "Formulaic Structure and Meaning in Early Downhome Blues Lyrics," was his least successful. Following John Fahey's "rejection of the romantic bias toward blues that characterized most of the writing at the time," Titon felt that his own interpretations of lyrics were too literal. Since Titon later felt this chapter needed revising, it is a shame he didn't rework this for the second edition.

Part III, "The Response," uses an American studies lens to examine the role of advertising in helping to define the blues. Titon gives a good analysis of race record advertisements and provides a number of black-and-white images of race record ads in the *Chicago Defender*, record company catalogs, and more.

The two appendices are interesting but odd. Appendix A—"Patterns of Record Purchase and Listening"—could have been worked into the body of the first chapter and not separated out. Appendix B is a transcription of Reverend Emmett Dickinson's 1930 sermon "Is There Harm in Singing the Blues?" While fascinating, Titon gives no explanation for it and provides no context. In the second edition's afterword, Titon writes about fieldwork and blues studies, discusses blues tourism, and gives a short survey of newer writings in the field. The afterword also includes images from nineteenth-century minstrel-song sheet music covers ("Jim Crow," "Zip Coon," etc.) that Titon felt he should have placed in the first edition.

The second edition has a companion CD of nineteen tracks, analyzed in chapter 3, that can be ordered; early printings of this edition included a CD. The first edition came with a four-song flexi disc (Soundsheet).

In addition to a good index, a bibliography, and detailed endnotes, the book includes 136 black-and-white photographs, charts, and figures (three more than in the first edition). The second edition includes a foreword by Alan Trachtenberg.

Early Downhome Blues remains a key work in our understanding of blues, particularly in terms of musical analysis.

Note: Between editions of this book, Titon had two editions of *Downhome Blues Lyrics: An Anthology from the Post–World War II Era* published (Twayne Publishers, 1981; University of Illinois Press, 1990). Despite the name, this excellent collection of blues lyrics isn't a supplement to *Early Downhome Blues*, as its contents are from the postwar era, whereas *Early Downhome Blues* focuses on prewar blues. —*GJ*

31. I've Got the St. Louis Blues

A Blues Life. By Henry Townsend as told to Bill Greensmith. (Music in American Life.) Urbana: University of Illinois Press, 1999. ISBN 0-252-02526-1 (paperback)

Henry "Mule" Townsend was a guitarist, pianist, and singer who lived through all of the major developments in the blues. As his

Mississippi Blues Trail marker proclaims, he was "the only blues artist to have recorded during every decade from the 1920s to the 2000s." Townsend wrote hundreds of songs and gave countless performances over his lifetime, though he was most active as a musician in the 1930s. In 1995, the National Endowment for the Arts honored Townsend by making him a National Heritage Fellow for his "contributions to our national cultural mosaic."

The body of *A Blues Life* comes from more than thirty hours of interviews conducted by Bill Greensmith, former member of the *Blues Unlimited* editorial board, photographer, and record producer. Greensmith edited the interviews to provide a chronological flow of the narrative, but other than the introduction, all of the words are Townsend's.

Henry Townsend was born in Shelby, Mississippi, in 1909, spent some childhood years in nearby Lula and later in Cairo, Illinois, where he ran away from home at the age of nine. Townsend then spent the remainder of his life living in the St. Louis/East St. Louis area, where he performed with, heard, and met many musicians, including Walter Davis, Big Joe Williams, Little Brother Montgomery, Peetie Wheatstraw, Leroy Carr, Scrapper Blackwell, Lonnie Johnson, and many lesser-known performers. His stories about his musical friends and acquaintances provide a wealth of information about the personal side of several prewar blues musicians and the music scene in the St. Louis area. From tales of the drinking habits of fellow musicians to reminiscences of being a teenager in trouble with the police, to illegally selling whiskey, to life hoboing, Townsend's stories about life are quite entertaining. Even at his advanced age during interviews, Henry Townsend's mind was sharp.

Some of Townsend's most interesting observations shed new light on his friend Walter Davis, so much that Greensmith writes that Townsend's "personal details of Davis's life will necessitate a major rewrite of his biography." He contradicts other accounts, including one by Big Joe Williams, of Walter Davis playing in nightclubs, saying, "Walter was very, very bashful when it came to public entertainment. . . . I've never known him to be booked on no job, not even no house party." He adds that Davis was just fine in the studio but was simply too shy to perform in public. A number of blues fans have assumed Walter Davis was forced to work as a hotel desk clerk because of hard times; Townsend's tales of him and Davis working at the hotel may shatter that myth.

While the life stories are captivating, *A Blues Life* doesn't focus that much on Townsend's actual music. It would be useful to have gotten to know more of Townsend's thoughts on songwriting, playing music, or musical inspirations, not just where he performed and with whom.

A Blues Life is one of the few works examining the much-neglected St. Louis and East St. Louis blues scene of the 1920s–1930s. Greensmith laments the lack of research into the St. Louis music scene: "The little knowledge we do possess only serves to illuminate how much we missed." (For more information on blues in St. Louis/East St. Louis, see Paul Garon's *The Devil's Son-in-Law: The Story of Peetie Wheatstraw and His Songs* [no. 32].)

A Blues Life includes a brief bibliography and a discography of Townsend's recordings, from his first side "Henry's Worry Blues" on Columbia in 1929 to his recordings for Blueberry Hill Records in 1997. This isn't a complete discography, as Townsend lived for another six years after the book was published. He was one of the featured artists recorded in 2004 on the Grammy-winning album *Last of the Great Mississippi Delta Bluesmen: Live in Dallas* (The Blue Shoe Project, 2007). Twenty-nine black-and-white photographs show not only Townsend but various people with whom he worked, places he lived, and records he made. There are detailed endnotes, but the index is fairly thin, limited to only names of people, places, and record labels.

A Blues Life is currently out of print, making new copies extremely expensive ($126–$189). Used copies can be purchased for as little as seven dollars or found at 380 libraries.

Townsend is quoted throughout Paul Oliver's *Conversation with the Blues* (1965; second edition, Cambridge University Press, 1997), and a two-part interview with Townsend appears in *Living Blues,* issues 164 and 165 (2002). For more life stories told by bluesmen, see the entries for Mance Lipscomb's *I Say Me for a Parable* (no. 83), Willie Dixon's *I Am the Blues* (no. 95), and David "Honeyboy" Edwards's *The World Don't Owe Me Nothing* (no. 45). —*GJ*

32. Oooh, Well, Well

The Devil's Son-in-Law: The Story of Peetie Wheatstraw & His Songs. By Paul Garon. London: Studio Vista, 1971. Revised and expanded edition, Chicago: Charles H. Kerr, 2003. 138 pp. ISBN 978-0-88286-266-8, $29.95

The music of Peetie Wheatstraw is little known today, though it was some of the most popular in the 1930s. With an output of 161 sides, Wheatstraw was one of the most recorded prewar blues artists; his popularity was so great that he even continued to be recorded through most of the Great Depression. He influenced countless musicians, including Robert Johnson, who, in contrast to Wheatstraw, recorded only twenty-nine songs and was relatively unknown during his lifetime but is quite well known today. Paul Garon contends that a large contributing factor to Wheatstraw's being largely forgotten is that the blues revival didn't focus on St. Louis piano music and that the "collecting establishment . . . preferred guitars to pianos and Gennetts to Deccas." Peetie Wheatstraw is the assumed name and persona of William Bunch (1902–1941), a piano player, singer, guitarist, and songwriter born in either Tennessee or Arkansas (Garon argues for the latter) and living most of his life in East St. Louis, Missouri's infamous "Valley" district. Despite the fact that the only known photograph of Wheatstraw shows him holding a guitar, he was more well known as a pianist. He cut his first side in 1930 and continued recording up to a month before meeting an early demise on December 21, 1941, when the car he was riding in crashed into a standing train.

In spite of Wheatstraw's popularity and large volume of recordings, relatively little information is known about his life. Other than a social security card application, a death certificate, and census records, little remains to flesh out a true biography of William Bunch. By the time Garon started research for the book, most of Bunch's relatives had died or could not be located. Only a few brief interviews with musicians and friends who knew Bunch (Henry Townsend, Ted Darby, and a few others) lend any personal accounts of his life. Garon readily admits that this isn't a full biography of Peetie Wheatstraw and that it is doubtful one can be written with such scant documentation of his life. Due to this fact, Garon devotes the majority of the book to analyzing Wheatstraw's songs, feeling that "there are other ways of finding out about bluesmen and their music . . . for the songs themselves constitute a meaningful picture of the blues singer." As lyrics aren't necessarily a window into how songwriters actually think and feel, Garon perhaps reads too much into the lyrics, particularly in his examinations of Wheatstraw's characteristic "Oooh, well, well."

It seems that the Peetie Wheatstraw and High Sheriff from Hell personas of William Bunch have lived on better than his music. The 1977 film *Petey Wheatstraw: The Devil's Son-in-Law*, starring blaxploitation star Rudy Ray Moore, clearly references Bunch, even if it is in name only. Garon devotes part of a chapter to examining the character Peter Wheatstraw in Ralph Ellison's *Invisible Man*. In one interview, Ellison claims to have known Peetie Wheatstraw and even to have played trumpet with him on a few occasions and that the book character was based on Wheatstraw's mannerisms and attitudes. In a later interview, Ellison makes no acknowledgment of having known Bunch and that the book character Peter Wheatstraw was only loosely based on "Afro-American mythology." While Ellison and others make mention of Peetie Wheatstraw existing as a figure in African American folklore long before William Bunch, they don't give any supporting evidence. Jon Michael Spencer in *Blues and Evil* (no. 98) writes of Peetie Wheatstraw's persona deriving from trickster figures in African mythology but never mentions any earlier characters by that name. Trudier Harris's article "Ellison's 'Peter Wheatstraw': His Basis in Black Folk Tradition" (*Mississippi Folklore Register* 9, no. 2 [1975]) also examines African trickster influences on the Wheatstraw character but doesn't offer any evidence of anyone using this name before Bunch.

Both editions contain a substantial number of photographs and illustrations (forty-eight in the 1971 edition and sixty-one in the 2003 edition). Most of the additional images in the revised book are surrealist drawings and paintings of Peetie Wheatstraw created by a number of surrealist artists, including Paul Garon and his wife, Beth. (While this inclusion may seem odd to some, Garon has long been involved in the surrealist movement and is the author of *Blues and the Poetic Spirit* [no. 87], an examination of blues through a surrealist lens.) The bibliography and discography are updated in the revised edition, and an index is added, making it a much more useful resource than the earlier edition. The most valuable addition is the inclusion of a twenty-four-track CD of Peetie Wheatstraw's music. Garon made few changes to the original text other than correcting transcription errors. He does expand several sections and adds an afterword. Despite these updates, there are several typographical errors in the new edition.

Garon succeeds in creating a compelling story of Peetie Wheatstraw despite a dearth of existing biographical data. The song analyses, transcriptions, and discography alone are useful references for blues scholars. —*GJ*

33. Where and When Pianos Are Preferred to Guitars

Deep South Piano: The Story of Little Brother Montgomery. By
Karl Gert zur Heide. London: Studio Vista, 1970. ISBN
0-289-70028-0

Often remembered as a blues player, Little Brother Montgomery
was an extremely versatile pianist, easily transitioning from barrelhouse playing to ragtime and then to jazz. With a seventy-five-year
performing career, he would influence countless blues and jazz
piano players. He is one of the major links between jazz and blues
piano playing.

Eurreal Wilford Montgomery was born into a very musical family in Kentwood, Louisiana, near New Orleans, in 1906. In addition
to the family singing at church, Eurreal's uncle Gonzy was the leader
of the Big Four Band, a local dance band. Most of Eurreal's nine
siblings also played an instrument, and he began playing piano at
the age of four or five. Due to his father owning a piano in the house
and also running a nearby honky-tonk, many pianists stopped by to
play, including Jelly Roll Morton. All of these musicians had a huge
influence on Little Brother Montgomery's development as a musician. He learned quickly and developed a strong ear.

Montgomery first began playing in barrelhouses in Louisiana
but soon was playing all over central and southern Mississippi at
turpentine and lumber camps. He later toured with the dance
orchestra Clarence Desdune's Joyland Revelers and led his own
jazz septet, the Southland Troubadours, both centered on Jackson,
Mississippi. In 1928, he moved to Chicago, where he would ultimately reside, though he did spend about eight years back in
Mississippi in the 1930s. Montgomery recorded for Paramount,
Broadway, Melotone, and Bluebird in the 1930s. In the 1960s, he
toured Europe extensively and even started his own record label,
FM Records. Montgomery performed right up to his death of con-
gestive heart failure on September 6, 1985.

While much has been written on blues in the Delta and northern Mississippi hill country, little has been done to document the
lower half of Mississippi. Montgomery's family moved to Norfield,
Mississippi, near Brookhaven, in the early 1920s. He recalls touring to different lumber camps and towns in Mississippi, where
the mills would provide a piano and hire a musician for a week or
more to entertain the workers. He performed all over the central

and southern portion of the state, spending time in Electric Mills, north of Meridian, and D'Lo and Sanatorium, between Jackson and Hattiesburg (where he also played). He even performed in Mobile and Birmingham, Alabama.

Deep South Blues isn't a great read. Like many others in the Paul Oliver Blues Paperbacks Series, zur Heide's work doesn't flow well or make any big conclusions. The strength of this and books like Bengt Olsson's *Memphis Blues* isn't in their narrative; it is that they were some of the few works to cover their respective subjects. Little Brother Montgomery had an incredible memory and related a wealth of information to zur Heide. The list of musicians Montgomery heard and worked with is staggering. Many of them are names that have never been recorded and are mostly forgotten: No Leg Kenny, Son Framion, Rip Top, Loomis Gibson, Papa Lord God, Sudan Washington, Leon Brumfield, Varnado Anderson, Ernest Haywood, Raggin' Willie Wells, Stiff Arm Eddie, Chicken Henry, Blind Jug, Blind Homer, and many others. Though *Deep South Blues* was published in 1970, zur Heide focuses on Little Brother Montgomery only up to about 1940; the remaining thirty years up to time of publication are cursorily summed up in a one-paragraph "Post-War Appendix." Thankfully, some later interviews in the *Mississippi Rag, Down Beat, Jefferson, Living Blues,* and other music magazines have fleshed out some of his later years, but a more comprehensive biography of Little Brother Montgomery is needed.

In the book's 112 pages, only the first fifty-three are the story of Little Brother Montgomery. The second half of this work contains a wealth of reference material. In addition to a discography, lyric transcriptions, and a name index, there is a "Who's Who" section that contains brief biographical entries on 121 of the musicians Montgomery associated with in his early years. This is the extent of what is known about a number of these figures. We are indebted to zur Heide for taking the time to create these short biographical sketches. This listing alone makes it clear that there have been more musicians performing throughout the South than we can ever possibly know. Those who were recorded represent only a small fraction of blues and jazz players.

Thirty-nine black-and-white photos help show some of the places Montgomery played and people with whom he performed.
—*GJ*

34. Going Where Robert Johnson
and Skip James Had Gone To

Searching for Robert Johnson. By Peter Guralnick. New York: Dutton, 1989. ISBN 0-525-24801-3 (hardcover), ISBN 0-452-27949-6 (Plume/Penguin/Dutton paperback), $12.00

Searching for Robert Johnson romanticized the blues for the 1990s as much as Samuel Charters's *The Country Blues* had for the 1960s. Printed a year before the two-CD Sony/Columbia reissue of Johnson's recordings, this little book was what was available in bookstores when the CD set's buyers sought something to read about the influential bluesman.

Sooner or later in his career, Guralnick was bound to write about Robert Johnson. In his 1971 book, *Feel Like Going Home* (no. 80), he mentions the bluesman only in passing, presumably because nearly nothing about his life was known. As a result, Johnson makes fleeting and ghostly appearances in the book's chapters on rock, blues, Muddy Waters, and Johnny Shines, but not in the profile of Skip James, an absence I think is interesting for a reason I will explain later.

As the 1970s proceeded, discoveries and speculations about Johnson's life were presented. Chief among them was Gayle Dean Wardlow's 1968 recovery of the 1938 death certificate, which provided the birth and death dates and some basic vital statistics information; it was made public in a 1971 article by Stephen Calt in *Blues Unlimited* magazine. Greil Marcus devoted a chapter in *Mystery Train* (1975) to Johnson, in which the lyric analyses of "Stones in My Passway" and "Hell Hound on My Trail" served to depict the singer whose "vision was of a world without salvation, redemption, or rest." Robert Palmer, for his remarks on Johnson in *Deep Blues* (1981), gave a Southern slant to the supernatural lore surrounding the bluesman. When it came time for Guralnick to weigh in on Johnson—for an illustrated article in *Living Blues* magazine (no. 53, summer/autumn 1982)—he had to give the principles of what Marcus and Palmer had tantalizingly suggested.

One of Guralnick's contributions was his report of the Johnson research done by Texas blues scholar Mack McCormick. Since McCormick's Johnson manuscript *The Biography of a Phantom* is still unpublished, everything we know about it is through Guralnick's essay. From McCormick's findings, Guralnick gives the earliest printed accounts of Johnson's parents, his birth, his two marriages and various lovers, and the surviving photographs. Taking what he calls "pieces of a puzzle, tantalizing clues," Guralnick combines them with previously published interviews with Johnson's contemporaries and recording associates. It was a remarkably comprehensive account of Johnson's life that needed no updating in 1989 when the article was published as the book. For many readers, it is one of the three main sources of biographical information about Johnson, the other two being Stephen LaVere's 1990 booklet notes for the two-CD Sony/Columbia Johnson reissue, *The Complete Recordings,* and Calt and Wardlow's article "Robert Johnson" for *78 Quarterly* (no. 4, 1989).

There are two matters in the study that seem incomplete. One is the gap in the chronology from 1931, when Johnson returned to the Delta after a year improving his guitar skills, to 1936 and his first recording sessions. Most writers since Guralnick have failed to account for what Johnson was doing, often just saying that "he rambled a lot during that time." While there may be seemingly nothing for his biography for those five years, there is a lot for 1931–1936 to be gleaned from the musical sources of his recorded repertory; Komara's *Road to Robert Johnson* (no. 35) was an attempt to fill that gap.

The other matter is the feeling that we cannot know everything about Johnson, and so we feel unsatisfied with what we do know. The irony of this unsatisfied feeling is that we possess more details about Johnson's life than we do for any other blues musician who had died in or by 1942.

Because the biographical record is fragmentary, Guralnick suggests that we should seek not the historical "what" of Johnson but the aesthetic source of his musical expressions. In this study, he begins his own search in African American blues culture as elicited through the interview quotations from Johnny Shines, Son House, and Robert Lockwood. But then, Guralnick steps from blues culture to the larger-scaled Western poetic culture, to which Guralnick likens the purported soul deal to the Faust legend and Johnson's lyrical facility to those of Catullus, Gerard Manley Hopkins, and John Donne. These poetic claims may risk seeming irrelevant to the subject of Johnson, but then again, they are no more outlandish than what Marcus and Palmer had claimed in their Johnson writings. Compare Guralnick and Marcus's explications of "Hell Hound on My Trail" to see what about Johnson each writer wants to convey to his readers. For his part, Guralnick seems to see romance not in the gritty life but in the cultural ideas found beyond the life; it is that romance that he stirs in his readers to seek for themselves. How that romance helps toward better appreciations of the records is a question left to the reader to solve.

Not to be overlooked is the discography that was added when the *Living Blues* text was reprinted as a book. One highlight of Guralnick's books—and of Marcus's *Mystery Train*, too—is the discography appendix, in which the comments to the citations are as informed and enthusiastic as anything in the main text. The record listing for *Searching for Robert Johnson* gives Guralnick's advice on reissues for Johnson, his "influences" (Charlie Patton, House, Tommy Johnson, Leroy Carr), "contemporaries" (Calvin Frazier, Johnny Shines, Muddy Waters), and "heirs" (Robert Lockwood, Elmore James, and Howlin' Wolf). Readers should not let the out-of-print status of the cited LPs keep them from enjoying the appraisals. For a wise example, about Skip James's complete 1931 Paramount recordings, Guralnick wrote, "As much as we look to Robert Johnson for vivid, sometimes startling originality of expression, so Robert must have looked to the deep, almost unfathomable blues of Nehemiah 'Skip' James." To be able to write that sentence in 1989 if not in 1971, Guralnick apparently realized (to paraphrase Skip James's forbidding statement in *Feel Like Going Home*) that "Robert Johnson has been and gone from places that Skip James had gone to." —*EK*

35. Listen at the Crossroad

The Road to Robert Johnson: The Genesis and Evolution of Blues in the Delta from the Late 1800s through 1938. By Edward Komara. Milwaukee: Hal Leonard, 2007. ISBN 978-0-634-00907-5 (paperback), $14.95

Robert Johnson is the subject of more books than just about any other figure in the blues. He is even the focus of a published screenplay (*Love in Vain* by Alan Greenberg) and a Japanese graphic novel (*Me and the Devil Blues: The Unreal Life of Robert Johnson* by Akira Hiramoto). Johnson's life has been so obscured by misinformation, myth, and legend that at least half the books written on him are attempts to "set the record straight." Each of these "clarifying" books makes valuable contributions to the scholarship while eliciting further criticism and elucidation from newer examinations of Johnson. The first decade in the 2000s saw a flurry of works critically reexamining various points in the life of Robert Johnson. Barry Lee Pearson and Bill McCulloch's *Robert Johnson Lost and Found* (University of Illinois Press, 2003) removes many of the myths to present a more historic figure. Patricia Schroeder's *Robert Johnson: Mythmaking and Contemporary American Culture* (University of Illinois Press, 2004) focuses on the myths and legends surrounding Johnson to "explore him in his larger role as a contemporary cultural icon." Elijah Wald's *Escaping the Delta: Robert Johnson and the Invention of the Blues* (no. 36) questions a number of false assumptions about Johnson's world and exposure to music outside the delta. Tom Graves's *Crossroads: The Life and Afterlife of Blues Legend Robert Johnson* (Demers Books, 2008) rethinks the crossroads lore and looks at issues related to Johnson after his death. Articles and letters in *Living Blues* magazine on Johnson and Ike Zimmerman (sometimes spelled Zinnerman) during this decade also help untangle the confusing web of Johnson's life (Tom Freeland, *Living Blues* no. 150 [2000]; Bruce Michael Conforth, *Living Blues* no. 194 [2008]; Stephen LaVere, *Living Blues* no. 203 [2009]; Jim O'Neal, *Living Blues* no. 204 [2009]).

Of all the books, the one that focuses most critically on Robert Johnson's music is Edward Komara's *The Road to Robert Johnson*. It was the last proposed work in a Hal Leonard series on Robert Johnson and was prepared in 2000 for a 2001 publication date, but production delays postponed its appearance until 2007.

Komara writes about Johnson's life, death, traveling, and recording sessions, as well as the record industry, the development of the blues, and life in the Delta, but the real theme of this book is that "no man is an island." Johnson didn't create his songs in a vacuum; he drew upon existing works of others and was influenced by popular styles of his day. Casual students of the blues know about the influence of Son House and Leroy Carr on Robert Johnson's music, but Komara gives melodic precedents for every song in Johnson's recorded oeuvre; he even shows twenty-five musical precedents for "Sweet Home Chicago." Musicians like Blind Blake, Peetie Wheatstraw, Roosevelt Sykes, Charlie Patton, Lonnie Johnson, and others certainly influenced Robert Johnson, as Komara convincingly details. Much has been written over the years of rock musicians "stealing" songs and ideas from blues musicians, but Komara points out a judicious amount of "borrowing" occurring among blues musicians. Much of *The Road to Robert Johnson* fleshes out the list of recorded melodic precedents to Johnson's songs that Komara prepared for *Living Blues* magazine (no. 129, 1996) and expanded in Gayle Dean Wardlow's *Chasin' That Devil Music* (no. 40). Komara doesn't just mention the names of melodic antecedents for Johnson's songs; he includes musical transcriptions. The transcriptions were done by Komara as well as a carefully crafted set by a team of transcribers led by Dave Rubin in *Robert Johnson: The New Transcriptions* (Hal Leonard, 1999).

From a musician's perspective, this book offers interesting insights into Johnson's music and technique. Komara gives detailed descriptions of various tunings most likely used by Johnson and how they were used for different songs. One of the most interesting sections in this book isn't about Johnson's life but about Dave Rubin and his music transcribing team obsessively trying tuning after tuning to determine the most likely tuning Johnson used for certain piano-based songs. Komara believes that the Aadd9 tuning (E-B-E-A-C#-E) they deduced was used by Johnson to "arrange [some] piano blues for the guitar." Komara examines probable tunings used by Johnson in relation to harmonica tuning and technique (Johnson started on harmonica before guitar) and how Johnson adapted piano technique to guitar. Komara also cleverly shows how Johnson musically took guitar blues from a more linear polyphonic approach to one that was more "vertical[ly] harmonic and homophonic."

The final chapter examines Johnson's influence after his death, particularly in the music of Calvin Frazier, Johnny Shines, Robert Junior Lockwood, and others. Komara clearly shows Robert Johnson as part of a blues continuum that "came before and continued after his performing years" but points to his unique talents as being a "musical catalyst, speeding up the rate of musical development among his contemporaries."

The book contains forty illustrations and fifty-seven musical transcription examples, a bibliographic reference list, a discographical reference list, and three appendices. Appendix I is a list of recorded melodic precedents to Robert Johnson's songs. Komara is careful to point out that he lists these as "precedents" and not "sources," as "there was no certain way to know if Johnson heard those melodies through individual records or from an imitator." Appendix II is a "suggested chronological order of composition of Robert Johnson's recorded repertory." Appendix III is a list of Johnson's "repertory by guitar tuning and technique."

The Road to Robert Johnson is recommended reading for anyone wanting to know more about the life of one of the blues' most intriguing figures. Musicians wanting insights into Johnson's probable technique or wishing to learn more about prewar country blues will want to read this book. It is unfortunate that the significant publication delay prevented the book from informing a large amount of Johnson scholarship for over half a decade. —*GJ*

36. Marketing the Delta

Escaping the Delta: Robert Johnson and the Invention of the Blues. By Elijah Wald. New York: Amistad, 2004. ISBN 0-06-052423-5 (hardcover), ISBN 978-0-06-052427-2 (paperback), $14.99

Elijah Wald is a musician and the author of a number of books on music and/in/as culture, including *Josh White: Society Blues* (Routledge, 2002), *The Blues: A Very Short Introduction* (Oxford University Press, 2010), *The Dozens: A History of Rap's Mama* (Oxford University Press, 2012), and more. Much like the work of Howard Zinn reexamining our ideas of American history, a key element in Wald's writings is overturning popular conceptions about music.

Wald's *Escaping the Delta* uses the life and music of Robert Johnson as a means of redefining blues not as an isolated purist romantic folk music but as pop music in constant dialogue with other popular musics. Upon publication, the book generated a lot of hype, mostly from one sentence: "As far as the evolution of black music goes, Robert Johnson was an extremely minor figure, and very little that happened in the decades following his death would have been affected if he had never played a note." (Wald isn't one to make soft statements; he is author of *How the Beatles Destroyed Rock 'n' Roll: An Alternative History of American Popular Music* [Oxford University Press, 2011].) Despite this statement, Wald focuses on Johnson because more people are likely to have access to his recorded works than most other blues performers and he is an example of a talented musician aware of popular music trends of his day and who incorporated many of them into his sound. Wald is interested in overturning what he claims to be false assumptions by most blues scholarship, but these assumptions aren't as strongly held as he claims. He is probably correct that Robert Johnson is held at the center of the blues universe by the general public, but a large amount of blues scholarship doesn't put Johnson on a pedestal over other prewar blues musicians.

Wald states that his main focus "is to try to look at the blues scene from inside, as it evolved, rather than to apply the standards of modern fans, experts, or academics." His point is that the framework we use to define and examine blues has been done almost exclusively by those not part of the culture that created the blues. While this is, of course, an interesting goal, his language seems disparaging of the many useful musicological/sociological examinations of blues. Blues scholarship has certainly given us more meaningful definitions of blues than Wald's "working definition of 'blues,' at least up to the 1960s [which is]: 'Whatever the mass of black record buyers called "blues" in any period.'" Elsewhere Wald does define blues in less vague terms, but he makes this strong statement, like others in the book, as a way of driving home the idea that prewar blues musicians saw themselves and their music in very different ways from what is often attributed by later scholars (the same could be said of all history).

The first section of the book, "The World That Johnson Knew," gives a framework to Robert Johnson's world by examining the popular music of Robert Johnson's time. A 1941–1942 joint study by Fisk University and the Library of Congress of music in Coahoma County, Mississippi, provides some of the most fascinating data in the book. Part of this study resulted in Fisk University student Samuel Adams's master's thesis, which looked at what music people in Coahoma County were listening to at this time. He surveyed people about their listening preferences and recorded the contents of jukeboxes in four different black cafés in Clarksdale around 1941. (A list of these jukebox records is included in an appendix; for a publication of the Adams thesis, see Gordon and Nemerov, *Lost Delta Found* [no. 43].) Part 2, "Robert Johnson," traces each of Johnson's songs to earlier commercial recordings as a means of showing how influenced he was by popular music of the day, particularly by artists such as Peetie Wheatstraw, Leroy Carr, and Lonnie Johnson. These explorations into the musical roots of Robert Johnson's recordings draw on Edward Komara's list of recorded melodic precedents to Robert Johnson's songs in Gayle Dean Wardlow's *Chasin' That Devil Music* (no. 40) and Bob Groom's articles in *Blues Unlimited*. (For a more thorough look at these sources, see Komara's *The Road to Robert Johnson* [no. 35].) "The Blues Roll On," the final section of the book, tackles a lot of the romantic, revisionist notions of the blues that developed through and after the blues revival. Wald's final chapter, "Afterthought: So What about the Devil?" examines our culture's fascination with stories of selling one's soul to the devil.

There are thirty-five pages of endnotes, a bibliography, and an index. There are no photos or illustrations.

In addition to some grand statements, there are some factual mistakes in the book. For instance, Little Milton was born near Inverness and raised in Magenta and later Greenville, not Jackson. Probably intended as a hook, the subtitle—*Robert Johnson and the Invention of the Blues*—is a bit misleading. The book isn't about the creation of blues as a style but more about the term "blues" as a label used by record companies for marketing and the sound white producers wanted from their black recording artists. Despite this, *Escaping the Delta* is an enjoyable read that challenges many romantic notions of blues and the life of rural bluesmen. (See the entry for *The Road to Robert Johnson* for other books written in this same period that challenge myths about Johnson and examine the image of Johnson in popular culture of today.)

Back to the Crossroads: The Roots of Robert Johnson (Yazoo 2070) is a companion CD to the book. It contains twenty-three song sources for Robert Johnson's music. *—GJ*

37. Pictures from the Dusty Blues Times

Hard Luck Blues: Roots Music Photographs from the Great Depression. By Rich Remsberg. Urbana: University of Illinois Press, 2010. ISBN 978-0-252-03524-1 (hardcover), $75.00, ISBN 978-0-252-07709-8 (paperback), $34.95

A good blues record can take your imagination far, but a good photograph can transport you the rest of the way. Unlike today's CDs and LPs, the blues 78s made before World War II were issued without photos. For faces of the blues artists, fans and researchers have scrounged for old record catalogs, dealers' lists, and promotional leaflets. For the everyday sights in prewar blues cultures, pictures taken by African Americans are rare, largely because most of them could not afford a camera or lived far from a photo-developing service. The photographs taken by the Farm Security Administration of the federal government between 1937 and 1941 provide us with most of the surviving images we have of the dusty blues times that we now romanticize.

It is odd that the Farm Security Administration is best known today for its documentary photographs of migrants, sharecroppers, their homes, and their environments. The administration had been formed in 1935 as the Resettlement Administration toward improving the situations of poor farmers on substandard lands. The photos were meant initially to record visually the farmers contacted by the government program, but later they were taken for press and educational uses. Led by Roy Stryker, several young photographers became legendary for their work for the administration, including Walker Evans, Dorothea Lange, Gordon Parks, and Marion Post Woolcott (who took many of the blues-relevant photographs in Mississippi).

Today the photographs are available digitally through the Library of Congress's American Memory website. The black-and-white images may be viewed for free at http://memory.loc.gov/ ammem/fsahtml/fahome.html, and the color images at http:// memory.loc.gov/ammem/fsachtml/fsowhome.html. However, the best images should not be viewed on a computer monitor but on good paper.

Rich Remsberg's *Hard Luck Blues* renders a great service to roots music fans and collectors by culling and presenting the music photographs worth a second look. They are presented geographically, starting in the Southeast, going west through the South, Louisiana and the Southwest, reversing direction in California, and heading eastward through the Northwest and the High Plains, the Midwest, Chicago, and the Northeast. The ethnicities are mixed together in the chapters: Caucasians, African Americans, Native Americans, and Spanish Americans. The now-dead practice of performing in blackface is given in a few shots, in one instance in a picture of grade-school white children applying blackface for a school festivity in South Carolina, placed jarringly opposite a photo of a middle-school black music class singing to piano accompaniment. In his selection, Remberg tenders no rosiness and offers no nostalgia.

For comparison among the geographic regions, Remberg tries to give a cross-section of images from public venues, private homes, playing for tips, playing for recreation, in school, and in church. The photos of white musicians should not be overlooked. Some are of brass bands, including a remarkable set of images of a Salvation

Army street band with a female member playing a gorgeous Gibson archtop guitar. In fact, guitars and fiddles are seen most often in the photos of white performers. Some photos allow several views of a cultural event, like a Cajun fais-dodo, an Alabama square dance, or an outdoor religious revival. The photos of various Spanish American and Mexican musicians performing at Penasco and Taos, New Mexico, bear close scrutiny.

Blues fans will find nearly every type of picture they are looking for in the Southeast, South, and Chicago chapters. There are two photos of musicians busking on street corners: one from Montgomery, Alabama, the other from Belzoni, Mississippi. In the selected images, the African American musicians appear to play a wide variety of instruments, including guitar, fiddle, wall one-string, harmonica, accordion, and piano, to name a few. The wide array of instruments available in their cultures is suggested in a 1939 photo of a Beale Street pawnshop, where guitars, banjos, and ukuleles are hanging in the window. Here and there recorded blues musicians pop up: Buddy Moss in a set of three photos from a Georgia convict camp; Lonnie Johnson in a small Chicago club; the Count Basie band at the Savoy Ballroom in Chicago. A curious shot suggesting a retention of nineteenth-century entertainment is of a minstrel troupe consisting of African Americans promoting their traveling show to a crowd of African Americans in New Jersey. The one set of photos that won't be found in this collection is Marion Post Woolcott's famous 1939 shots of the couple dancing in a Mississippi Delta juke joint. However, there are a few pictures—only a few, so all the more remarkable—of whites and blacks intermingling: around a white guitarist on a West Virginia street; and performers of each race taking turns to perform at an Oklahoma union meeting. Otherwise, the races and cultures stayed separate, even in the shot of the Chicago nightclub of African American dancers and jazz band performing to what appears to be an exclusively white audience. Such pictures communicate the pre-1942 era of segregation like very few blues records can. —*EK*

38. The Best Woman Guitarist
That Big Bill Broonzy Ever Heard

Woman with Guitar: Memphis Minnie's Blues. By Paul and Beth Garon. New York: Da Capo, 1992. ISBN 0-306-80460-3 (out of print)

Though women constituted the bulk of early blues recordings, there have been relatively few female blues guitarists until fairly recently. In 1930–1931, female singer-guitarists Geeshie Wiley and Elvie Thomas recorded fewer than five songs for Paramount Records. Laura Dukes of the Memphis Jug Band played mandolin, banjo, ukulele, and banjolele on recordings from the 1930s to the1970s. Though she wasn't recorded until the 1950s, Piedmont musician Etta Baker began playing guitar (and later banjo) in 1916. The most popular, though, was Memphis Minnie, who played guitar on 212 sides from 1929 through 1959. Big Bill Broonzy called her "the best woman guitarist [he] had ever heard," but several stories of her winning guitar contests against Broonzy, Muddy Waters, and others show her as one of the greatest guitarists of the 1930s and 1940s, male or female. Her music influenced countless performers, from Koko Taylor, "Bukka" White, and Johnny Shines to Chuck Berry, Lucinda Williams, and even Led Zeppelin. She was inducted into the first class of Blues Hall of Fame recipients in 1980.

Memphis Minnie was born Lizzie Douglas in Algiers, Louisiana, in 1897 and moved to Walls, Mississippi (Desoto County), several years later. (Paul and Beth Garon state that she moved in 1904, but recent research by Jim O'Neal points out that the US Census lists her as living in Tunica County, Mississippi, in 1900 and 1910.) She received her first guitar in 1905 and later, as a teenager, she began performing as "Kid" Douglas around northeast Mississippi and Memphis, playing for house parties, on street corners, and even for the Ringling Brothers Circus. She ultimately began performing as Memphis Minnie, the name used on almost all her recordings. She married "Kansas" Joe McCoy in 1929 and recorded her earliest sides with him that same year. Two of these first sides would remain some of her most popular: "Bumble Bee" and "When the Levee Breaks" (later covered by Led Zeppelin). The couple soon moved to Chicago, where Minnie's career would really take off. In the late 1930s, she married another guitarist, Ernest Lawlars, "Little Son Joe." She recorded prolifically during the 1930s and 1940s, with several hits like "Me and My Chauffeur Blues," "What's the Matter with the Mill?," and "In My Girlish Days." She was one of the early blues guitarists to play a steel-reso-nator National guitar and was also one of the early blues adopters of electric guitar. By several accounts her most wild guitar playing was reserved for live audiences; the studios reined in her technique for recording sessions. Minnie suffered a stroke in 1957, effectively ending her musical career. Her and her husband's declining health forced them to move to Memphis. Memphis Minnie passed away in a nursing home in 1973.

Woman with Guitar by husband and wife Paul and Beth Garon is the first and, so far, only book-length biography of Memphis Minnie and analysis of her music. Similar to Paul Garon's earlier book, *The Devil's Son-in-Law* (no. 32), *Woman with Guitar* is divided into two sections: biography and song analysis. The first section follows fairly standard biographical structure while carefully placing Memphis Minnie's life in larger social contexts. Interviews (and stories told secondhand) with Minnie's younger sister Daisy Douglas and sister-in-law Ethel Douglas provide good information and insights into Memphis Minnie's life. The second half of the book is less straightforward than the biographical section. The Garons analyze the lyrical content of Minnie's songs "to reveal the unheard side of Minnie's entire realm so that we might recover the power of her achievement in a way that addresses the urgent needs of humankind today." They manage this through "a contemporary surrealist lens, focused on the past, for it is the ceaseless reevaluation of the past that enables us to step more confidently into a provocative future." Quotes by André Breton and other surrealists may make this section difficult, strange, or even irrelevant for casual readers wishing only to know about Memphis Minnie's life and guitar technique. But this section offers much to the patient reader. Among the many good analyses in the latter half of this book, the Garons' examination of issues of prostitution offer very interesting insights into not only Minnie and her lyrics but typical white music critics' handling of issues like sex for money and drug use. Perhaps the authors see more in some lyrics than what is likely there, but their deep thinking about lyrics is important and shouldn't be outright discounted as intellectuals reading too much into "simple" lyrics. Their analyses through the lenses of surrealism, psychoanalysis, folklore, critical theory, and more help us more fully flesh out our understanding of blues.

In addition to an index and extensive endnotes, the Garons have provided an excellent discography that updates the entries in *Blues and Gospel Records 1902–1943* (no. 41). They correct a number of recording dates as well as instrumentation and personnel information. The book also includes fifty black-and-white photographs and images from various business documents. There are some typographical errors, and the 332 pages could have been reduced by stronger editing, but the work is important to anyone wanting to know more about one of the blues' most important guitarists, male or female.

Though currently out of print, used copies of *Woman with Guitar* can be found for approximately twenty dollars or in a number of academic libraries.

Readers wanting to learn more about early female electric guitarists may enjoy Gayle Wald's *Shout, Sister, Shout! The Untold Story of Rock-and-Roll Trailblazer Sister Rosetta Tharpe* (Boston: Beacon Press, 2007). Those wanting to better understand the analytical lens used in the book's second half may want to consult Paul Garon's *Blues and the Poetic Spirit* (no. 87). —GJ

39. Sing the Blues in Church to Cry Out "Holy, Holy, Holy"

The Rise of Gospel Blues: The Music of Thomas Andrew Dorsey in the Urban Church. By Michael W. Harris. New York: Oxford University Press, 1992. ISBN 0-19-506376-7, ISBN 0-19-509057-8 (paperback), $39.99

To some in the church, blues has long been the "devil's music." From tales of souls sold to the devil to the "devil's son-in-law" of Peetie Wheatstraw to Son House's inner conflict of whether to sing the blues or preach the gospel, blues is often described as music antithetical to the church. But the gap between blues and gospel music isn't as wide as many often think. Blind Willie Johnson's songs were musically blues but lyrically spiritual. Today, Rev. John Wilkins, pastor of Hunters Chapel in Como, Mississippi, sings powerful gospel words to the sound of hill country blues. Known as the "Father of Gospel Music," Thomas Dorsey once performed hokum blues as Georgia Tom.

It is Thomas Andrew Dorsey who serves as the central figure in Michael Harris's book *The Rise of Gospel Blues: The Music of Thomas Andrew Dorsey in the Urban Church.* Dorsey was a pianist, composer, and arranger born in Villa Rica, Georgia, in 1899 to a minister father and church organist mother. His family moved to Atlanta in 1908, where Dorsey was exposed to the music of Ma Rainey. He began playing piano for theaters, house parties, and brothels at the age of twelve. At sixteen, Dorsey moved to Chicago and studied at the Chicago School of Composition and Arranging. This led to him composing and arranging for J. Mayo Williams's Chicago

Music Publishing Company and for Paramount. His early years in Chicago were an interesting time, as Dorsey was playing and composing both sacred and secular works. Inspired at hearing W. M. Nix (incorrectly listed as A. M. Nix by Harris) sing at the National Baptist Convention in 1921, Dorsey started writing religious music and briefly served as music director for New Hope Baptist Church. It wouldn't be for another decade that Dorsey's musical career would ultimately turn religious. The blues reigned for Dorsey in the 1920s. He served as bandleader and arranger for Ma Rainey's Wild Cats Jazz Band. Georgia Tom recorded and performed with a number of blues musicians, including Big Bill Broonzy and Tampa Red, the latter cowriting the hit song "Tight Like That" with Dorsey. Rigorous touring schedules and internal conflict led Dorsey to two nervous breakdowns. The 1932 death of his wife during childbirth helped solidify Dorsey's decision to devote his life to religious music. This event also inspired the song "Take My Hand, Precious Lord." This and his "Peace in the Valley" have been covered by numerous black and white musicians and now appear in various denominational hymnals.

The Rise of Gospel Blues uses the life and music of Thomas Dorsey to explain the creation of modern black gospel music. Like W. C. Handy and Jimmie Rodgers, other musicians touted as "fathers" of blues and country music, Dorsey wasn't the sole creator of the gospel music genre. Dorsey never claims to have invented gospel music (the term itself was widely used in the late nineteenth century), but his sound was so popular that many people referred to works in his compositional style as "dorseys" before they became popularly known as gospel music or gospels. While he does make mention of those innovators, such as Charles Tindley, who were doing similar musical fusions much earlier than Dorsey, Harris doesn't give them enough credit or attention.

Through exploring the life and compositional techniques of Thomas Dorsey, Harris gives excellent insights into tensions between blues and sacred music. Many larger urban black churches in the 1920s and 1930s tried hard to blend into white society, favoring the music of Beethoven to the "rougher" sounds of some rural black singing traditions with hand clapping, call and response, and shouting. Dorsey's background in blues and understanding of jazz, combined with his schooling in composition and arranging, put him in the perfect position to help create a new sound, fusing more staid hymn singing with more emotionally expressive elements from the blues. Dorsey in some ways created musical analogues to the sermons delivered by the Reverends J. M. Gates and W. M. Nix, particularly in contours of climaxes. Extensive interviews with Dorsey and Harris's own analyses give clear musical insights into how Dorsey crafted these songs.

Harris does a good job examining the preacher-bluesman relationship, looking into the roles each played in society. He also gives a good overview of the record industry, particularly between 1926 and 1932, the "sermon era" of recorded music, when more than 750 sermons were produced on 78 rpm discs. These sermons on record were extremely popular; Rev. J. M. Gates's sermon "Nebuchadnezzar" outsold 1926 Bessie Smith releases fourfold.

Despite a tension many felt between blues and sacred music, Dorsey saw a neutrality to the blues: "There's no such thing as a blue note. Blues don't own no notes. The world of music owns the notes and sounds on the piano . . . [the seventh] can be in anything. It's up to the individual to know how and when to bring it out." In some ways, he saw blues and gospel as two sides of the same coin: "Blues is as important to a person feeling bad as 'Nearer My God to Thee.' I'm talking about popularity; I'm talking about inside the individual. This moan person. . . . When you cry out, that is something down there that should have come out a long time ago. Whether it's blues or gospel, there is a way. . . . A man or woman singing the blues in the church will cry out, 'Holy, holy, holy.'"

The Rise of Gospel Blues was adapted for book form from Harris's 1982 dissertation at Harvard, where he received a PhD in music and American church history. As such, it can prove awkward reading for those not used to reading academic texts. His musical analyses are excellent but could be confusing to readers not familiar with music theory. As Harris's book is mainly concerned with the beginnings of modern black gospel music, the story ends in 1933. Dorsey would go on to live another sixty years, dying in 1993, one year after the book was published. It would be nice to know more about his life in these later years, though these would involve virtually no blues.

Harris provides an excellent index, thorough bibliography, and extensive endnotes. Only nine black-and-white photographs are included in the book. The twenty-three music notation examples are extremely clear and easy to follow.

For more information about Dorsey's years playing blues, see Jim O'Neal and Amy Van Singel, "Georgia Tom Dorsey," in

The Voice of the Blues: Classic Interviews from "Living Blues" Magazine (no. 91) or the same interview in *Living Blues* no. 20 (March–April 1975). —GJ

40. Knocking on Doors and Talking with People

Chasin' That Devil Music: Searching for the Blues. By Gayle Dean Wardlow. San Francisco: Miller Freeman, 1998. ISBN 0-87930-552-5 (paperback), $19.99

As blues fans begin learning more about the musicians who created and performed the music, they will eventually start learning the names of those who have helped uncover and rediscover this music. At the height of the blues revival in the 1960s, many white fans became obsessed with locating blues artists who had helped create the genre in the 1920s and 1930s. Collectors began searching for then "undiscovered" 78s of prewar blues artists, hoping to find rare Robert Johnson recordings or an even more elusive Willie Brown 78. Many of these discoveries made their way into the pages of music collector magazines like *78 Quarterly* or blues fan publications such as *Blues Unlimited* or *Blues World*. Some of the most important discoveries reported in these publications were contributed by Gayle Dean Wardlow.

Born in Freer, Texas, in 1940, Gayle Dean Wardlow spent his early years in Bienville Parish, Louisiana, and moved to Meridian, Mississippi, at age seven. At fourteen he actively began searching for country and hillbilly records. Samuel Charters's *The Country Blues* (no. 63) inspired Wardlow and others to seek out any information that could be found on pioneering bluesmen. Wardlow literally went door to door around the South asking people whether they had any old records to sell. His inquiries were rewarded with thousands of 78 rpm discs as well as finding people who knew musicians like Charlie Patton and Tommy Johnson. He later rediscovered Ishmon Bracey and through him learned of H. C. Speir, the Jackson furniture store owner and talent scout who made test pressings of some of the most important bluesmen like Skip James and Robert Johnson, as well as Patton, Tommy Johnson, Bracey, and many more. Wardlow is also the researcher who discovered Robert Johnson's death certificate.

Chasin' That Devil Music compiles over twenty-five of Wardlow's articles published in *78 Quarterly, Blues Unlimited, Blues Revue*

Quarterly, Guitar Player, Living Blues, Storyville, and more. Some of the chapters come from liner-note articles Wardlow wrote for Origin Jazz Library issues. Several of the chapters were originally written with other authors, like Stephen Calt, Bernard Klatzko, Mike Leadbitter, Pat Howse, and Jimmy Phillips. Some of the chapters have been modified from their original printings. The book also includes three articles that had previously been unpublished.

The book is divided into five sections plus a prologue, epilogue, and additional materials. Part 1, "Initial Inquiries and Encounters," contains a fascinating article where Wardlow describes his process of locating 78s in the South: "I had the best luck with older women who had flowerpots on the porch. . . . The pots indicated that someone had lived at one location for a long time." In another chapter ("Memphis City Directory Blues") Wardlow describes the skills he learned as a reporter for the *Meridian Star* and how he learned to fully utilize city directories in his research. These early collecting and research skills are fleshed out in part 2, "Tips, Leads, and Documents." Wardlow began conducting oral histories with musicians. These resulted in a number of important finds. Wardlow's journalism skills helped him locate Robert Johnson's death certificate and later determine that there was more printed on the reverse side of the certificate. Oral histories with family and friends of musicians form the heart of part 3, "Witnesses." H. C. Speir's importance in recording bluesmen from Mississippi was so great that he is the sole focus of part 4. The articles in the final section, "Retrospectives," comment on some of the earlier research and shed new light on older findings.

This isn't the best starting book for those just getting into the blues. A general history or introduction to the blues might be best as a prerequisite to *Chasin' That Devil Music.* Names like King Solomon Hill, Geeshie Wiley, Rube Lacy, and "44" Charlie Taylor are well known to longtime blues fans and scholars, but some blues esoterica could prove overwhelming for newcomers to the blues who haven't gained a good general understanding of blues history. The many stories of discovery and speculation are infectious and exciting and have inspired others to seek out new information on the blues.

Edward Komara edited the book, wrote an introduction, and prepared a list of recorded melodic precedents to the recordings of Robert Johnson. This list was influential to Elijah Wald's book *Escaping the Delta* (no. 36) and was later expanded upon in

Komara's *The Road to Robert Johnson* (no. 35). Komara also provides an explanation of the system of grading record conditions. In addition to works cited and an index, the book also includes a listing of Wardlow's associates involved in the blues revival and their locations in the 1960s through the 1980s, a detailed list of 78 rpm record issues cited, an index to 78s, a list of Ishmon Bracey 78s reconstructed from Dixon, Godrich, and Rye (no. 41), a list of interviews cited, and a brief essay on music reissues with an alphabetic listing of artists and descriptions of which labels have reissued their works.

There are over one hundred black-and-white photographs in the book. The book is accompanied by a twenty-five-track compact disc containing six interview clips and nineteen rare blues songs. "Liner notes" to the CD are printed as part of the book.

Outside of a small number of academic libraries, it is difficult to find complete runs of magazines like *Blues Unlimited* and *78 Quarterly. Chasin' That Devil Music* makes it possible for readers to more easily access these early Wardlow articles. The book is also available in an e-book edition. In 2006, *Chasin' That Devil Music* became a "classic of blues literature" in the Blues Foundation Hall of Fame. —*GJ*

41. What Is a "Blues" Record?

Blues and Gospel Records, 1890–1943. Fourth edition. Compiled by Robert M. W. Dixon, John Godrich, and Howard Rye. Oxford: Clarendon Press, 1997. ISBN 0-19-816239-1, $170.00

This volume may be the most expensive of the Blues 100, but it is worth the cost. It may also be the largest, too, measuring at 6" wide × 9½" high × 2½" thick. As explained in our appendix about "the books behind the Blues 100," discographies are essential tools for collecting blues records and for checking who played what song on which date. *Blues and Gospel Records 1890–1943*, or "Dixon, Godrich, and Rye" as blues scholars call it, is not only the sole discography of blues and black sacred music of the prewar era, but it is also exemplary of the discographer's craft. If a blues reader feels he cannot afford a copy, he should see whether a library near him has one.

The stuff of discographies are recordings, which for prewar blues are 78 rpm records, those black and brittle discs that contain

only one song per side. There are two ways of organizing them into
lists. One is by record label. The other way, which Dixon, Godrich,
and Rye prefer, is by recording artist, then by recording session
and (if known) date. For the most part, the logbooks and ledgers
maintained by the prewar blues labels that could have made easy
the compiling of the discography are missing, destroyed, or inac-
cessible. Therefore, the discographers have had to cull a staggering
variety of data from record labels, record retail catalogs, newspaper
ads, and the recording musicians themselves. One historical circumstance that did ease the data compilation was that blues and
black sacred records before 1942 were issued in separate "race
catalogs" with distinct retail serial numbers; therefore, there was
little need to search for African American music within listings of
records by white pop artists. In addition, the Library of Congress
field recordings through 1943, radio transcriptions, and records
made outside the United States are included and described.

When using Dixon, Godrich, and Rye for the first time, one
should take the time to read the sections at the beginning of the
book. The introduction states the purpose and limits of the discography, and it poses the not-so-easy-to-answer question, "What is a
'blues' or a 'gospel' record?" The "Race Labels" section describes
the various record firms, their studio practices, and their out-of-
town recording trips. If you can't get enough of early blues recording lore, you should seek out Dixon and Godrich's little classic
Recording the Blues (New York: Stein and Day, 1970; reprinted
complete in the collection *Yonder Come the Blues* [Cambridge:
Cambridge University Press, 2001]), for their history of the blues
recording industry.

The body of *Blues and Gospel Records* is the listing by artist of
the recordings. If you are one who listens to blues from mp3 files
or via audiostream, this discography will supply you the artist, title,
and recording date information. As one flips through the pages,
one becomes aware of several things. One is that the "good" and
"intense" bluesmen like Robert Johnson and "Bukka" White didn't
record nearly as much as unlegendary artists like Bo Carter and
Bill Broonzy. Another is that pianists were as likely to accompany
singers as guitarists; despite being out of today's blues fan tastes,
piano-backed performances deserve fair hearings today. A third
observation is that many dates are conjectural because many documents have been long gone; as a matter of fact, some of the dates
have been deduced from the known recording dates of other

records. One more awareness to mention here is that many recordings are either lost, or they are field recordings maintained at the Library of Congress (LC). Many of those LC recordings are accessible for listening through the library's American Memory website (www.loc.gov), and they can be retrieved with the proper spellings of names and locations provided by Dixon, Godrich, and Rye.

John Godrich (d. 1991) published discographies in blues and jazz periodicals but earned his living in the Merchant Navy of England and at the Swansea dock. Robert M. W. Dixon is a professor of linguistics in Australian universities. They had published the first two editions of *Blues Records* in 1964 and 1969. While they were preparing the third edition in 1982 for Storyville, they were assisted by Howard Rye to such an extent that he became a de facto third editor. Rye has had a distinguished and prolific career in blues and jazz discography, contributing the entries on pre-1942 record labels for both the *New Grove Dictionary of Jazz* and the Routledge *Encyclopedia of the Blues.*

It is pointless to acquire any of the first three editions to avoid the cost of the fourth edition, because used copies start at $95 and then rise sharply to $200 and higher. If by chance a copy of one of those early editions comes your way, it is worth keeping, especially the 1969 edition, which has the separate listing of LP reissues of prewar blues. But the fourth edition is the first one to have a title index, a feature that eased greatly research into blues antecedents of lyrics and melodies. There are also indexes to singers and accompanists that will guide you to all recordings by your favorite performer, even those that were issued originally with odd and misleading pseudonyms. These indexes alone are worth the extra cost above the prices of used older editions. —*EK*

42. Tell Me Why You Like Roosevelt

Roosevelt's Blues: African-American Blues and Gospel Songs on FDR. By Guido van Rijn. Jackson: University Press of Mississippi, 1997. ISBN 0-87805-937-7 (hardcover), ISBN 0-87805-988-5 (paperback), $22.00

In his poem "Questions from a Worker Who Reads," Bertolt Brecht observed, "Caesar beat the Gauls. Did he not have even a cook with him?" It was his way of wondering about the common men behind the great men in history. Blues lyrics contain many comments from

African American men and women. What would they be regarding a president of the United States?

In *Roosevelt's Blues*, Guido van Rijn sought to discover why Franklin D. Roosevelt was popular among black voters of the 1930s and 1940s. When Roosevelt was elected president in 1932, he seemed far removed from black interests. He was born in New York state in an affluent family. He belonged to the Democratic Party, not to the Republican "Party of Lincoln" in which most black voters were then registered. In fact, in 1932, he was elected president despite receiving less than one-third of the black vote. Yet during his reelection in 1936, he received an overwhelming majority of their votes, especially in New York, where 81 percent of the ballots cast by blacks were for him. How to explain this swing of votership? To answer this question, van Rijn made use of blues and black sacred records about the president as resources of opinion and comments. The result was a distinctive 1995 doctoral dissertation at Leiden University, the Netherlands (titled "Roosevelt's Blues: African-American Blues and Gospel Artists on President Franklin D. Roosevelt"), which was soon published as an academic book by the University Press of Mississippi.

For his study, van Rijn gathered 349 blues and black sacred performances recorded between 1901 and 1945 whose lyrics referred to the social and political situations of African Americans. Then he selected 128 of those records for lyrics transcription, examination, and explication. As he wrote in the introduction (xviii), van Rijn wasn't merely concerned with what the singers sang about Franklin Roosevelt and the presidents before him. He also asked what factors influenced the political content in each recording, how the singers learned of the news (whether in print, through radio or theater newsreels, or orally), and what political and topical subjects were mentioned (and if so, with what personal opinion, if offered). Overall, he asked what effects Roosevelt's presidency had on "his popularity among blacks."

The first two chapters establish the disenfranchisements of civil rights and voting rights from African Americans, who were then disregarded by most twentieth-century presidents through Herbert Hoover (1929–1933). But the hard economic times brought by the 1929 Wall Street crash affected everyone regardless of race, and it was not alleviated in the early 1930s by the policies and actions of Hoover. When Roosevelt was elected president in November 1932, new jobs for the unemployed were among the expectations for him. Work agencies like the Civil Works Administration (1933–1934), the National Recovery Administration (1933–1935), the Works Progress Administration (1935–1943), and the Public Works Administration (1933–1939) employed black labor along with whites on projects, including roads and civic buildings. How did blacks view these efforts? They had mixed feelings about the CWA and the NRA but more positive ones for the WPA, and for many black children PWA stood for "Papa's Working Again."

World War II interrupted these work programs, and yet the increase in demand for metals and munitions toward the war effort resulted in more jobs than ever for African Americans, especially for those living in the cities. At the same time, large numbers of young black men served in the armed forces, although in segregated units. Nonetheless, for those who were abroad and survived combat, the war was a broadening experience which changed their expectations for living. Shortly before or during their trips home, many veterans learned of Roosevelt's death, which for the black soldiers seemed to end an era of positive change.

The Roosevelt era coincided with rapid musical changes in black music on records, from acoustic bluesmen to blues bands, and from preachers giving three-minute sermons to full-fledged gospel music. For *Roosevelt's Blues*, van Rijn compiled a companion CD on his label Agram (*Roosevelt's Blues*, Agram 2017, 1997), containing twenty-three songs recorded between 1933 and 1949. It begins with Walter Roland's "Red Cross Blues" (1933), which uses a melody that blues fans will recognize as precedent to Robert Johnson's "Sweet Home Chicago." There are blues—happy and thankful blues, if ever such blues existed—about the CWA, the WPA, and the PWA. A few rarities are included, especially Rev. R. H. Taylor's (of Hattiesburg, Mississippi) sermon recording on the 1936 bonus payout to World War II veterans. Six or so tracks are devoted to World War II, the most memorable of them being a black oral toast recorded by the Library of Congress in 1942 that relates the abuse the speaker would inflict if he were to ever lay his hands on Hitler. The anthology ends with Otis Jackson's two-part gospel song "Tell Me Why You Like Roosevelt," which was covered by other artists and then updated for later presidents, including Barack Obama (see Chick Willis's "Obama," CDS CD 1007, 2008).

The University Press of Mississippi published *Roosevelt's Blues* initially in a hardcover edition but now only in paperback. If you need to borrow this book through your library's interlibrary loan program, be sure to specify any of the University Press of Mississippi printings. The dissertation version for van Rijn's Leiden degree was well known enough to have been ordered and acquired by some twenty libraries worldwide, but the American book publication is preferable for the updates and better printed appearance.

In his 1997 book introduction, van Rijn stated that he had drafted chapters for the presidents including the then-current president, Bill Clinton. While *Roosevelt's Blues* was prepared as a stand-alone work, its references to later presidents John F. Kennedy and Richard M. Nixon raised readers' hopes (at least my hopes) for sequel volumes. Indeed, five such volumes with companion CDs have appeared, the last of them ending with the first term of Barack Obama as the nation's first African American president. But this opening installment about Roosevelt is worth purchasing and reading often, for the political and social issues it presents from the blues-class perspective, the historical questions that it poses, and the great music and lyrics on records that it features. —*EK*

43. The Delta in 1941–1942 as Work, Jones, and Adams Reported It

Lost Delta Found: Rediscovering the Fisk University–Library of Congress Coahoma County Study, 1941–1942. By John W. Work, Lewis Wade Jones, and Samuel C. Adams Jr. Edited by Robert Gordon and Bruce Nemerov. Nashville, TN: Vanderbilt University Press, 2005. ISBN 0-8265-1485-5 (hardcover), $29.95

Lost Delta Found presents pioneering research, by African American scholars, of black music and culture in the 1940s Mississippi delta. Partially inspired by Fisk University's sociology chair Charles S. Johnson's *Growing Up in the Black Belt: Negro Youth in the Rural South* (1941), Fisk University and the Library of Congress joined forces "to document adequately the cultural and social backgrounds for music in the community," by examining Coahoma County in the heart of the Mississippi Delta. Scholars from the two institutions conducted a series of research trips in 1941–1942. Much of the research from these expeditions remained lost for more than sixty years, only partially and sometimes incorrectly referenced by folklorist Alan Lomax in his book

The Land Where the Blues Began (Pantheon, 1993) (no. 44) . While conducting research for his book *Can't Be Satisfied: The Life and Times of Muddy Waters* (no. 48), Robert Gordon uncovered some of this research from the 1940s Delta trips. He teamed up with Bruce Nemerov to make sure this important research by John Wesley Work III, Lewis Wade Jones, and Samuel C. Adams Jr. could finally be made publicly accessible. In publishing *Lost Delta Found*, the editors offer an important historical corrective.

The preface and introduction by Gordon and Nemerov explain the rediscovery of the Coahoma County research and give context to this research. Here the editors give their perspective on the Fisk researchers' complex relationship with Alan Lomax, as well with some members of the Fisk administration. Other than the preface, introduction, afterword, and introductions to each section, Gordon and Nemerov present the original research essays as written by Jones, Work, and Adams. With the exception of slight copyediting, the editors left the manuscripts as they appeared in their final draft form and note that "these manuscripts were always *intended* for publication, [but] never *prepared* for publication" (emphasis theirs). The 1941–1942 Coahoma study resulted in three manuscripts written by Fisk University scholars that comprise the bulk of *Lost Delta Found*. The work was never fully completed due to several of the researchers being drafted into the military and disagreements between Fisk and the Library of Congress about portions of the study. The first section, "The Mississippi Delta," by social sciences instructor Lewis Wade Jones, serves as a good introduction to the Coahoma County study. Though Jones initially intended to write a larger manuscript documenting changes in the Mississippi Delta from 1860 to approximately 1940, through focusing on transportation by river, railroad, and highway and how these shaped folk culture, he only wrote on the early river period, stopping just before the twentieth century. While it would be wonderful if Jones had finished this section, his work provides an excellent introduction to the broader study.

The middle, and arguably most important, section of the study is the report by John Work, an ethnomusicologist, composer, and choral director, who was born into a very musical family. His grandfather was a choir director, his father was a music professor (as well as Latin and history) at Fisk, his mother was a singer, his uncle collected folk songs, and his brother was a composer. (Work's Columbia University thesis, "American Negro

Songs and Spirituals," was published by Bonanza Books in 1940 and was reprinted as *American Negro Songs* by Dover Publications in 1998.) The editors list this simply as "John Work's Untitled Manuscript." Work divides his study into two parts, the first examining sacred music and the latter addressing secular music. Work discusses music in the church, paying most attention to Baptist and Methodist congregations.

The majority of this section (approximately one-third of the entirety of *Lost Delta Found*) consists of musical transcriptions copied from microfilm at Fisk University's Franklin Library (the originals are lost). These were all handwritten, in great detail, by John Work, who was gifted as a musical transcriber. Included are transcriptions of gospel quartets, spirituals, children's game songs, and even an entire sermon, painstakingly notating the speech-song vocal patterns. Of more interest to blues scholars and fans are transcriptions of songs by Son House, Honeyboy Edwards, Muddy Waters (at the time of this study, he went by Muddy Water), and William Brown, as well as a holler by Thomas Jones and songs by Sid Hemphill. Work's general index, included right before the transcriptions, doesn't line up with the ordering of the actual transcriptions; readers need to use the editors' index, in the back of the book, potentially leading to some confusion. The editors present only 138 (plus two additional variations on one song) of the 158 Work transcriptions preserved on microfilm. No explanation is given for why twenty transcriptions are excluded.

The final, and only completed, section of the study is Samuel Adams's 1947 sociology master's thesis, "Changing Negro Life in the Delta." Adams examined changes in rural Coahoma County by looking at the effects of "urbanization" on the county's largest town, Clarksdale. He examines changes in church and secular life through a number of means, but primarily through information gleaned from questionnaires completed by one hundred families. Adams's "Appendix 5: List of Records on Machines in Clarksdale Amusement Places" lists the artists and song titles of records in five locations that Lewis Jones wrote down in 1941. This information was used as part of the core of Elijah Wald's *Escaping the Delta* (Amistad, 2004) (no. 36).

In an attempt to rightfully bring the long-forgotten research of John Work to the fore, the editors are quick to place Alan Lomax in a negative light. Much of this is presented carefully, but occasionally their arguments don't make sense. In their introduction to Work's manuscript, the editors mention one of Work's transcriptions, stating, "The gambler explicitly states that music was not an integral part of [gambling]; yet this knowledge doesn't stop Lomax from persistently asking interview subjects, 'What kind of songs do men sing when they gamble?'" In Work's transcription, the interviewee never makes a statement about music not being a part of gambling. In fact, he apparently sang two gambling songs, which Work transcribed and included in the text. Readers will want to compare *Lost Delta Found* with Lomax's presentation of this study in *The Land Where the Blues Began*.

Gordon and Nemerov have done American music scholars a major service by publishing highly important research that may have otherwise remained lost. This study by African American researchers was conducted almost twenty years before "pioneering" works on the blues by Samuel Charters and Paul Oliver. The research of John Work, Lewis Jones, and Samuel Adams has finally gotten some of the respect it deserves. —*GJ*

44. The Delta in 1941–1942 as Lomax Remembered It

The Land Where the Blues Began. By Alan Lomax. New York: Pantheon, 1993. ISBN 0-679-40424-4 (hardcover). New York: Delta, 1994. ISBN 0-385-31285-7 (paperback). Reprint, New York: New Press, 2002. ISBN 1-565-84739-3 (paperback), $23.95

Alan Lomax followed in the footsteps of his folklorist parents, John and Ruby Lomax, to become one of the world's most prolific folk song collectors, oral historians, and promoters of folk music. He worked at the Library of Congress Archive of Folk Song from 1937 to 1942. Lugging a "portable" (five-hundred-pound) aluminum disc recorder, he conducted field recordings around the world, capturing many performers and songs that would, in many cases, never have been known. In 1983, Lomax created the Association for Cultural Equity at Hunter College.

Though he recorded and produced many albums, wrote and cowrote a number of books about music, including *Our Singing Country* (1941), *Mister Jelly Roll* (1950), *The Leadbelly Songbook* (1962), and *Cantometrics* (1976), it may be surprising that Alan Lomax didn't write an in-depth examination of the blues until 1993 with *The Land Where the Blues Began* (henceforth *The Land*). The book is, in part, Lomax's memoirs of his time conducting fieldwork in the American South from around 1940 through the 1970s (he leaves out the 1930s expeditions with his parents).

The Land is a frustrating book. It was the winner of the National Book Critics Circle Award and is a compelling but lengthy (539 pages) read. Lomax gives excellent explanations of the links between music and culture, he provides an interesting description of the evolution of community-based participatory music to the professional musician, he provides good analyses of work songs and hollers, he explains eroticism within the blues and its relation to West African dance, and there are great interviews and anecdotes. His chapter "The Hills" is a good introduction to the music of the North Mississippi hill country, particularly African American fife-and-drum traditions. However, there are many factual errors and a lack of drawing upon the vast amount of scholarship done by others. Much of his most important early fieldwork was conducted in 1941 and 1942 in a joint project between Fisk University and the Library of Congress studying musical and social changes in Coahoma County, Mississippi. Perhaps too much time had elapsed between this study and writing *The Land,* or maybe he wanted to simplify the narrative, but Lomax conflates the series of studies over two years into one summer trip. Lomax's writing gives the impression that some of the coresearchers on this project, particularly John Wesley Work III and Samuel C. Adams Jr., were there in a secondary capacity or leaves them (Adams) out entirely (except in the acknowledgments). (For a lengthy explanation of this trip and a report by the Fisk University researchers, see *Lost Delta Found: Rediscovering the Fisk University– Library of Congress Coahoma County Study, 1941–1942* [no. 43].)

At another point he confuses Jefferson Davis with Joseph Davis (his brother). There are other small errors, like getting the date of a major Muddy Waters performance wrong, but there are larger problems as well. Those wanting documentation of interview dates and other events will find them lacking in much of *The Land.* Lomax gives little attention to blues women, writing, "Few delta women sang or composed the blues precisely because they did not live the blues in the sense that their men did." He goes on to give a weak argument justifying this position. In his descriptions of racism in the South, Lomax repeats the story of Bessie Smith bleeding to death because she was refused admittance to three hospitals because of her skin color, even though Chris Albertson shattered this myth in 1972. With all of the genuine racism Lomax experienced and fought against on his trips into the South, he could have used a thousand honest examples rather than perpetuating a false story and potentially undermining the good points he tries to make about racism. (For an interesting examination of race and authenticity in *The Land*, see Aaron N. Oforlea, "[Un]veiling the White Gaze: Revealing Self and Other in *The Land Where the Blues Began*," *Western Journal of Black Studies* 36, no. 4 [2012]: 289–300.)

Originally published by Pantheon Books, *The Land Where the Blues Began* was reprinted in 1995 by Delta, a division of the Bantam Doubleday Dell Publishing Group. The New Press reprinted the book in 2002. There are forty-two excellent black-and-white photographs and a good index. There are also "A Brief Book List," "A Brief Discography," and "A Brief Filmography," which are very telling in what they choose to include and what is left out. For instance, Lomax lists Edward Albee's play *The Death of Bessie Smith* but doesn't list Chris Albertson's biography *Bessie*.

The Land is a fascinating read of the journeys of a song collector in the segregated mid-twentieth-century South and of life in one of the United States' financially poorest but culturally richest areas. Lomax gives some particularly useful insights into music and culture. As with anything, readers are urged to read this with a critical eye, knowing there are some factual errors.

Twenty-eight recordings discussed in the book are available on a compact disc also titled *The Land Where the Blues Began* (Rounder CD 82161-1861-2). Samples of other tracks can also be heard on various compilation albums.

The Land Where the Blues Began is also the name of a documentary Lomax wrote, directed, and produced, which originally aired on PBS in 1979 and was rebroadcast in 1990. It is available on VHS by Pacific Arts Video/PBS Home Video and DVD by Media-Generation. It features some great performances of Othar Turner, Napoleon Strickland, Jack Owens, Bud Spires, Sam Chatmon, and many others. —*GJ*

45. Spanning Most of the Known Blues History

The World Don't Owe Me Nothing: The Life and Times of Delta Bluesman Honeyboy Edwards. By David "Honeyboy" Edwards. Chicago: Chicago Review Press, 1997. ISBN 1-55752-275-4 (hardcover), $26.00, ISBN 1-55652-368-8 (paperback)

Living to almost ninety-six, David "Honeyboy" Edwards's life (1915–2011) spanned most of known blues history. This singer and guitarist from Shaw, Mississippi, wasn't widely known for most of his life, but his story is nonetheless significant to our understanding of the life of a rural itinerant bluesman. Edwards knew and performed with many blues musicians and is our best source of information about a number of people and events. The best information we know about Robert Johnson's death was told by Edwards, who was present the night he was poisoned. Edwards was friends with the poorly documented Tommy McClennan and traveled around with Big Walter Horton and Little Walter Jacobs, among many others.

The World Don't Owe Me Nothing is a fascinating read. The stories Edwards weaves are colorful and filled with detail; his incredible memory makes his story so much richer than many others'. The words are all Honeyboy's but were compiled and edited from many hours of interviews he gave to Janis Martinson and Michael Frank, his longtime manager and founder/owner of Earwig Music Company. Martinson and Frank arranged the various interviews into a more or less chronological narrative that flows well and reads as though it were told in the manner presented, allowing the reader to "hear" Honeyboy's voice.

Edwards's life in music began as a young boy. Soon after receiving a guitar from his father, he began playing music at house parties. At fourteen he set out on the road, hoboing around the country with Big Joe Williams. Big Joe provided the foundation for Honeyboy's career, teaching him about the blues, how to hop trains, and how to hustle. Honeyboy's vivid memories of traveling from town to town in train boxcars, playing street corners or country store porches, and encounters with the law in the segregated South give some of the best stories of life as a rambling musician.

Apart from recording a few sides for Alan Lomax on behalf of the Library of Congress in 1942 and a few sides in the 1950s, Edwards didn't really begin recording until the late 1960s. He mentions several times how he wishes he'd gotten recorded earlier, seeing the success of those musicians who did get records cut and played on jukeboxes and the airwaves.

Stories about gambling and hustling are just as prevalent as the stories of music making. In fact, Honeyboy saw his guitar as his meal ticket, but his real source of money was gambling: "I had three ways of making it: the women and my guitar and the dice." These stories are often less than honorable. Edwards tells how he used loaded dice and other tricks to cheat people out of their money. Edwards saw this as a way of making it in a world where others were trying to cheat you. In response to his cousin telling him that he "ain't done nothing in [his] life but rob people's money," Honeyboy responds, "He thinks I'm lazy, but I wasn't lazy. I know what I done: I made it."

Despite all his stories of hard times, Edwards felt very fortunate that he learned how to be a musician, seeing this as his ticket out of a life of manual labor. All the stories of jail time on county farms, death of loved ones, and poverty ultimately end with the words "the world don't owe me nothing." Edwards was very satisfied with his life and felt that he had it much better as a musician than many other folks.

Edwards gives little information about his later years when he stopped playing music and when he revived it in the 1970s. It would be interesting to know more about his thoughts on touring around the world on airplanes and traveling in style as a juxtaposition to his tales of hoboing or to hear his insights on how he saw blues evolving over his lifetime. But analysis isn't the point of this book. Anecdotes of a past way of life, whether true or exaggerated, are the heart of this work.

In addition to an index, bibliography, and foreword by Albert Murray, the book contains three useful appendices. The first one, "Miscellany," is an alphabetical listing of terms/phrases, nonmusician people, and places mentioned by Edwards. The second appendix is an alphabetical listing and brief biography of every musician whom Edwards mentions in the text. The third appendix is a list of every song he mentions in the book, along with their recording dates, songwriters, and other pertinent information if known. Most of the photographs were taken by Cedric Chatterley between 1990 and 1995; Chatterley followed Edwards's journey from a rough draft of this book. Others are from Edwards's personal collection.

The World Don't Owe Me Nothing is an accessible book for a general audience wanting to learn more about the life of an itinerant blues musician and for the devoted blues fan looking for stories from someone who has lived through it all. For musicians, Edwards gives good information about what keys he and others often played in and what tunings were used. This book is about much more than music, though. Honeyboy Edwards gives personal accounts of the 1927 flood of the Mississippi River, life in the Great Depression, racism in the old South, and much more. —*GJ*

46. A Classic Gateway into the Blues

Deep Blues. By Robert Palmer. New York: Viking, 1981. Second printing, New York: Penguin, 1982. ISBN 0-14-006223-8, $16.00

Deep Blues is a bit of a two-edged sword. It has its flaws, some serious, but it has served as perhaps the major gateway into the world of blues research, significantly outselling similar books. *New York Times* music critic, musician, and blues fan Robert Palmer takes readers deep into the world of down-home blues. While the book does cover Chicago and other areas of the northern blues diaspora, primary focus is in the jukes, cotton fields, and other landscapes of the Mississippi Delta. Palmer's colorful language and respect for the music and musicians of this region transport readers into the early years of the blues through the migration north to Chicago and surrounding areas and back to the Mississippi and Arkansas deltas.

Reading the pages of *Deep Blues*, readers can almost hear Robert Johnson and Charlie Patton speaking. Palmer's ability to bring these people to life is perhaps one of the most intriguing facets of the book. It is also one of the more problematic. It is easy for the casual reader to think that these are the real voices, real thoughts, and real motivations of blues musicians long past. Jeff Todd Titon writes, "He identifies so completely with his subjects that he divines their thoughts and writes from their point of view . . . when Palmer tells me what Son House (a man I know) [. . . was] thinking in the 1930s and even puts words in their mouths, I resist."

Much of Palmer's history is a synthesis of the research done by others. Here he is not alone, as all modern blues histories are indebted to the early works of Paul Oliver, Samuel Charters, and others. His descriptions are fleshed out by his own trips to the Delta, his time living in Memphis, and personal interviews with blues musicians.

Perhaps the most troubling part of the book is that Palmer perpetuates the story, told by Homesick James and Sonny Boy Williamson II, of Lillian McMurry of the Trumpet label secretly recording Elmore James's "Dust My Broom" and releasing it without his permission. As business documents from Trumpet, located at the University of Mississippi, point out, James had signed a contract the day before the recording session and received advance royalties. Until her death in 1999, Mrs. McMurry received angry e-mails about this false story. (Note: For a good summary of the history of this myth, read "Appendix One" of *The Amazing Secret History of Elmore James* by Steve Franz [no. 55].)

Palmer devotes the most time to the early years of the blues. In his attempt to be comprehensive, the later sections feel as though he is trying to cover too much ground. While no one wants to leave out key figures in the blues, there are a lot of them and not enough space to do it. Either the book should have been longer to cover what Palmer feels is important, or he should have bitten off less subject matter. There is a feeling that he starts rushing through the stories of later musicians, whom he obviously cares deeply about but doesn't have the space to do justice to.

In a way, *Deep Blues* is a bridge between an academic examination of country blues and a popular culture introduction to the blues. Probably in an attempt to reach a popular music audience, the work unfortunately lacks any end- or footnotes. It does, thankfully, include an index as well as a discography and bibliography.

Deep Blues, despite the aforementioned problems, is one of the best paths into the world of blues. Palmer's romantic style is easy to read, and the story he weaves is mostly accurate, but most important, it is compelling. You want to learn more about the people he celebrates.

Note: The 1991 film *Deep Blues* by Robert Mugge and written by and featuring Robert Palmer is different in concept from the book. It is more of a musical pilgrimage for Dave Stewart of the Eurythmics and Robert Palmer into then relatively unknown areas of Mississippi blues. While the North Mississippi hill country blues is barely mentioned in the book, it receives significant attention in the film. —*GJ*

47. The First Serious Work on Chicago Blues

Chicago Blues: The City & the Music/Chicago Breakdown. By Mike Rowe. London: Eddison Press, 1973. American edition, New York: Da Capo Press, 1975/1981. ISBN 0-306-80145-0, $16.50

Since its origins in the Deep South, the blues diaspora has spread far and wide; indeed, there are blues fans and musicians in practically every country throughout the world. As blues spread, various regional styles emerged: Delta blues, Piedmont, Texas blues, West Coast, and so on. In the middle decades of the twentieth century, the Chicago sound dominated the blues world. Southern African Americans flocked to the city during the first and second Great Migrations of the twentieth century, bringing along their foodways, stories, and musical traditions. Some of the most famous and influential blues musicians made their names in Chicago: Muddy Waters, Howlin' Wolf, Big Bill Broonzy, Tampa Red, Little Walter, Jimmy Reed, Junior Wells, and Sonny Boy Williamson.

While the earliest years of Chicago blues (indeed all blues) weren't documented in any depth by contemporary scholars, we are fortunate that the 1960s saw a true development of blues scholarship, with pioneering works by Samuel Charters and Paul Oliver and the emergence of blues magazines documenting each new blues discovery. The British *Blues Unlimited* (1963–1987) and especially the Chicago-based (now Oxford, Mississippi) *Living Blues* (1970–present) magazines really followed the contemporary Chicago blues scenes. It was these publications, along with works like Big Bill Broonzy's 1955 autobiography (with Yannick Bruynoghe) *Big Bill Blues* (no. 57), interviews and articles by Tony Russell and Gayle Dean Wardlow, and others that informed much of the research behind the first monograph focused solely on blues in Chicago.

First published in London as *Chicago Breakdown* for Tony Russell's Eddison Bluesbooks series in 1973, Mike Rowe created the first in-depth work on blues in the Windy City. The book was released two years later by Da Capo as *Chicago Blues: The City & the Music* in 1975 and reprinted in 1981. Other than the title and publisher, nothing is changed in the American edition. In the first chapter, Rowe gives a good introduction to prewar blues in Chicago, looking at musicians like Big Bill Broonzy, Tampa Red, and Bumble Bee Slim. Much of the chapter examines the great influence businessman Lester Melrose had in defining the overall sound of blues in 1930s and 1940s Chicago. Melrose worked for Paramount, Gennett, and later RCA Victor and Columbia. It was with RCA Victor's subsidiary Bluebird that Melrose is most associated. Rowe refers to this era as the "Melrose Mess," not liking the formulaic sounds that Melrose cultivated in Chicago artists and produced on record. For better or worse, Melrose's consistency for recording sessions helped establish an urban blues instrumentation of vocals, guitar, bass, drums, and piano as a core band, with harmonica or saxophone sometimes thrown in.

Rowe next examines, in great detail, the population dynamics of the two Great Migrations of the twentieth century (1910–1930 and 1940–1970). Census data are analyzed to great effect to show the patterns of African American migration to various areas in the United States. Rowe manages to bring the raw data to life through stories of musicians leaving their southern homes for the promise of work in cities like Gary, Indiana, Detroit, Michigan, and Chicago, Illinois. Much of the rest of *Chicago Blues* tells the stories of the musicians, record labels, and clubs that helped define the Chicago blues sound. The ebb and flow of new musicians coming onto the scene and changing styles is well documented through interviews and data collected from *Cashbox*, jukebox playlists, and the records themselves. Rowe, of course, gives most emphasis to titans like Muddy Waters, Howlin' Wolf, and Sonny Boy Williamson (I and II), but it is often the stories surrounding slightly less famous musicians like J. B. Lenoir, Jimmy Rogers, Junior Wells, and Magic Sam that are most useful in furthering blues research. It is especially help-ful that Rowe devotes significant time to still lesser-known artists like Little Willie Smith, Lazy Bill Lucas, Willie Nix, Jody "Guitar" Wilson, and many others.

Rowe organizes most of these artists by the labels on which they recorded. Most attention is obviously given to the story of the Chess Brothers' (Phil and Leonard) labels Aristocrat/Chess/Checker and their many artists. As multiple books have since been written on Chess Records, it is Rowe's attention to the smaller labels that is most useful to the greater blues scholarship. Chicago labels like J.O.B., Opera, Chance, States, United, Parrot, and others often recorded artists who didn't fit the Chess mold.

While Mike Rowe gave us the first serious work on Chicago blues, his clear biases for country blues–based Chicago blues are strongly worded throughout the book. Like many authors on blues, Rowe's musical descriptions are often more poetic than musico-logical: "There was a suspense and agonised tension to his music as he dragged out the notes . . . he tortures the words with his crying . . . the band groaning and heaving in the background." In the last few chapters, "Decline and Fall," "The West Side," and "Chicago Today," he also paints a fairly bleak picture of the state of blues in Chicago: "The feeling that the blues are marking time in the city is inescapable; as the older artists die or retire the young ones, ham-pered by the dictates of changed social and economic pressures, seem unable to make a significant breakthrough to give a cohesion and form to a new style of Chicago blues." He also predicts for blues in general that "any change in the direction of the blues will be through the super-eminence of a new blues hero—a new B. B. King, for instance—and the trend is almost certain to be towards larger and more jazz-influenced groups." If the huge success of Fat Possum artists in the 1990s and early 2000s is any indication, the pendulum has certainly swung in the opposite direction.

David Whiteis's *Chicago Blues: Portraits and Stories* (no. 99) gives an excellent update to the thirty years of the Chicago blues scene following where Rowe left off. —*GJ*

48. Hearing His Own Voice

Can't Be Satisfied: The Life and Times of Muddy Waters. By Robert Gordon. Boston: Little, Brown, 2002. ISBN 0-316-32849-9 (hardcover), $21.00. Reprint, Boston: Back Bay Books, 2003. ISBN 0-316-16494-1 (paperback), $17.00

Muddy Waters, born McKinley Morganfield, was one of the most important and influential figures in the history of blues. He and his music served as a major link from the sounds of Robert Johnson and Son House to the electric Chicago blues, which Muddy Waters helped create, and rock and roll; the Rolling Stones even took their name from his song "Rollin' Stone."

Although Morganfield was long thought to have been born in 1915, author Robert Gordon makes a compelling case that he was born in 1913 in Issaquena County, in the southern half of the Mississippi Delta. He gained the nickname Muddy from his grandmother and Water(s) from friends. Like others born in the Delta, Muddy Waters grew up in a sharecropping family. At a young age, he moved to the Stovall Plantation outside of Clarksdale, where he chopped cotton, plowed, and did all else that comes with life working on a plantation. Muddy received a harmonica as a boy and began learning music on that as well as on a homemade guitar he cobbled together. He borrowed and bought some blues records to play on his grandmother's phonograph, immersing himself in the sounds of Blind Lemon Jefferson, Barbecue Bob, Blind Blake, Roosevelt Sykes, and Little Brother Montgomery. At fourteen, Muddy Waters first heard Son House and was blown away by his skill and powerful performance, leading him to purchase his first guitar three years later.

On August 31, 1941, Alan Lomax from the Library of Congress and John Wesley Work III, a music professor from Fisk University, arrived at Stovall Plantation in part to document "the cultural and social backgrounds for music in [an African American] community" in the Delta. Among the people recorded on this expedition was Muddy Waters. The recording technology allowed Muddy Waters to hear the recordings shortly after they were made. Hearing his own voice was the turning point away from life on the plantation to one as a musician. Thinking back to that moment, Muddy Waters said, "Man, you don't know how I felt that afternoon . . . I thought, 'Man, I can sing.'" Two years later, he would leave Stovall Plantation to realize his dream in Chicago, where he worked what jobs he could by day and played blues with musicians like Little Walter, Jimmy Rogers, and Otis Spann at night. He was soon recorded on the Aristocrat/Chess labels and propelled into the prime blues spotlight, where he influenced countless blues and burgeoning rock musicians.

The first book to devote significant space to Muddy Waters was James Rooney's 1971 work *Bossmen: Bill Monroe & Muddy Waters*, which examines two quintessential bandleaders of bluegrass and Chicago blues. The next book devoted to him came out five years before Gordon's biography: *Muddy Waters—The Mojo Man* (1997), by Sandra B. Tooze.

Can't Be Satisfied contains an excellent index, extensive notes (seventy-three pages), bibliography, foreword by Keith Richards, and useful appendices, including a list of records in Muddy Waters's collection, his repertoire as of July 29, 1942, and a guide titled "How to Buy Muddy Waters and Other Related Recordings." The book features over thirty photographs and illustrations, less than half the number in the Tooze biography. Gordon does not include a discography, perhaps because Sandra Tooze's book reprints a sixty-seven-page discography compiled by Phil Wight and Fred Rothwell and originally published by *Blues & Rhythm* in 1991.

There are some small errors in the text, but nothing substantial. For instance, Gordon writes of W. C. Handy's first encounter with the blues as hearing a man play guitar with a bottle, when Handy clearly wrote that it was a knife.

Gordon's account of Alan Lomax is quite negative. He writes about Alan Lomax keeping John Work "at arm's length" and not giving him any credit for his role in the recording expedition that would first record Muddy Waters. Gordon even writes that in *The*

Land Where the Blues Began (no. 44), "Lomax relegates John Work to a single mention, an aside in the preface," when he is in fact mentioned three times in the book and is thanked in the very first sentence of the acknowledgments. Also, the LP *Afro-American Blues and Game Songs* (1956), produced by the Library of Congress, clearly lists the songs recorded on that expedition as "Recorded by Alan Lomax and John Work." (To read more about the Lomax/ Work issues, readers may wish to consult Ellen Harold's "Fanning the Flames: Defending Alan," *Sing Out! The Folk Song Magazine* 46 (Winter 2003): 103–105 and *Lost Delta Found: Rediscovering the Fisk University–Library of Congress Coahoma County Study, 1941–1942* (no. 43), edited by Robert Gordon and Bruce Nemerov.) Despite his perhaps unfair assessment of Lomax, Gordon does rightly point out that John Work has not received the proper amount of credit he deserves. In this, Robert Gordon should be applauded for bringing some overdue attention to the role of Work and others involved in the Coahoma County study.

Despite the abovementioned problems, *Can't Be Satisfied* is the best book on Muddy Waters to date. It is compelling reading, informative, and well researched. Robert Gordon does an excellent job of objectively examining Muddy Waters's great talent and accomplishments while not glossing over his womanizing. Gordon sets a high bar for music biographical writing.

Robert Gordon and Morgan Neville also directed the documentary *Muddy Waters—Can't Be Satisfied* (Winstar, 2003), that could be seen as a companion to the biography. —*GJ*

49. Capturing Some of the Deepest Blues on Record

Spinning Blues into Gold: The Chess Brothers and the Legendary Chess Records. By Nadine Cohodas. New York: St. Martin's, 2000. ISBN 0-312-26133-0 (hardcover), ISBN 0-312-28494-2 (paperback)

Chess Records of Chicago occupies a central place in the history of the blues. It recorded the best performances of the cream of the postwar Mississippi bluesmen: Muddy Waters, Howlin' Wolf, Sonny Boy Williamson II, Robert Nighthawk, and Elmore James. It also was a midwife for the best African American contributions to the earliest rock and roll, especially those made by Chuck Berry and Bo Diddley. In the 1960s it helped to bring about the next generation of blues and soul, introducing singers Buddy Guy and Koko Taylor and developing into mature artists Etta James and Little Milton. Lovers and historians of the blues cannot avoid the Chess legacy. Through the 1990s, parts of its story were told in magazine articles and book chapters. In 2000, Nadine Cohodas published her all-encompassing narrative, not just of the blues recordings but also of the successful jazz releases, the 1960s psychedelic albums, and radio station ownership.

The central figures were the Chess brothers, Leonard (1917–1969) and Phil (born 1921), two Jews who emigrated from Poland to Chicago with their mother and sister in 1928. Leonard was the brother who was driven to succeed and grow in business, and his early enterprises in the South Side were the 708 Liquor Store and the Macomba Lounge. In 1947, he began assisting Charles and Evelyn Aron with Aristocrat Records, leading its first significant recording sessions with African American musicians. He became part owner of Aristocrat in 1948 and then sole owner in December 1949, eventually changing the label's name to Chess in 1950. For the next nineteen years, Leonard and Phil Chess developed an operation that performed every step in the music record process, from music recording and song copyright registration to record pressing and sales distribution. During the 1960s, the brothers enjoyed additional commercial success through radio station ownership, but Leonard's sudden death in 1969 prevented their entry into television.

In the overall sweep of the Chess brothers' successes, the music would seem incidental by comparison, except that Chess captured some of the deepest blues on record, including Muddy Waters's "Still a Fool" (1951), Howlin' Wolf's "Smokestack Lightnin'" (1956), and Elmore James's "The Sun Is Shining" (1960). Also, at times, Leonard Chess would pique and cajole his musicians with some of the saltiest language heard on dry land, as in this long-notorious exchange with Aleck Miller, "Sonny Boy Williamson II," from 1957, which Cohodas gives in transcription (149):

> Williamson (SBW) (singing during a take): "Little village, too small to be a town" (repeats the lyric)
>
> Leonard Chess (LC) (interrupting the take): What's the name of that?
>
> SBW: Little Village, Little Village, motherfucker. Little Village.

LC: There isn't a motherfuckin' thing in there about a village, you sonofabitch. There's nothin' in the song that has anything to do with a village.

SBW: Well, it's a small town.

LC: I know what a village is.

SBW (yelling): Well, all right, goddammit. You don't, you don't need no title. You name it after, after I get through with it, you sonofabitch. You name it wha'ch you want. You name it your mammy if you want.

During his early jobs, Chess absorbed the tough street talk into his everyday speech, but like great football coaches, he also used it to draw what he wanted from his musicians, employees, and associates. Blues historians have been long amazed or appalled by the "Little Village" session tape, but the coarseness reflected the tough, scrappy business world of commercial recording after World War II. Either you survived, or you didn't, and Cohodas includes cautionary examples of those who didn't, from Lillian McMurry of Trumpet Records, which ceased active operations in 1955 after prolonged difficulties with distributors, to the GRT Corporation, which bought Chess Records from the brothers in 1969 and soon mismanaged it into near oblivion.

In addition to giving practical advice on how to survive assertively in the record business, Cohodas also shows the necessary formal and legal processes in which songs are copyrighted and how royalties are prepared and paid. However, she shows in what ways the Chess brothers did not follow what we today would call "best practices." To their artists through the 1950s, they paid out royalties according to an individual artist's needs, not to what the sales of his or her records had earned (this was less the case with the jazz artists in the 1960s). Sometimes they used Chess funds to get an artist out of a personal problem, whether it was a paternity suit or a jail stay. To some readers, these kinds of payments may seem paternalistic, but to others, they may be understandable if the artists come from lower economic classes and broken homes, trying to find their ways through their lives while achieving their fame.

Once acquired, this book will be the main reference to which a critical reader should compare and weigh all other writings about Chess Records. As of this writing, it is out of print, but used-book dealers offer their available copies (hardcover and paperback) from eighteen dollars on up. —*EK*

50. Death of a Bluesman

Stormy Monday: The T-Bone Walker Story. By Helen Oakley Dance. With a foreword by B. B. King. Baton Rouge: Louisiana State University Press, 1987. ISBN 0-8071-1355-7 (hardcover), ISBN 0-8071-2458-3 (paperback), $24.00

To some blues fans, *Stormy Monday* may seem to be a wasted opportunity to document the importance of T-Bone Walker (1910–1975). He was among the first musicians to adopt the electrically amplified guitar, and he was the one who gave the new instrument a central role in the blues. He was a foundational influence on the guitarists who played in Louis Jordan's Tympany Five (especially Bill Jennings and Carl Hogan) and on Chuck Berry, all of whom copied Walker's licks and string bends to form the "vocabulary" for rhythm and blues and rock and roll. His run of popular hit records lasted some fifteen years (1940–1955), through which he established in the blues repertory the standards "Stormy Monday," "T-Bone Shuffle," and "Mean Old World." Culturally, in the late 1930s he emerged as a star through the clubs on Central Avenue in Los Angeles, and in so doing he contributed toward establishing that avenue as the entertainment strip for African Americans in that city. Most of these achievements are not described in this book, and the few that are included are given passing mentions. Helen Oakley Dance (1913–2001) was the wife of jazz historian Stanley Dance, so she witnessed and knew much about jazz and, to a respectable extent, rhythm and blues. Maybe she had a different sort of book in mind than a biography.

The subtitle of the book says "story," not "life" or "biography." To be sure, Oakley does not present a straightforward narrative. On its surface, the book is about her visits to Walker during the last eighteen months of his life. The first nine chapters document her conversations at the musician's bustling home with him, his family, and their friends around April 1974. The next nine chapters are presented from the perspective of her research conducted from 1975 through the mid-1980s. At chapter 19, she pulls us back to before the time of the book's beginning, to the end of 1973, when she decided to write Walker's "story." From there through the twenty-fourth chapter and the epilogue, the book is a memoir of Walker's last performances, physical decline, and death in March 1975. Within this first-person structure, she gives the facts of Walker's life as they were conveyed to her by family and friends. Walker himself didn't tell her much. First, during his interviews with Dance, he was simply too restless, often getting up and having someone else talk about him. A friend admitted in Walker's presence that "Bone don't like a lot of gab," which could not have boded well for Dance's attempts to interview him. Also, as Dance documented in the later memoir chapters, Walker experienced minor lapses of memory, the most troubling of them occurring onstage. The resulting book is a scramble, demanding the reader to piece together Walker's life despite Dance's shifts of perspective from 1974 to the late 1970s and 1980s and then back to 1974–1975. One maddening aspect is Dance's frequent omissions of dates from her presentations of individual events. Yet if the reader keeps track on a sheet of paper the coverage of life in each chapter, determining from context, clues, and the appended discography as to what year each event happened, one finds that just about every year is represented.

At the end of the final chapter, about Walker's funeral, Dance seems to hint at what she has intended her book to be (228): "One by one the ministers whom the family had invited to speak proceeded to the front of the chapel and stood, solemn, erect, in purple and black, before the expectant congregation. Those who anticipated a storybook account of his career were instead exhorted to pray, as T-Bone, no longer a public but now a private man, was consigned to his Maker and laid to rest. This was perhaps fitting, for in his estimation T-Bone was indeed a family man." What she wrote is definitely not a storybook. Instead it seems more a requiem, meditating not on the life, but on the decline and death of a bluesman. In such a function, her interviews read like testimonials, and Walker's musical stature seems to take second place to the personal memories of him.

The memories that were conveyed by family and friends were of him being too human: the drinking, the gambling, the children with his wife and other women, too. Their acknowledgments of his human weaknesses are what enliven this book. The passages about Walker's gambling led me to think some about the closeness between blues and gambling. Oliver in *Blues Fell This Morning* (no. 64) devotes a chapter to gambling, which has pervaded labor-class African American culture. Many juke joints usually had a card game or craps being played. Certainly many African American men gambled because some banks refused them accounts or the ability to cash large checks; gambling was a way to enjoy disposable income or else risk its theft. On a larger scale, as Robert Pruter pointed out in *Chicago Soul* (no. 88) regarding Vee Jay, the record industry had its "gambling types," risking much money on whether a record release would be profitable or not. Walker's gambling manner is interesting, as Dance describes it. Yes, he was a habitual gambler, perhaps compulsive, playing in nearly every city and town he performed in. Yet when he won big outside his home city of Los Angeles, he often "returned" some of those winnings to the other players, either by "losing" intentionally in a small bet or by simply giving some dollars back. However he did so, it showed he didn't want to strip a town of all of its money; he seemed to make sure it kept a little cash to invite him back for another gig and another game. If so, that may be unique among the gambling bluesmen I have read about. —*EK*

51. When the Blues Became Rhythmic, Hot, and Fun

Honkers and Shouters: The Golden Years of Rhythm and Blues.
By Arnold Shaw. New York: Collier, 1978. ISBN 0-02-610000-2 (hardcover), ISBN 0-02-061760-7 (paperback)

For many years, *Honkers and Shouters* by Arnold Shaw (1909–1989) was the main narrative about postwar blues and rhythm and blues through 1960. Since the mid-1990s, some of its chapters about individual recording firms have been superseded by book-length histories, such as Nadine Cohodas on Chess Records (*Spinning the Blues into Gold*, no. 49) and Fox on King Records (*King of the Queen City*, no. 60). If the book is to be reprinted, some of Shaw's factual statements will have to be corrected and some of his emphases rebalanced, according to the research published since *Honkers and Shouters'* publication in 1978. It has been out of print for some years. What makes it worth seeking and reading is Shaw's overall sweep of twenty years of music history, grounded in his personal experiences as fan, composer, and music publishing executive.

Admittedly, it takes about fifty or so pages of the 555-page book for Shaw to find his stride. That initial section, "The Roots," attempts to give some 1920s and 1930s antecedents for rhythm and blues. Blues fans who love postwar blues may wonder over the relevancies of Blind Boy Fuller, Big Bill Broonzy, John Lee "Sonny Boy I" Williamson, and Champion Jack Dupree. But the sections devoted to Leroy Carr, Roosevelt Sykes, Sunnyland Slim, and the boogie-woogie piano masters Meade "Lux" Lewis and Albert Ammons are not to be overlooked. Carr was among the first (if not the very first) African American singers to talk and croon to the recording microphone, not project his voice forcefully at it. Roosevelt Sykes reinforced much of Carr's performing styles as singer and pianist, especially through the lean recording industry years of 1932–1933 and after Carr's 1935 death. The meters and loud volume of boogie pianists would serve as models for the subsequent small bands that "jumped" the blues, including those led by Jay McShann and Louis Jordan.

Once Shaw presents Louis Jordan, he begins exploring in earnest rhythm and blues. While ushering in this new kind of city blues, Jordan instilled a sense of fun about life through his humorous lyrics and musical bounce. The kind of fun was not merely gentle humor or entertainment but sometimes over-the-top, rollicking slapstick. Jordan's early agent, Berle Adams, remembered one of the "first engagements"—about 1941—during which the Three Stooges (presumably with "superstooge" Curly Howard) had difficulty performing after a Louis Jordan set. This theme of fun runs throughout the book, ending with disc jockey Hunter Hancock admitting that he left radio in the mid-1960s because radio management was selecting what records were to be played—likely very few rhythm and blues singles among them—and so "it was no longer much fun."

The main portion of the text may be summarized in a remark that Atlantic producer Jerry Wexler gave to Shaw (414):

> Many fans think of R & B in terms of the 1950s, but it was really hot in the forties. World War I started bluesmen moving up North, and [World War] number II made it a mass migration. There were three paths. Up from Mississippi and Alabama, the center of America, they headed into Chicago—and we had the strong Delta influence on Chess Records. From Oklahoma, Texas, and the Southwest, they went to California—that was T-Bone Walker and the honky-tonk, jazz combo influence. And

from the Carolinas, Florida, and Georgia, they came up to New York, giving us a mix of gospel and pop.

I cannot give a more succinct précis of *Honkers and Shouters* than that. But I should give a few names of who "they" were among the innovators of the rhythm and blues era. There was Cecil Gant, whose 1945 hit record "I Wonder" showed entrepreneurs that African Americans were willing to buy records and what kind of records they would buy. T-Bone Walker was one of the first soloists on the electric guitar and the composer of the postwar blues standard "Stormy Monday." There were the singers Wynonie Harris and Dinah Washington and a flock of honking saxophonists, from Big Jay McNeeley to King Curtis.

Shaw proceeds to survey the music from the West Coast through the Midwest to New York, with a brief look at the South. Instead of looking primarily at the individual recording acts, he groups them by the labels that recorded them. Therefore, to describe the California styles, he concentrates on Art Rupe's Specialty label, the Bihari brothers' Modern/Meteor/Flair group, the Messners' Aladdin, and the Bay area productions of Bob Geddins. For the Midwest, there were three giant firms: Syd Nathan's King Records, the Chess brothers' Chess Records, and Vee Jay Records. For New York firms—with whom Shaw had worked personally for music publishing rights—he focuses on Herman Lubinsky's Savoy and on Atlantic Records with the Ertegun brothers and Jerry Wexler, although he also presents interviews with the owners of small labels like Herald, Old Town, and Baton.

What nurtured rhythm and blues as commercial music was the demand from African American buyers, the lack of interest from the major record labels in recording the music, the speed with which independent record people acted in the place of the major labels, and the accessibility of tape recorders and disc-pressing equipment to the new "minor labels." As the appeal of the music grew and spread across the racial cultures, the attitude of independent and minor labels evolved from the 1940s' "maybe white people will buy this record release, too" to the 1950s' "white people had better buy this." Assimilation of African American rhythm and blues into American mainstream music was taking place, whether through sales of the African American records to white buyers or the rerecording of African American songs by mainstream pop singers. When the radio networks shifted their programming to television in the late 1940s, music records filled the radio airtime. With limited programming time available for the large numbers of new pop and rhythm and blues records, it became consequential that label owners had to resort to payola to disc jockeys to have the records played on the air. In the closing chapters, Shaw looks unflinchingly at the payola scandals and court trials of the late 1950s, showing them as bringing about the end of the rhythm and blues era.

Because of Shaw's perspective from the music industry of rhythm and blues, he ran the risk of describing too impersonally the music, its artists, and their times in the spotlight. To prevent that risk, throughout the book he gives twenty-five interviews with performers, producers, and industry types, who all talk about how much they loved the music even when they were at times consumed with its creation and marketing. For some interviewees, like producer Ralph Bass, their transcribed talks with Shaw serve as the autobiographies they never got around to writing. These engaging conversations may be the most enduring parts of the book. —*EK*

52. Where the Great and the Good Traveled

The Chitlin' Circuit and the Road to Rock 'n' Roll. By Preston Lauterbach. New York: Norton, 2011. ISBN 0-393-07652-0 (hardcover), $27.00, ISBN 0-393-34294-8 (paperback), $17.00

The term "chitlin' circuit" has been used for so long a time that its origins seem indistinct. Who coined the term is forgotten; maybe it was thought of not by a person but by people. To what extent the chitlin' circuit has been a formal circuit wasn't known until Preston Lauterbach wrote *The Chitlin' Circuit and the Road to Rock 'n' Roll,* his first book. He quotes the great soul performer/bluesman Bobby Rush's claim of being "The King of the Chitlin' Circuit" (4), but certainly the venues where Rush performs now are different places from where he had established his career over fifty years ago. Today's rounds for blues and soul musicians may rely a great deal on word of mouth and handshakes. Where the great and good traveled may be viewed in hindsight with some facts and features from Lauterbach's research. Person by person, venue by venue, he reconstructs the early years of the so-called circuit, from the 1930s through the 1960s, from Indianapolis to Houston.

Lauterbach's history is framed by the career of Denver Ferguson, an African American veteran of World War I who settled in Indianapolis, Indiana. For many years, he ran the local numbers gambling in the African American neighborhoods (for its relevance to the blues and its culture, see Paul Oliver's *Blues Fell This Morning* [no. 64]). Meanwhile, Walter Barnes parlayed his contacts and his musical talents to blaze for his bands some pioneer tours of the South. His profitable efforts showed that there were audiences for touring African American bands. Barnes died in the calamitous 1940 Natchez, Mississippi, Rhythm Club fire (Howlin' Wolf's recording "The Natchez Burning" was among the various memorials in song and tales).

Ferguson opened the Sunset Club in 1938 in Indianapolis as a leading venue for entertainment for blacks. A year after Barnes's death, Ferguson and his brother established the Ferguson Brothers Agency to book gigs for blues acts, toward meeting the audience appetite across the South that Barnes had shown. World War II demand for gasoline and other materials hampered touring for musical acts; at the same time, the innovations in sound amplification helped a small group like Louis Jordan and the Tympany Five become as loud as a full big band. At the end of the 1940s, Ferguson Brothers was beginning to decline, but Don Robey in Houston was beginning his rise to regional domination. It is interesting to note that the Ferguson brothers and Robey left the daily details of their performance agencies to women: Twyla Mayfield ran the office for the Fergusons, while Evelyn Johnson supervised the Buffalo Booking Agency.

Ferguson died in 1957, when Robey was nearing his peak of control of the rhythm and blues scenes in Houston and Memphis. Nonetheless, as Lauterbach points out, some small cities and towns managed to nurture some young musicians at the outset of their influential careers, such as Macon, Georgia, where Little Richard and James Brown received their first important career breaks.

In the 1960s, partly as a result of the Great Migration of black labor (and audiences) and partly as a result of postwar urban renewal initiatives, many venues were closed and/or torn down, and the surrounding African American communities were displaced. Lauterbach gives Memphis as a case example, where Beale Street was mostly dismantled in the 1970s, and the main clubs for African Americans were to be found in South Memphis, such as the

Club Paradise. There ends this story of the chitlin' circuit for the past forty years, for which one hopes for a sequel.

One critical distinction that Lauterbach makes is that the chitlin' circuit was not the successor to the Theater Owners Booking Association, on whose circuit many of the classic blues singers had toured in the 1920s. He also shows how—and with whom—Denver Ferguson in the early days of his agency had coordinated performances with the so-called territory circuit that existed in Texas and Missouri in the 1930s (89). The chitlin' circuit carried a variety of touring musicians—some great, many good, some not so good, and a few perhaps memorably awful. One of the by-products of this book are the memorable characters. There is Sax Kari, the elder veteran who served as the author's guide to the circuit as it was before 1960. There were the Sweethearts of Rhythm, an all-girl big band from central Mississippi. The legendary promotion man Dave Clark is seen as a young man arranging for the advance publicity for the Jimmie Luncefond bands in each town on its 1930s southern tours. In Memphis was Sunbeam Mitchell, whose hotel in the 1950s was more home to some musicians than where their families lived.

Overall, though, Lauterbach focuses on a select few acts for their influences on American popular music. One of the outcomes of an extensive network of clubs and venues across wide swaths of the United States is an impact on the national musical tastes. For Lauterbach, that impact is the emergence from rhythm and blues to rock and roll, with the accompanying crossover from black audiences to white. Throughout the narrative, Lauterbach presents portraits of circuit legends Jimmie Lunceford, Big Joe Turner, Wynonie Harris, Louis Jordan, Johnny Ace, and B. B. King. But Lauterbach devotes a whole chapter to the keystone figure Roy Brown and his song "Good Rockin' Tonight," which the author views as both a timely hit record calling for good times and a timeless product of the circuit on mainstream musical influence. —*EK*

53. A Victim of the Business of Rhythm and Blues

The Late Great Johnny Ace and the Transition from R&B to Rock 'n' Roll. By James M. Salem. Urbana: University of Illinois Press, 1999. ISBN 0-252-02444-3 (hardcover), ISBN 0-252-06969-7 (paperback), $26.00

The only good thing about Johnny Ace's life was his music. Everything else stank, from his soured relations with his family in Memphis to his business deals with Don Robey in Houston. His success as a recording artist became a curse, resulting in long, bleary performing tours from coast to coast. Even the memories of him are misguided, emphasizing not his records but his surprise death from gunplay on Christmas night 1954. The stink emanates from the business of rhythm and blues that gripped Johnny Ace, a system that soon made a complete transition to the business of rock and roll. James Salem tells Ace's career so thoroughly that the young singer's death seems inevitable, perhaps a welcome release.

Salem's chapters on the business of music and on Don Robey describe the system which Ace could not control once he was caught in it. In the early 1950s, live entertainment for African Americans was in high demand, partly because television at that time broadcast mostly programs for whites. Black entertainers and musicians found themselves with lots of work, which increased with successes on records and radio. By this time, the so-called chitlin' circuit of roadhouses, clubs, ballrooms, and theaters provided what most radio and nearly all television could not and would not.

The African American Don Robey's tight-fisted toughness earned him an oft-remembered reputation as a "black Jew" (the more one learns about Robey, though, the less fair this comparison is to blacks and Jews). When his fist wasn't holding his wallet, it was holding a gun; one artist remembered Robey pulling out a pistol during negotiations. He began in the music business as owner of the Peacock Club in Houston, Texas. When he discovered guitarist Gatemouth Brown in 1947, he decided to enter the field of talent management. To maximize his profit in managing Brown, Robey started the Peacock record label to make and sell records of his artist. To maximize Robey's record profits, his right-hand assistant, Evelyn Johnson, began the Buffalo Booking Agency to organize and book tours for Peacock label artists to capitalize on and promote their record releases. Their success on records fed into success on the road, which then fed back into opportunities for continued success on records. Merely surviving in such a commercial circle—never mind thriving—was emotionally and physically demanding on the performers. None of that mattered to Robey, who back in Houston was learning and taking advantage of every way of maximizing his investments. Not only was he copyrighting under his name songs he didn't write—which many other label owners did also—but he quickly arranged for cover versions of his artists' songs on other labels by white performers as well as by black.

Enter Johnny Ace. He was born John Marshall Alexander Jr. to a poor yet industrious African American family in Memphis. As a teenager he showed himself a natural at music, and he was often found at a piano at home and at school. By 1950 he took the stage name Johnny Ace and was pianist for a local group, the Beale Streeters, which also included guitarist B. B. King and singer Bobby Bland. When King left Memphis to pursue his big break at national stardom, Alexander inherited the band. It soon had an opportunity to record for a new Memphis label called Duke. However, when the then-illiterate Bland nearly jeopardized the band's first recording session by failing to read the lyrics to some new songs, Ace stepped in to record the vocals to the ballad "My Song." He had a pleasing high baritone voice and a singing style that may be heard now as part gospel crooning, part proto-doowop. The resulting release was a sizable hit, but Duke founder David Mathis had trouble collecting money from the record distributors. Needing capital to make another record, Mathis entered into a partnership with Robey, who then appropriated Duke under his sole control. And then he appropriated Johnny Ace.

At first, under Robey, Ace enjoyed a string of hits within two years: "Cross My Heart" (1952), "The Clock" (1953), and "Saving My Love for You" (1953). To make the most of each increasing success, Ace embarked on tours set up by Johnson's Buffalo Booking Agency. It seems unbelievable today, but at the height of Ace's fame, venue owners wanting to book him had to agree to take B. B. King and Bobby Bland as well, then unknowns but now elder statesmen of blues and soul. In 1954, though, Ace was no longer on the rise. To be sure, his record releases that year were still profitable. But the toll of living on the road and living up to commercial success was wearing him down. Communication with his family, including a wife with whom he had two children, became nonexistent. Whenever he came to Memphis, he stayed not with his parents and wife but at the Mitchell Hotel, the popular hangout for musicians on Beale Street. His health was weighed down literally by overindulging on road food, and the resulting paunch and a newly grown mustache rendered him nearly unrecognizable from his publicity photos. In Florida he bought a gun, with which he often used to play pranks on friends and bystanders. And so it was on Christmas night 1954, between sets, that Ace tried to prove to some friends that his gun wasn't loaded by pointing it to his head and squeezing the trigger—and it fired. Oops. The news of Ace's ignoble end—it was widely reported as death by Russian roulette—fueled the sales of his "Pledging My Love," released only the previous week and eventually selling a million copies.

The shame of this story is that the only lesson learned is that performing artists can be exploited commercially in death as well as in life. Don Robey didn't formulate that lesson, but he showed by example that in 1954 it was still viable and extremely profitable. That morbid lesson was carried over when young white musicians and their audiences adopted for rock the business, along with the music, of rhythm and blues. It was easy to adopt those practices. When enough white teenagers bought records by black artists in numbers beyond the typical rhythm and blues market sales, the recording artists were then booked to play white venues. The most popular of these artists were then signed to the major labels selling to white buyers, the successes of those releases leading to more lucrative bookings. Once white rock and rollers achieved the level of appeal of their black R & B counterparts, they, too, followed them into that all-consuming circle. Johnny Ace was a black casualty of the success with black audiences. Sam Cooke became in 1964 a black casualty of the success with black and white audiences. Elvis Presley became in 1977 a white casualty of the success with white audiences. As described by Salem, this transition in business terms from "R&B to Rock 'n' Roll" is merciless. —*EK*

54. The Scariest, Most Deliciously Frightening Bit of Male Testosterone

Moanin' at Midnight: The Life and Times of Howlin' Wolf. By James Segrest and Mark Hoffman. New York: Pantheon, 2004. ISBN 0-375-42246-3. Revised edition, New York: Da Capo Press, 2005. ISBN 978-1-56025-683-0 (paperback), $17.95

Howlin' Wolf was one of the true giants of the blues. While he was a physically imposing man (accounts vary from six feet three inches to six feet six inches and anywhere from 260 to 300 pounds, with either a size 14 or 16 shoe), his music and onstage persona were something most people had never seen. Various accounts of his performances have him walking on the bar, crawling on all fours, howling like a man possessed, and pounding the floor. Of meeting Howlin' Wolf, Bonnie Raitt said, "He was the scariest, most deliciously frightening bit of male testosterone I've ever experienced in my life." Even fellow male blues musicians were enamored with Howlin' Wolf; Johnny Shines says, "I thought he was a magic man" who must have sold his soul to the devil. His music has influenced countless musicians, blues and rock alike.

For such a prominent figure in the blues world, it is odd that it took almost thirty years after his death for a biography to be written. If authors James Segrest and Mark Hoffman hadn't started research when they did, much of the rich information on Wolf's life would have been lost. Having never met Chester Burnett, the authors conducted an extraordinary amount of research to bring Howlin' Wolf to life.

On June 10, 1910, Howlin' Wolf was born Chester Arthur Burnett in White Station, a small community just outside of West Point, Mississippi. Experiencing a rough early childhood, neglected by his mother and beaten by his great-uncle, Chester ran away at age thirteen to live with his father in the Mississippi Delta, near Ruleville. Here he met Charlie Patton, who introduced him to the guitar. Enamored with Patton's music-making skills, Chester began seriously practicing guitar and developing as a musician. After serving in the army during World War II, Wolf moved to West Memphis, Arkansas, and began playing throughout the region. In 1951 and 1952 he recorded several sides (including "Moanin' at Midnight") at Sam Phillips's Memphis Recording Service for the RPM and Chess labels. Wolf moved to Chicago in 1953, where he would become one of the icons of not only the Chicago sound but blues in general. He recorded a number of Willie Dixon songs that became huge hits for the Chess label, including "Back Door Man," "Evil," "I Ain't Superstitious," "Little Red Rooster," "Spoonful," "Wang Dang Doodle," and more. These recordings would have a profound influence on many 1960s rock bands, such as the Rolling Stones, Led Zeppelin, and the Doors. Howlin' Wolf's gravelly voice and distinctive howl influenced the singing of Captain Beefheart (Don Van Vliet) and the radio persona of Wolfman Jack (Robert Weston Smith).

Through extensive research and interviews with more than 250 people acquainted with Wolf, Segrest and Hoffman provide a wealth of previously unknown information about his life. The sections on Wolf's early life are particularly useful for the historical record. In addition to Wolf's onstage persona and impressive showmanship, the authors paint a good picture of Wolf's personal life and mannerisms outside the spotlight. Readers are shown the determination of a man lacking formal education in his formative years but bettering himself through studying to learn how to read music and taking adult education classes (Billy Boy Arnold says that Wolf would study during gig breaks). He had a strong work ethic and didn't put up with his band getting sloppy drunk.

Clearly enamored with the mythos of Howlin' Wolf, the authors tend to highlight all of the colorful stories that surround Wolf. In an attempt to leave nothing out, the same story gets repeated over and over, told from various perspectives. While often interesting, many of these are not significantly different enough to warrant their inclusion in the book. For fans, the more tales the better, but the book could be significantly pared down without the loss of any real material.

In addition to an introduction by B. B. King, there are forty excellent black-and-white photographs of Wolf, various family members, and important musicians in Wolf's career. The authors provide excellent endnotes, a detailed index, a useful bibliography, and a discography of Howlin' Wolf recordings available on compact disc. A sessionography lists all known Howlin' Wolf studio recording sessions; live album "sessions" are excluded.

Casual blues fans may get bored with lists of tour and recording information. Others may wince at repeated wolf imagery (e.g., references to his "lairs"), though some of this is probably inevitable, given Burnett's own emphasis of the wolf persona. Despite this, *Moanin' at Midnight* is extremely well researched and provides an excellent biography of one of the blues' most popular and influential figures.

A revised edition was published by Thunder's Mouth Press in 2005 and is now available from Da Capo Press. This edition corrects name and date information in the sessionography and other areas. While these corrections are important, the photo reproduction suffers in the revised edition, with images appearing faded and grainy.

Readers enjoying this book may also wish to read Robert Gordon's *Can't Be Satisfied: The Life and Times of Muddy Waters* (no. 48). Containing interviews with Hubert Sumlin and ten other former band members, *Living Blues* issue 174 (2004) is almost entirely devoted to Howlin' Wolf. —*GJ*

55. The Bluesman versus the Union

The Amazing Secret History of Elmore James. By Steve Franz. St. Louis: BlueSource, 2002. ISBN 0-9718038-1-1 (paperback)

Records made Elmore James (1918–1963) famous. They also turned his life into a legend before it (the life) could be documented adequately. During his short life, James himself gave little help to prospective biographers. He gave only some perfunctory answers when French writers Jacques Demetre and Maurice Chevard asked him some questions in 1959 on behalf of *Jazz Hot* magazine. After his untimely death from a heart attack in 1963, there wasn't much known about him, even though his records "Dust My Broom" and "The Sky Is Crying" were big hits and remained in print for many years. Reporting what they could learn were magazines *Blues Unlimited* (1972), *Soul Bag* (1983), and *Blues Revue Quarterly* (1994). Still, there were many published reminiscences to be gathered. In 2003, Steve Franz published *The Amazing Secret History of Elmore James,* for which he researched thoroughly every published reference and transcribed spoken remark he could find. For the first time, James was given a complete biography that ranks with Gordon's Muddy Waters (no. 48) and Segrest and Hoffman's Howlin' Wolf (no. 54).

Elmore James was born in Mississippi in 1918; among his cousins were the bluesmen Boyd Gilmore and "Homesick James" Williamson. He had only a fourth-grade education, yet at age twelve he showed an interest in music by playing on a one-string "diddley bow." It isn't certain when he began playing guitar in public, but he was known to have been playing it in the mid-1930s. It remains an unsolved mystery as to whether James learned "Dust My Broom" from Robert Johnson or vice versa; the records favor Johnson as the originator, but oral testimonies indicate James. At any rate, James recorded the song in 1951 as his first and only record for Trumpet Records in Jackson, Mississippi, and in storybook fashion, it was a hit upon its public release. From 1952 through 1960, his band, the Broomdusters, was one of the heavies on the Chicago blues scene, led by James with his trademark bottleneck-slide guitar riffs and his high, blunt style of down-home singing.

One resource Franz used that his predecessors lacked is the collection of American Federation of Musicians (AFM) union documents on James that were gathered by researcher Scott Dirks (coauthor of the Little Walter biography *Blues with a Feeling*, no.

74). While union monitoring of musicians was lax in many areas of the rural South, it prevailed as mandatory in Chicago. In addition to aspects of the business of the blues, the AFM papers give some precious hints of James's personality. Some musicians remembered him as affable. But the AFM recorded that James did not hesitate to fire a musician, even when that musician had not been at fault. Sometimes he was shameless enough to leave one paying club appearance whenever a competing venue promised more money. It is no wonder, then, that the union suspended James's membership in 1960, and it was three years before the musician paid the fines and made amends. By then, his days on earth were numbered. Reportedly, at the time of his sudden death, he was preparing to join the American Folk Blues Festival tour in Europe for 1963; the boost to his career would have been huge. Instead, the missed opportunity enhanced the legend.

Franz also devotes his attention to the sidemen and some side issues. He looks at the lives of the Broomdusters, namely pianist Johnny Jones, tenor saxophonist J. T. Brown, and drummer Odie Payne. Later, he counts James's disciples through the song "Dust My Broom," his first and most imitated hit record, and so he assesses the contributions of B. B. King, Hop Wilson, Little Milton, Sonny Rhodes, Bo Diddley, Hound Dog Taylor, John Littlejohn, J. B. Hutto, and "Homesick James" Williamson to the Elmore legend. Turning from men to matters, Franz tackles several rumors. The main one is whether James's hit version of "Dust My Broom" for Trumpet Records was recorded without his knowledge during a rehearsal. This tale had been first told by Homesick James Williamson to a British writer, and repeatedly through the years it was retold in print without verification. As Franz affirms, James knowingly recorded the song during a formal recording session, and he had copyrighted the song beforehand with the assistance of Trumpet owner Lillian McMurry. More tantalizing is the possibility of film footage of James. Supposedly some film was shot by his Atlanta manager toward promoting live appearances. If indeed true, that reel has been long lost, and no other film has yet surfaced. So the only visual record of James consists of still photographs, many of which are reproduced in *The Amazing Secret History*.

The discographies in the final third of the book should not be ignored, at least for the reproductions of rare record labels placed throughout. In the "Career Discography," Franz presents all of James's records in the order in which they were made, listing the studio locations, the band members, song titles, and label releases. There are also various chronological lists of James record releases, so a reader can use them to play the James records in the order in which they were issued on a 78 or a 45 rpm single, and in that way the freshness of each song may be reexperienced.

Copies of *The Amazing Secret History of Elmore James* are available from the publisher BlueSource as a third-party dealer on Amazon.com. It has been published only in paperback; to my knowledge, there has been no hardcover edition. If later in time you have to purchase a copy from a used-book dealer, remember that the original price was forty dollars, and consider the asking prices accordingly. —*EK*

56. Youth and a Golden Age

Upside Your Head! Rhythm and Blues on Central Avenue. By Johnny Otis. With an introduction by George Lipsitz. Hanover, NH: Wesleyan University Press, 1993. ISBN 0-8195-5263-1 (hardcover), ISBN 0-8195-6287-4 (paperback), $20.00

Johnny Otis (1921–2012) was a drummer, bandleader, and composer in Los Angeles rhythm and blues for over sixty years. He became famous as leader of the revue "The Johnny Otis Show," in which he presented integrated bands, including the top African American musicians he could hire. He was also a first-rate scout of singers, discovering Etta James, Little Esther Phillips, and Marie Adams. During the 1950s, he recorded several national hits, including "Willie and the Hand Jive" (Capitol Records, 1958). Although born in a Greek family in California, he lived among the African Americans with whom he worked, broke bread with, and loved. Therefore, he was also a longtime activist for African American civil rights and, for a time, the pastor of the interdenominational Landmark Community Church in Los Angeles. Like the best rhythm and blues musicians, Otis elicited and shared exuberance and joy during his performances. But he also knew firsthand the social pains that his fellow African Americans experienced, and in later years he became outspoken whenever civil unrest flared up. His first book, *Listen to the Lambs* (1966), was written shortly after the riot fires of Watts had smoldered down. This one, *Upside Your Head!*, was strongly influenced by the 1992 Los Angeles riots upon the court dismissal of the policemen who had beaten Rodney King. Otis did not intend the title to be entertaining but rather as hard hitting as a policeman's billy club.

It is not an uplifting book. Its overall tone is pensive; its theme is about loss. In Otis's opening chapter, "Central Avenue," he remembers a conversation in the early 1990s when he and a few African American music veterans reminisced about the 1940s glory days on Central Avenue in Los Angeles. But then the trombonist John "Streamline" Ewing cut through the haze of memories by saying, "We had it all to ourselves." It stopped the talk that night. Otis wrote about what that stillness meant:

> To begin with, it was about the pensive mood of oldsters when they reflect upon the loss of their youth. There was also the sense of loss at the passing of a golden age. But the deeper and more pervasive source of the pain was the knowledge that racism was the primary factor in the deterioration of African American culture and, mourn that we may, that we are powerless to undo the damage. The silence and sadness that night was finally about bewilderment. . . . How, with things seeming to be moving in the right direction as they were in the forties and fifties, could we lose it all so completely?

What was lost? First, the economic prosperity that came with the swing-shifts during World War II. There were plenty of jobs available for those who had migrated west and north, and at good pay, too. Gradually, and by the late 1980s, the labor class in the cities was nickeled and dimed to bare subsistence. Also lost was a sense of civic responsibility, which had melted into apathy and then frozen into individual selfishness during the "Me Decade." As a result, there were fewer resources to share and fewer role models to guide young African Americans during the 1980s. The communality and warmth among African Americans seemed to wither for lack of heat during what seemed like a very cold social climate.

There is also the question of what African Americans may never have possessed. As close as Otis admits in this book, there may have been only a little sense of history in the sense of retaining the cultural heroes from one era to the next. Otis gives a personal example. His first serious experience as a professional musician was in the early 1940s as a drummer in a little jump band led by Otis Matthews. At that specific time, Otis shared with many people the opinion that the swing bands were playing the popular music that mattered and that the popular black stars of previous eras like Louis Armstrong, Jelly Roll Morton, and Bessie Smith, among others, were "relics of the past." Then bebop jazz hit Los Angeles in late 1945 and 1946, whereupon (in Otis's words) "the music of Duke [Ellington, Jimmie] Lunceford, and [Count] Basie . . . was seen as old hat by a new generation of young snobs. I felt very defensive. . . . I came to realize that bebop enthusiasts' scoffing at Duke and Basie was quite the same as what we had done to artists such as Satchmo and Jelly Roll."

If this discarding of cultural memory as Otis and his cronies realized in the early 1990s had occurred due to the political and economic undernourishment of their civic communities and cultures, what may be done in response? One answer was to riot. Otis well understood the feelings behind why people felt the need to revolt violently, which after the Watts riots he had tried to present and explain in *Listen to the Lambs* and try yet again in *Upside Your Head!* after the 1992 Rodney King riots. The other answer, which Otis provided by example as family man, musician, and pastor, was to love his wife and family, feed the poor, affirm the discarded heroes of previous eras, and criticize the leaders of the current times. To be sure, George Lipsitz describes Otis's deeds in this book's introduction and in his biography of Otis (*Midnight at the Barrelhouse: The Johnny Otis Story* [Minneapolis: University of Minnesota Press, 2010]). But blues readers need to read Otis's own words to feel their sting, fervency, love, and incitement to interact and share with humans of all races. —*EK*

57. A Blues Life Told in a Blues Way

Big Bill Blues: William Broonzy's Story. By William Broonzy as told to Yannick Bruynoghe. Brussels: Editions des Artistes, 1955. London: Cassell, 1955. Paris: Barclay, 1956. London: Jazz Book Club, 1957. Paris: Ludd, 1987. English language text reprint, New York: Oak Publications, 1964; New York: Da Capo Press, 1992. ISBN 0-306-80490-5 (paperback)

If you are a bluesman, and if you have an opportunity to tell one story about yourself, would you tell it according to the events that happened only to you personally? Or would you tell it according to the events that happened to your neighbors, your audiences, and your people?

William "Big Bill" Broonzy (1903–1958) took that opportunity in 1953, writing a set of vignettes during a stay in Belgium which were then prepared for publication by Yannick Bruynoghe. There were very few books about blues singers at the time, and those few concentrated on the city singers in New York and Kansas City. Broonzy was born in the Deep South and lived in Chicago for nearly his whole adult life, as had his friends. In his preface to the first American edition, Bruynoghe remembered that Broonzy initially wanted to title it *The Truth about the Blues.* Since there was a lot of "truth," it would have to be told quickly and broadly. And since bluesmen sing in the first person about events that could have happened to them if they had happened, so, too, did Broonzy write in a blues way, about what could have happened if not actually happened to him personally. As he wrote in his "envoi" closing the book, Broonzy admitted, "I would love to pick up a book and read a story about Big Bill Broonzy. . . . I would enjoy reading it because it could be true."

The book is organized in three parts: Broonzy's life to 1928, a discussion of fourteen songs, and presentations of fifteen blues "friends." Let us look first at the section about "My Friends." For the most part, they consist of blues musicians active in Chicago during the 1930s and 1940s. Some names will be recognizable to today's blues fans (Memphis Minnie, Lonnie Johnson, Tampa Red, and Sleepy John Estes), and others may be forgotten now (Washboard Sam, Tommy McClennan, Lil Green, Georgia White, John Lee "Sonny Boy" Williamson, Dr. Clayton, Joe McCoy, and Big Maceo). The remainder are as obscure today as they might have been in the early 1950s. Broonzy wrote of traveling to East St. Louis in 1937 to pick up two blues singers for a recording session, knowing them only as Red Mike and Black Mike. From the titles of the songs that Broonzy remembered them performing, Red Mike would be Mike Bailey, but the identity of "Black Mike" remains a mystery. Curtis Jones was a fine boogie pianist from Oklahoma who came to Chicago in the 1930s; in 1962 he would move to London. Some of the stories Broonzy tells about the others are entertaining, but upon thinking them through, they may be close to unbelievable. One story is of Sleepy John Estes as a caller for a railroad track-lining gang, the events of which may be plausible except that Estes was already half blind at the supposed time. Another story—famous in this instance—is of Broonzy claiming Washboard Sam as his half-brother, sharing a common father. Maybe the purpose behind Broonzy's outlandish stories is to have others seek these people to ask whether Broonzy was right, thus "rediscovering" them in the process.

For the presentation of the fourteen songs, the lyrics were transcribed, to which Broonzy added commentaries and stories. Among the songs are some of his most famous and provocative ones, like "Black, Brown and White," "When Will I Get to Be Called a Man," and "Just a Dream." Others are given odd interpretations. For example, one would expect "Blues in 1890 (Joe Turner Blues)" to be one of the many versions of the song about Joe Turney, whose job was to escort black prisoners to the Tennessee state penitentiary in Nashville during the 1890s. But Broonzy's Joe Turner was a benefactor assisting black farm families after droughts and floods. For other songs he draws from culture and personal anecdotes, such as the lover shared with a friend in "Partnership Woman." Some lyrics serve as springboards for Broonzy's observations, such as "Old Man Blues" and his remarks on May-December romances.

What of Broonzy himself? In the opening section, "My Life," he states that his parents were born as slaves, he was born in 1903 in Mississippi, he served in World War I, and he had worked since an early age at manual day jobs. It sounds believable. If he had not experienced those events in his life, others he knew had. For him, the events he claimed for himself were the core experiences of his generation. The attentive reader may realize through the disparities among years and facts within the book that maybe Broonzy had not done some of the acts he recounted, but that is not to say that those acts had not been done by someone else. This is true writing of a folk and blues sort, and as such it makes for one of the most precious books in the blues literature.

Big Bill Blues had a curious early publication history. Since no English publisher wanted to publish it, the manuscript was translated into French, given an introduction by Hughes Panassie, and published in Belgium, Bruynoghe's native country. The British jazz critic Stanley Dance gave much help toward the first English-language edition, which was published by Cassell in 1955 with illustrations drawn by Paul Oliver, an introduction by Dance replacing the one by Panassie, and a discography by Albert McCarthy. In 1964, Oak Publications issued what is now the standard edition that was reprinted in 1992 by Da Capo Press: the 1955 introduction by Dance, a new introduction by Bruynoghe, a study "Big Bill and the Country Blues" by Charles Edward Smith, Broonzy's chapters and envoi, and McCarthy's discography enlarged by Ken Harrison and Ray Astbury. —*EK*

58. A Book Big Bill Broonzy Would Enjoy Reading

I Feel So Good: The Life and Times of Big Bill Broonzy. By Bob Riesman. Chicago: University of Chicago Press, 2011. ISBN 0-226-71745-3 (hardcover), $27.50

One may think that *Big Bill Blues: William Broonzy's Story* (no. 57) would tell all that need be known about that great Chicago blues-man. After all, it is an autobiography, isn't it? However, there may be more to Broonzy's life than what he wrote for that book. He told some truths, sure, but they may not be any more autobiographical than the blues Broonzy sang. Over the years since his 1958 death, his records have been collected and reissued, the lyrics transcribed, and his family and friends found and interviewed. Glimpses of the man underneath the bluesman may be seen. What of the whole man?

To answer that question for himself, Bob Riesman had to dismantle the persona that Broonzy had constructed for himself, and then he had to find and affirm the actual life that was lived. In his preface, Riesman tells how his interview with Broonzy's Dutch lover and mother of his son led him to find the musician's sister in Arkansas. With their help, he found plenty of information to help him assess what Broonzy had written in *Big Bill Blues*:

- That his parents were not slaves but born after the end of the Civil War and Emancipation
- That he was born not in 1893 in Mississippi but in 1903 in Arkansas
- That he had not served in World War I
- That he began playing not around 1903 but more likely during the mid-1910s
- That his birth name was not William Broonzy but Lee Conley Bradley

Why did Broonzy make these claims, despite the facts that Riesman uncovered? I think Broonzy wanted to place himself not as man but as bluesman in the center of African American culture and post–Civil War history. To claim a familial memory of slavery still vivid, it was better to claim parents as slave-born rather than grandparents. By saying he was born in 1893 in Mississippi, he could claim that he was born in the same land at the same time as the blues. By claiming a birth year of 1893, he would need to claim also to have served in the world war and hence have some experience of life outside the United States. Why he adopted the name of Broonzy is unclear, but no matter; it is a rarely used name that is still most associated with him.

In his published "story," Broonzy told of his life through 1928 through chronologically arranged tales and from then through the early 1950s through descriptions of his songs and musician friends. For this biography, Riesman had to proceed systematically through the whole factual life, from the years as a leading figure in Chicago blues to the performances as folk figure across the northern United States and Europe. As it turned out, even the best-documented periods have some mystery. For example, Broonzy took many opportunities to participate in commercial recording sessions in Chicago as featured singer and as sideman guitarist during the 1930s. Yet he claimed to have been working day jobs during the same period. But the sheer number of the sessions documented with his presence suggests to me that either he was earning enough from music alone not to have a day job or he had a sympathetic and flexible boss at the day job. Another mystery is why he chose to be a mentor to young bluesmen on their arrivals in Chicago, for he seemed not to have had a mentor when he arrived there in the early 1920s. There are just some things that remained private with the person and that will never be known.

In his songs and writings, Broonzy presented himself as rooted in African American cultures in the South and Chicago yet taking the opportunity after World War II to bring those cultures in a first-person blues way to white Americans and Europeans. However, Riesman brings forth a racial cross-current in Broonzy's later life. The postwar Chicago blues scene with the new formulations of electrically amplified bands rendered obsolete the prewar bluesmen for younger African Americans in that city, however much that Broonzy recognized and encouraged the leaders of those bands, like Muddy Waters and Elmore James. At the same time, the blooming folk music efforts being nurtured by William Stracke and Studs Terkel in Chicago and the affirmation of blues as a jazz antecedent by Hughes Panassie and Yannick Bruynoghe in Europe needed for credibility Broonzy and his central blues persona. It takes a tall man to put and keep one foot in each racial culture, but Broonzy did that without selling out commercially. If Riesman had to deconstruct the mythical status that Broonzy claimed as a bluesman, he succeeded in recognizing and showing the bridging of cultures that the great man in his postwar career did quietly and without self-acknowledgment. —*EK*

59. Give My Regards to Sixth Street

Going to Cincinnati: A History of the Blues in the Queen City. By Steven C. Tracy. Urbana: University of Illinois Press, 1993. ISBN 0-252-01999-7 (hardcover), ISBN 0-252-06709-6 (paperback)

Any tour of a city's blues history with a local resident as a guide is valuable for its street smarts. Although Steven Tracy is a professor of Afro-American studies at the University of Massachusetts, he grew up in Cincinnati, Ohio. It was there during the late 1960s as a teenager that he began exploring local African American culture and its blues. What he reports in *Going to Cincinnati* is not merely local lore but of considerable interest for any blues lover, whether of the post–World War II era or of the prewar era.

The blues press doesn't think of Cincinnati as a black migration destination as often as it does of Chicago and Detroit. But Cincinnati is a river town that was also a major stop on the Illinois Central Railroad. While there are written records of African American presence from the 1790s, their arrivals in large numbers occurred during and after World War I. They settled in the so-called West End of Cincinnati, whose streets included George Street, where a red-light district was located until World War I, and Sixth Street, a central thoroughfare for blacks that is mentioned in several early Cincinnati blues records.

It is interesting to read Tracy's account of verifying the claim that the first blues singer on phonograph records, Mamie Smith, had come from Cincinnati. To his surprise, he couldn't locate any written record of her having been born or residing there nor any oral testimony from the older residents he had interviewed. So his local blues history begins with Sam Jones, "Stovepipe No. 1," a songster who recorded for the commercial labels from 1924 through

1930. Although Jones did not record after 1930, he was seen playing music for tips on Cincinnati streets into the 1960s. In a thorough chapter, Tracy untangles a cluster of prewar record releases that had been issued under the names Kid Cole, Walter Cole, Kid Coley, Bob Coleman, Walter Coleman, and Sweet Papa Tadpole. On the basis of performance style and lyric analysis, he concludes that behind these six names were only two singers, one for the Kid Cole and Bob Coleman sides, another for the rest. His "good guess" (72) is that the Bob Coleman and Walter Coleman listed in the city directory as living at the same address in the West End section may be the two singers that he deduced from the 78s. Even if this "good guess" isn't provable, it is tantalizing enough to make one listen anew—or for the first time—to these recorded performances.

Early in his explorations, Tracy met several older musicians who came to enjoy "discovery" careers, if they had not been famous enough previously to qualify as "rediscoveries." Chief among them were pianist Pigmeat Jarrett, harmonica player James Mays, and boogie pianist Big Joe Duskin. With Tracy's assistance, Jarrett and Duskin would take offers to travel to and perform at selected festivals in the United States and Europe. But all three men would tell Tracy of the musicians active in Cincinnati before World War II, indicating that the 78s by Stovepipe No. 1 and the Cole/Coleman singers were merely slivers of what had been heard around the West End.

To open the postwar half of the book, Tracy gives a lengthy history of King Records. Syd Nathan may have engaged for his label mostly national blues talent from outside Ohio, but he did retain a number of local rhythm and blues instrumentalists for his "house bands." One of the chief services of this book is to identify those King musicians who had been raised and were living in Cincinnati. The King Records story is told more expansively in Jon Hartley Fox's *King of the Queen City* (no. 60), but the function of Tracy's chapter is to record some local perceptions of what had been a nationally distributed label.

For many years, the Cotton Club, previously a ballroom, was Cincinnati's showplace for black music acts. One performer who came there and then stayed in town was jump-blues singer/pianist H-Bomb Ferguson. He was one of the few city-based musicians who did record for King Records. Guitarist Albert Washington may have been born too late for the Cotton Club or for King Records, but nonetheless he was the city's premier blues guitarist until his death in 1998. In a loving chapter, Tracy describes Washington's career through his records, the earliest of which are the 45 rpm singles that Ace Records recently collected in a CD reissue (Albert Washington, *Blues and Soul Man*).

Today, there is a large "Cincy Blues Fest" which is hosted by the local blues society. The surest way to verify any claims made from the festival's stage that a musician is a Cincinnati legend is to find his or her name in the index to Tracy's book. It is hard to believe that, at the time of this writing, *Going to Cincinnati* was published twenty years ago but is now out of print; remainders and used copies may be purchased for ten to twenty dollars. This book deserves a reprint with a new chapter on the chief blues performers who have sustained the city's blues tradition since 1990. —*EK*

60. Little Caesar and the Godfather of Soul

King of the Queen City: The Story of King Records. By Jon Hartley Fox. With a foreword by Dave Alvin. Urbana: University of Illinois Press, 2009. ISBN 0-252-03468-8 (hardcover), $30.00

On the surface, the story of King Records is heartwarming. It was founded and run in Cincinnati by a Jewish entrepreneur who had concerns for "the little guy." He hired alike white and black employees. He accepted alike white and black musicians as artists. The white musicians recorded songs previously recorded by the black musicians, and the blacks recorded those previously done by whites. Sales were often very good, and there were even a few hits. For nearly a quarter century, King Records thrived as an independent label, holding its own in competition with the other independent labels and the major firms RCA Victor, Columbia, and Decca.

However, Sydney Nathan, the founder and owner of King, ruled as "Little Caesar," the title that singer James Brown conferred on him. Smoking cigars as short and fat as he was, asthmatic, often screaming as if each word would be his last, his diatribes during recording sessions were scary, yet they became legendary in the retellings afterward. John Hartley Fox's book on Nathan and King opens with an account of the February 1956 recording session for James Brown's "Please, Please, Please." "Stop the tape! Stop the tape!" Nathan yelled. "This is the worst piece of shit I've ever heard in my life. Nobody wants to hear this crap. All he's doing is stuttering, just saying one damn word over and over. . . . No, I'm going to put this out nationally to prove what a piece of shit it is." Nathan was up there with Leonard Chess of Chess Records and Herman Lubinsky of Savoy Records for speaking out memorably.

Yet by being King Records' toughest critic, Nathan made enough money to run an impressively large-sized business, and record by record he built a catalog that still merits rediscovery. For some reason, King hasn't caught the imaginations of blues fans in the same ways that Paramount Records and Sun Records have. This situation is a little surprising, because writers have long recognized the label's legacy. Arnold Shaw took pains to include King in *Honkers and Shouters* (no. 51), and Steven Tracy devoted a lengthy chapter in *Going to Cincinnati* (no. 59). Jon Hartley Fox presented a public radio series about King Records in 1986, and then this book in 2009. Still, there hasn't yet been a theatrical film about King Records and there is hardly likely to be one unless a biopic is made about James Brown.

When Nathan founded King in 1943, his first sessions were of country music artists who were heard by the white people living in the Kentucky Appalachians. Therefore, the first hits were by the Delmore Brothers, Merle Travis, and Grandpa Jones (who did perform as "Grandpa" even though as a King artist he was in his early thirties). When original material ran out, Nathan allowed some of his country music artists to record some blues and black popular repertory, which were either played as Western swing or as straight-up country. In later years, when he was losing his country artists like Homer and Jethro to the major labels, Nathan broadened the country catalog by engaging bluegrass musicians, most notably the Stanley Brothers and Reno and Smiley.

Before starting King, Nathan had operated a record shop in Cincinnati, through which he learned of the blues and rhythm and blues tastes of his African American customers. And as King grew, Nathan hired Henry Glover, an African American from Alabama, whose businesslike demeanor in the studio helped to reassure musicians after Nathan's blow-top moments. Glover was key to facilitating hit-making sessions for black—and white—performing acts. Moreover, he brought songs previously recorded in King country sessions to the black rhythm and blues sessions. Wynonie Harris is known today for his cover of Roy Harris's "Good Rockin' Tonight," but he also recorded a hit version of "Bloodshot Eyes" previously done by Hank Penny. Bull Moose Jackson had hits not only with "My Big Ten-Inch" but also with Wayne Raney's country song "Why Don't You Haul Off and Love Me."

From this cross-pollination would emerge some originality, the most radical of which was brought by James Brown. Despite Nathan's vociferous doubts, Brown's first record, "Please, Please, Please," was a national hit, becoming big enough to keep Brown in King's recording studio when his next few singles were duds. The patience paid off (even if Nathan's might have been sorely tested) when a run of hits came for Brown in 1959–1961. However, Brown's idea of recording one of his 1962 Apollo Theater shows was seen as a huge risk—this having to be issued on a twelve-inch LP instead of a seven-inch single—but its rampant sales success in the cities showed there was a market for contemporary soul and rhythm and blues albums. Guralnick in *Sweet Soul Music* (no. 81) tells the story of *Live at the Apollo* in dramatic fashion, but Fox sets it firmly in the context of King business. Credit for Brown's development should go mostly to Brown and Nathan, of course, but some should also go to Nathan's self-built network of King sales offices across the country to distribute and sell records that had become immediately and whimsically in demand. Nonetheless, in the wake of the live album's commercial success, Brown did extract from Nathan some justly earned rewards, including a set of offices for himself and his own staff. Fox observes that if Nathan had ruled King as emperor, Brown in the mid-1960s ran his suite of offices as cult leader, levying fines for rules broken, even if unwittingly.

As Fox tells in the final chapters, Nathan died in 1968. King was sold to another independent label, Starday, and then to Polydor Records. Since 1975, the King recordings have been reissued by GML, Inc., owned by Moe Lytle. In a closing irony, Fox points out that Lytle has owned the King recordings longer than had Nathan. But he also shows the ways that Lytle has reissued on CD not only the albums but also the songs that had been released by Nathan only on vinyl singles. The present reissues on CD are much easier to find and cheaper than the original pre-1968 vinyl issues. There is a lot of King music as great as that recorded by Sun and Chess to be rediscovered by fans and writers, and the history of postwar blues can be still rewritten in the King way. —*EK*

61. The Crescent City as a Musical Melting Pot

Walking to New Orleans: The Story of New Orleans Rhythm &
Blues. By John Broven. Sussex, England: Blues Unlimited,
1974. Republished as *Rhythm & Blues in New Orleans.*
Gretna, LA: Pelican Publishing, 1978. ISBN 0-88289-125-1
(hardcover), ISBN 0-88289-433-1 (paperback), $18.00

Popularly known for its Dixieland jazz, New Orleans has had a
major role in shaping the sound of American popular music. This
port city was in many ways a magnification of the American "melt-
ing pot" of different cultures; Caribbean, African, and European
sounds merged to create new styles of music. Figures such as Buddy
Bolden, Jelly Roll Morton, and Louis Armstrong helped popular-
ize the emerging sounds of jazz that would greatly shape American
music. With the emergence of musicians like Professor Longhair,
Champion Jack Dupree, and Fats Domino in the 1940s and 1950s,
New Orleans would produce some of the United States' most influential rhythm and blues and rock and roll artists.

Originally published by Blues Unlimited in 1974 as *Walking to
New Orleans: The Story of New Orleans Rhythm & Blues,* John Broven's
seminal work was released in the United States as *Rhythm & Blues in
New Orleans* for Pelican Publishing Company in 1978. In this vari-
ously titled book, Broven examines the rise and decline of rhythm
and blues and rock and roll to the growth of newer musical styles
in New Orleans. From Professor Longhair and Fats Domino to Dr.
John and the Meters, John Broven catalogs the New Orleans music
scene from 1946 to 1973.

Broven, a longtime writer for the British blues magazine *Blues
Unlimited,* wrote *Walking to New Orleans* after realizing how little had
been written about New Orleans and its "vast contribution to rhythm
and blues and rock 'n' roll." Seeing the far-reaching influence of
recorded music, Broven focuses most of his attention there by examining New Orleans record labels and the recordings of the Crescent
City's many artists. While extensive use of *Billboard* charts provides
significant data, the most interesting portions of the book come from
interviews Broven conducted on a trip to New Orleans in 1970. The
real stories of the New Orleans music scene come from Professor
Longhair, Cosimo Matassa, Earl King, Allen Toussaint, Clarence
"Frogman" Henry, Johnny Vincent, and many others.

Like many British-authored books on music written in this
period, *Walking to New Orleans* feels at times like an extensive cata-

loging of recording sessions. Those interested in the history of New Orleans record labels and recording studios will find a wealth of information here. Interviews with J & M Studio owner and recording engineer Cosimo Matassa provide excellent insights into the music scene, as the majority of New Orleans rhythm and blues recordings from the 1940s through the 1960s were made in his studios. The focus on recordings and hit records overshadows the many other facets of music.

Walking to New Orleans is divided into four sections: "Rhythm and Blues, 1946–55"; "Rock 'n' Roll, 1955–59"; "The Local Record Scene, 1955–63"; and "The End of an Era, the Start of Another . . . 1963–73." The book also includes an appendix showing influences on the music of New Orleans and its impact on other sounds, birthdates of musicians born in New Orleans, a list of major New Orleans R & B bands and recording personnel, a list of the top-selling New Orleans singles from 1946 to 1972, and a discography of albums. Broven also includes an index of names.

The body of the American printing, *Rhythm & Blues in New Orleans*, is virtually unchanged from the original British printing, but there are a few minor variations—most notably, the inclusion of an afterword mentioning New Orleans musical developments from 1973 to 1978. Oddly, the photo examples in the 1978 printing are of lower quality than those in the original, while the illustrations are clearer.

Anyone interested in rhythm and blues or nonjazz popular music in New Orleans from the 1940s through the 1970s will find this book extremely useful. While Broven's aesthetic biases resonate throughout, *Walking to New Orleans* is well researched and fills many information gaps that were missing in previous writings on the subject.

I Hear You Knockin': The Sound of New Orleans Rhythm and Blues by Jeff Hannusch (no. 62) is a nice supplement to Broven's work. Hannusch gives a series of profiles of the many musicians and record producers that made New Orleans famous. —*GJ*

62. The Second Line Matters, Too

I Hear You Knockin': The Sound of New Orleans Rhythm and Blues. By Jeff Hannusch, a.k.a. Almost Slim. Ville Platte, LA: Swallow Publications, 1985. ISBN 0-9614245-0-8 (paperback), $20.00

John Broven's *Walking to New Orleans* (no. 61) is the overarching narrative history of postwar Crescent City rhythm and blues through 1970. In *I Hear You Knockin'*, Jeff Hannusch singles out those performers a reader should stop to enjoy. Through thirty-one profiles, Hannusch covers nearly sixty years, from the beginning of pianist Tuts Washington's career in the 1920s to the mid-1980s when the book was published. Some of the "usual suspects" are presented: Professor Longhair, Allen Toussaint, Dave Bartholomew, and Cosimo Matassa. As explained in an appendix, Fats Domino was omitted because Hannusch had given his notes on him to John Broven, who was researching the pianist toward a biography (still yet to appear). Irma Thomas and Ernie K-Doe have been the subjects of recent lengthy articles, but Hannusch's chapters on them describe them as they were in the early 1980s, when the futures of their careers may have seemed a little uncertain. The personalities of the remaining twenty-five people range from cult to character, but they are treated so sympathetically that I took interest in them, and I kept checking the discography appendix and Amazon.com to see whose records have been reissued.

Most captivating for me are the lesser-known subjects—"the second line" as Hannusch described them. For example, there was James Booker, whose pianism I recently came to know through a recent reissue. Until reading the chapter about him, I had little idea of the severity of mental illness and alcoholism that clouded his last years before his 1983 death; for those reasons, it was fortuitous that Hannusch met Booker and obtained a quotable conversation from him. The profile on composer Dorothy LaBostrie is as remarkable for how Hannusch met her after years of searching for her as for the story behind her writing the song "Tutti Frutti," which became a landmark record hit for Little Richard. In one chapter, Jessie Hill is having a hard time fielding a band for his gig that very night at the club Tipitina's. In another, singer Johnny Adams seems to have a harder time getting his band members to show up on time.

Overall, though, there were records to be made and sold, and a New Orleans recording artist was going to have to be strong enough to survive the risk behind laying down his or her most catchy songs or else be ground up in the gears of the music industry system that could cheat them of success. It seems exceptional now that Lew Chudd, Dave Bartholomew, and Fats Domino produced a continuous stream of hits for about ten years, starting with

"The Fat Man" in 1949. For success seemed to come to those who didn't care one way or another, like Lee Dorsey. It eluded those who desired it greatly, like Huey Smith. What the typical musician was going to have to do in order to maintain a performing career was to continue making new records, regardless of the record label and the chances of high sales. Johnny Adams learned that lesson, Irma Thomas was beginning to learn that, and Smiley Lewis had not. Hannusch's profile on Lewis (1913–1966), who had recorded the song "I Hear You Knockin'" that serves as the book's title, combines many of the themes that appear singly in other chapters. Lewis was of New Orleans and for New Orleans, but as a recording artist he didn't get the breaks that others felt his talent deserved. If he failed to succeed on a national scale, it wasn't for lack of effort or musical achievement. Then again, as Hannusch documents, Lewis's musicians said that the local and regional successes went to their leader's head and, as a result, made his behavior on performance tours difficult to tolerate. Sometimes, the moral seems to be that there can be such a thing as too much success.

Upon its publication, *I Hear You Knockin'* became an instant classic, receiving the American Book Award in 1986. To my knowledge, there was never a hardcover edition. The paperback remains in print, along with Hannusch's follow-up, *The Soul of New Orleans: A Legacy of Rhythm and Blues* (Ville Platte, LA: Swallow Publications, 2001). Readers who cannot get enough of Hannusch's writings should view his blog on the Ponderosa Stomp website, http://www .ponderosastomp.com/blog/author/jeff-hannusch/, and his many magazine articles and LP/CD notes; the best of them deserve to be collected and reprinted as his third book. —*EK*

63. The Book That Launched the Rediscovery Era

The Country Blues. By Samuel Charters. New York: Rinehart, 1959. London: Joseph, 1959. London: Jazz Book Club, 1959. Munich: Nymphenburger, 1962. Reinbek: Rowohlt Teschenbuch, 1982. Second printing, New York: Da Capo Press, 1975. ISBN 0-306-80014-4 (paperback), $16.95

A lot has been written on blues over the years, and new discoveries ensure that more will continue to be written. Researchers can now easily access thousands of recordings, books, articles, and videos on and of the blues. When Samuel Charters's *The Country Blues* was published in 1959, very little research had been done into the blues, and recordings from the 1920s and 1930s were extremely difficult to locate. In the original introduction, Charters writes, "It is difficult writing the first extended study of any subject, and it has been especially difficult writing a first study of early blues singers and their recordings." Howard Odum had conducted research on African American folk music in Lafayette County, Mississippi, as early as 1905, identifying a number of songs as "blues." Other writings on blues were produced during the first half of the twentieth century, but no one had written a large-scale examination of the subject. Articles on blues had appeared in magazines like *Jazz-Hot*, *Matrix*, *Discophile*, *Jazz Journal*, *Jazz Publications*, and *Jazz Monthly*. Charters drew heavily on blues articles in *Record Research* magazine as well as recordings in the collections of Pete Whelen, Ben Kaplan, and Pete Kaufman. His own extensive field research rounds out the sources for *The Country Blues*.

In writing *The Country Blues*, Charters admits some anxiety in tackling the subject, saying, "There has been . . . an over-riding sense of responsibility toward the material," and an awareness of the difficulties: "a further difficulty of a first study is that there will be considerable error." In the preface to the 1975 printing, Charters writes, "I shouldn't have written *The Country Blues* when I did; since I really didn't know enough, but I felt it couldn't afford to wait." Modern readers will find a number of errors and much incomplete information in this book, but we are informed by over fifty years of research that came after Charters's pioneering work. In the 1975 preface, Charters tells of the two major reasons for writing *The Country Blues*: "It was a romanticization of certain aspects of black life in an effort to force the white society to reconsider some of its racial attitudes, and on the other hand it was a cry for help. I wanted hundreds of people to go out and interview the surviving blues artists. I wanted people to record them and document their lives, their environment, and their music—not only so that their story would be preserved but also so they'd get a little money and a little recognition in their last years."

The book inspired many young white blues fans to begin seeking out old recordings, interviewing performers, and documenting these findings in articles, books, sound recordings, and documentaries. Charters notes in the 1975 preface, "I was trying to describe black music and black culture in a way that would immediately involve a certain kind of younger, middle-class white American. They were the ones most ready to listen, and they were the ones, also, who could finally force some kind of change." It was *The Country Blues* that partially inspired Gayle Dean Wardlow to begin searching for old blues records and the men who made them. Indeed, with the exception of W. C. Handy's *Father of the Blues* (no. 12) and Big Bill Broonzy's *Big Bill's Blues* (no. 57), all the books in *100 Blues Books* owe much to the pioneering work of Samuel Charters. Despite the errors and incomplete data, Charters notes in the 1975 preface, "What I was doing wasn't academic, and it wasn't scholarly, but it was effective."

It is interesting to read some of the assumptions Charters held in 1959. In the original preface he writes, "Two singers, Rabbit Brown and Robert Johnson, have been discussed at length, despite their minor roles in the story of the blues." It is interesting to see how much has been written on Johnson, including Charters's own *Robert Johnson* (Oak Publications, 1973), since the first publishing of *The Country Blues*. Charters focuses on marketing and record sales as a means of objectively focusing on the blues in relation to its audience. He eschews musical and sociological examinations of the blues, stating, "The blues audience is capricious and not in the least concerned with musical or sociological concepts." This narrow and perhaps condescending view is one of the faults with the book. Later studies through musicological and sociological lenses have given us much better information by which to form our understanding of the blues.

The Country Blues gives good introductions to jug-band music and the record industry in the 1920s and 1930s, and it provides some of the earliest biographical sketches of important blues musicians. There are thirty-six black-and-white photographs and two appendices devoted to those who have recorded the blues and who have been involved in 1950s reissues of early blues recordings. The index has a number of page omissions.

In the same year as the book was first published, Charters also produced an LP titled *The Country Blues*. Charters states in the liner notes that this record "is intended as an appendix to the Rinehart book." A follow-up, *The Country Blues*, volume 2, was produced in 1964. Several of the artists on this second volume were largely unfamiliar until after the book *The Country Blues* came out. In these liner notes, Charters writes: "As the years pass, and more and more of the older singers die, it will be less possible to learn much about the lives of the singers who are still unknown, but with so much added to the knowledge of the blues in only a few years it will perhaps be only a short time before the country blues will become one of the best known, instead of the least known of the rich musical styles that the Negro has created in America."

The Country Blues truly inspired generations of research into arguably the United States' most important musical legacy. It is a quick read and worth reading to get a sense of the excitement it generated in young blues fans in 1959 and 1960 who were eager to learn more. —*GJ*

64. What Is Real for the Blues?

Blues Fell This Morning: Meaning in the Blues. By Paul Oliver. With a foreword by Richard Wright. London: Cassell, 1960. Second edition, Cambridge: Cambridge University Press, 1990. ISBN 0-521-37437-5 (hardcover), ISBN 0-052137793-5 (paperback), $45.00

Blues Fell This Morning may be the most influential book about the blues. If Samuel Charters's *The Country Blues* inspired American readers to rediscover bluesmen and their music, this Oliver volume inspired British readers to study the blues and its surrounding cultures. Later, when blues became a subject of college courses on both sides of the Atlantic, *Blues Fell This Morning* was often the textbook assigned to students. It may be said that nine out of ten books published since 1960 about the blues are merely commentaries to this one. Every writer who studies African American culture through blues lyrics has to contend with Oliver's shadow; indeed, many of the other ninety-nine books we discuss will be compared to what Oliver first wrote here.

Until Charters and Oliver, most writing about the blues treated those performed and recorded in cities often as current reportage with little context. Raised and living in England, Oliver did not know and could not take for granted the slang, names, terms, and places in the lyrics sung by bluesmen on records. What the words were was one matter; what they were referring to—what they "meant"—was what Oliver explored. The resulting study presented the topical and social contexts assumed by bluesmen and their listening audiences.

The introductory chapter related a thumbnail history of blues recording, a short description of the early blues styles based on what information was then known, and some observations on the challenges of studying blues from commercial records. From there, a succession of topics was discussed in ten chapters: farming and labor (ch. 1), mobility and migration (ch. 2), physical attraction and love (ch. 3), sex (ch. 4), religion, superstition, and cultural magic (ch. 5), gambling, liquor, and drugs (ch. 6), urban life and crime (ch. 7), punishment (ch. 8), forced labor in disaster relief and wars (ch. 9), and health (ch. 10).

If you haven't yet read it, then whenever you acquire this book, I urge you to read it from cover to cover; you have the rest of your life to reread favorite bits. But first, read it whole. That way, you can grasp the full sweep of Oliver's arrangement of topics. For example, the frustration of work conditions in chapter 1 leads to the migration to where the work is in chapter 2. The chapters on love and sex—topics that Oliver discusses frankly and which most writers on blues still shy away from even acknowledging—are followed in turn by the beliefs behind superstition and ritual, including those intended to lure new lovers. The way these topics follow one another from the first chapter through the last is something I admire.

The guts of the text consist of lyrics selected and transcribed from 350 blues records (mostly pre-1941), with Oliver setting up context or commenting. He acknowledges the blues singer for each song but not necessarily the composer. The apparent reason for this view is that for this study, Oliver is viewing blues as a folk music conveying more of the surrounding culture at a particular time (here, African American blues, mostly in the American South, before 1950) than individual blues achievement. Such a view is allowed only as long as it is taken strictly for a cultural study within a limited historical scope.

Indeed, according to his 1960 introduction, *Blues Fell This Morning* was intended to be paired with a history of the blues, which was completed and published in 1969 as *The Story of the Blues* (no. 2). Those who followed Oliver in this approach often slipped, and even fell, because they did not acknowledge the creating composer along with the re-creating singer when appropriate, or they did not take the historical context hand in hand with the social context (especially the anthropologists and folklorists who often write of historical blues with present-tense verbs, as if the blues has never evolved).

If this classic book has any flaws—and its imitators may choose to see none—it may be due mostly to Oliver's heavy-handed tone, especially in the second half of the book. To be sure, while he was writing the book during the late 1950s, African American blues received scant attention in print and condescending passive attention at that. Throughout the text, Oliver tries to persuade the reader that the blues was and is worth studying, and he tries to incite serious study of the culture, if action toward the easing of the culture's burdens is not possible for the reader. At times, he incites almost to the point of absurdity. For example, in chapter 9, "Going Down Slow," he writes: "Black doctors had no hope of treating white patients and white doctors would often refuse to treat Blacks. Consequently, black doctors were overworked and had to serve families that were unable to meet their bills. The medical profession held little attraction for doctors in the South." The first two sentences state baldly and without flinching the lack of proper health care for African Americans, but the third sentence is puzzling.

Oliver asserts (in ch. 2, "Railroad for My Pillow") that "the blues acted as a catalyst for the anger, humiliation, and frustration that tended to demolish the moral codes and spirit of a man, and the act of creating blues brought satisfaction and comfort both to him and to his companions. Essentially the blues singer is a realist and often his statements are accurate portrayals of his state of mind, uninhibited in their self-expression." That much should be acknowledged. Yet I can't imagine that there weren't small joys and loves that were celebrated to a good blues. The great African American novelist Richard Wright's foreword to *Blues Fell This Morning* gives a wider sense of "realism" through the blues than what Oliver described: "Yet the most astonishing aspect of the blues is that, though replete with a sense of defeat and down-heartedness, they are not intrinsically pessimistic; their burden of woe and melancholy is dialectically redeemed through sheer force of sensuality, into an almost exultant affirmation of life, of love, of sex, of movement, of hope. No matter how repressive was the American environment, the Negro never lost faith in or doubted his deeply endemic capacity to live. All blues are a lusty, lyrical realism charged with taut sensibility." These wise words are worth remembering.

Copies of the book may be split into two groups, those based on the 1960 first edition, and those on the 1990 second revised edition. The first printings were done in England by Cassell in 1960 and in New York by Horizon Press in 1961. There was a special edition from the Jazz Book Club series issued in 1963 by Sidgwick and Jackson in London. A 1963 reprint by Collier Books was titled *The Meaning of the Blues*. The second edition in 1990 has been handled by Cambridge University Press, whether through its regular imprint or through its Canto paperback series.

There was a companion LP issued in 1960 by Philips Records, titled *Blues Fell This Morning*, on Philips BBL7369. It presented fourteen blues recordings made between 1927 and 1940, made by artists who were forgotten (like Barbecue Bob, Texas Alexander, and "Bukka" White) if not downright obscure (Lewis Black). This was issued only in England and hence may be difficult for American collectors to find. Happily, in 2011, JSP has produced *Meaning in the Blues: The 50th Anniversary of "Blues Fell This Morning"* (JSP 77141), a splendid four-CD set containing 103 of the songs whose lyrics are cited in the book. —*EK*

65. The Blues in Chains

Living Country Blues. By Harry Oster. Detroit: Folklore Associates, 1969. Reprint, New York: Minerva Press, 1975. ISBN 0-30810-236-3 (paperback)

When Harry Oster's *Living Country Blues* was published, many libraries purchased it for their music sections. However, it has not been reprinted since 1975, not even during the blues boom of the 1990s when many less accomplished blues titles were reappearing in print. Some writers still consult it with regard to Oster's famous 1950s recordings of Robert Pete Williams and other inmates at Louisiana State Penitentiary at Angola. In some academic opinions, its uses of folklore and anthropology as approaches to studying blues seem to have been supplanted by Evans's larger-scale advocacy for those disciplines in his *Big Road Blues* (no. 14). I suspect that many of Oster's readers have read mostly the first ninety-five pages, which contain the overview statements, dipping only casually into the remaining 350 pages presenting the transcriptions of song lyrics. If they have done so, they have denied themselves the full impact of his presentation. For if the first hundred pages present a long submarine sandwich, so to speak, the other 350 pages eat that sandwich bite by delicious bite. For this reason, at least, *Living Country Blues* may be a book worth rediscovering.

Harry Oster (1923–2001) published *Living Country Blues* while teaching at the University of Iowa. But his fieldwork for the book was done previously while he was at Louisiana State University. He had collected approximately 400 songs, of which 230 appear in lyric transcriptions in the book. Many of them were recorded in performances of prisoners at Angola. It has been believed by folk music researchers that prisons are where many songs and chants have long been practiced, although in the book's first chapter Oster acknowledges that commercial music was filtering in by way of prison radios, televisions, and movie showings. Still, he was willing to listen for and identify folk practices where they were exercised at Angola. Indeed, he found some master exercisers of blues and folk music, namely Robert Pete Williams, Roosevelt Charles, Hogman Maxey, and Butch Cage.

Before examining each blues in his collection, Oster takes care to describe the folk blues as a whole. First, he relates a sketch history of the blues, which was necessary because Oliver's *Story of the Blues* (no. 2) had not yet appeared. For Oster, the lyrics as the vocal expression of emotion are central to blues history, and the twelve-measure, three-phrase blues chorus is the conventional structure. While so-called city blues is a part of the blues, Oster wants to look at and listen more closely to "country blues" as the "spontaneous expression of thought and mood." To that purpose, in chapter 3 he gives some topical themes and social functions of country blues toward a "sociological picture": love and infidelity, sickness and death, work and bosses, trains, alcohol, crime, and punishment. Finally, he ends his overview with some conventions of blues as poetry: personification, metaphors and similes, and rhetorical devices in successive blues lyric phrases. By describing the history and listing the means of expression, Oster tries to convey in general terms what has abided in the blues and what of it may endure in the future.

But timely notes about specific songs and singers are needed for a balanced presentation of the blues, not just generalities in timeless terms. That is what the massive fifth chapter, "The Songs," provides. The 230 songs are grouped according to the topics and functions listed in chapter 3. Each song's lyrics are given in transcription, with Oster's notes on context and history, antecedent songs, previous commercial recordings, and references to LP issues of the transcribed performance. Every song's singer is acknowledged; there are no anonymous folk in "The Songs." Even some performances by master Snooks Eaglin early in his career are presented. The serious reader has to read this chapter carefully to see to what extent the selected songs illustrate the general statements made in the previous chapters.

As an appendix, Oster lists nine LPs that he issued of performances discussed in the book. Some of these records are now classics, such as *Angola Prisoner's Blues* (originally issued on Louisiana Folklore Society LFS A-3, 1959, and later reissued on Arhoolie Records), featuring Robert Pete Williams's "Talking Prisoner's Blues" and Snooks Eaglin's *New Orleans Street Singer* (originally issued on Folkways FA 2476, 1959). It is likely that owners of *Living Country Blues* use their copies as a text companion to their LP and CD issues of Oster's recordings. For an updated web discography of Oster's tapes, see Stefan Wirz, "Dr. Harry Oster Recordings," http://www.wirz.de/music/osterfrm.htm (accessed January 9, 2013).

One vexing question is about the place of artists in folk cultures, especially of those whose "spontaneous expressions" on LPs and CDs sell in considerable numbers. Oster (95) asserts that blues singers are of two sorts: the majority are "imitators" who combine common verses and phrases as if stitching a patchwork quilt, and the remaining few are "gifted and imaginative" singers whose "artistic creations . . . have the impact and vividness of deep personal involvement." However, David Evans in *Big Road Blues* (103) points out that some of Oster's named "imitators" have performed regularly in public in and around Baton Rouge while the "gifted and imaginative" singers like Williams "have performed most of their lives only for their own benefit and enjoyment." Therefore, to Evans, "their [the imitators'] songs deserve special attention" because they (quoting from Oster's p. 95) "reflect the basic elements and attitudes of the folk Negro environment." Evans makes a good point, because in *Living Country Blues,* Oster rarely mentions audience, because he recorded many of his performances in secluded places like prison rooms and because he studied and wrote about those performances with an ear to artistic expression. However, if one were to defend Oster, one would need to page through "The Songs" chapter, note how many and which songs were transcribed from performances by "imitators," then see to what extent Oster's overview can be affirmed with only those imitators' songs. Then again, one could simply answer Evans's question by asking, "How many folks are permitted to listen together and still be identified as a 'folk group'?" That answer may be the same or fewer than the number of persons with Oster in the designated recording spaces within Angola.

Many American libraries have *Living Country Blues* for borrowing. Readers wishing to purchase their own copies can find some priced in the fifteen-dollar to thirty-dollar range among the online used-book dealers. Those desiring a hardcover should purchase the 1969 Folk Associates edition, as the 1975 Minerva Press reprint was in paperback. —*EK*

66. Iconic Moments in Memphis Music

The Memphis Blues Again: Six Decades of Memphis Music Photographs. By Ernest C. Withers and Daniel Wolff. New York: Viking Studio, 2001. ISBN 0-670-03031-7

From the Memphis sanitation workers' strike to the last speech of Dr. Martin Luther King Jr. to the funeral of Emmett Till, Ernest Withers captured some of the most iconic images of the American civil rights movement. Withers was also an important photographer of Negro league baseball and thoroughly documented the images of the Memphis music scene. While many general readers might not be familiar with Withers's name, they have probably seen his iconic photo of a young B. B. King posing with a young Elvis Presley, his photo of Martin Luther King Jr. blocked by police at the funeral of Medgar Evers, or any number of photos that help define the civil rights movement.

Ernest Withers worked as a professional photographer in his lifelong home of Memphis after leaving the army in 1946. At first he shot public events for Nat D. Williams, teacher, journalist, editor, and first African American radio announcer in Memphis. He later set up his own studio. In addition to portraits of Memphians, Withers was granted access to the top clubs, where he captured shots of the country's hottest acts. It was this access that allowed Withers to document the world of Memphis music behind the scenes.

The Memphis Blues Again features almost 160 stunning black-and-white photographs of music in Memphis from the late 1940s through the 1980s. His compositional technique in capturing these photos is impeccable. His style provides a physical depth to photographs that is lacking in many others from this period. These photos capture music history in Memphis like no others. A shot of Ruth Brown singing at the Hippodrome captures the rapt attention of audience members.

One can feel the energy as Tina Turner and an Ikette practically dance off the page. A shot of Rufus Thomas and Elvis Presley dancing onstage at the WDIA Goodwill Revue in 1956 exudes joy. The gravity of history is captured in photos of James Brown arriving for Otis Redding's funeral, the Staple Singers standing at the spot where Martin Luther King Jr. was killed, or the faces of mourners at Sam Cooke's wake. There are also humorous photos of Howlin' Wolf and his band clowning in a posed photo of them picking cotton, Roscoe Gordon posing with a chicken on his shoulder, and Rufus Thomas and Nat D. Williams in a goofy embrace at the Mid-South Coliseum.

Though the title suggests that the photographs will all be of blues performers, the images represent the diverse styles popular in Memphis over Withers's photography career. There are images of jazz stars like Louis Armstrong, Lionel Hampton, Dizzy Gillespie, Count Basie, and Duke Ellington; gospel greats like Mahalia Jackson, the Clara Ward Singers, and the Reverend Cleophus Robinson; rock and roll figures such as Elvis Presley, Jerry Lee Lewis, and disc jockey Dewey Phillips; and soul, funk, and R & B artists like Al Green, Isaac Hayes, James Brown, and Roberta Flack. There are even photographs of country singer Charley Pride and the contralto Marian Anderson.

Some of the photo captions give very limited information. For instance, a caption for a photo showing some of the members of the Memphis Jug Band performing simply reads "Opening of the Al Jackson, Sr., Esso Servicenter, 1963." Another caption mentions only Isaac Hayes, but doesn't list Helen Washington. A photo caption for an image of Chico Chism, James Cotton, Little Walter, Howlin' Wolf, Big Bill Hill, and an unidentified man reads only "Howlin' Wolf Band, Brinkley, Arkansas, ca. 1961." With a career photographing thousands of people for almost sixty years it is understandable that Withers couldn't identify all subjects, but these images were selected by Daniel Wolff, who also wrote the text. In Withers's book *Pictures Tell the Story* from the previous year, some of these same photos do provide fuller captions. Other than the captions, the only text is a ten-page essay on Withers and Memphis music written by Wolff.

In 2010 it was discovered that Withers worked for the FBI as an informant during critical years of the civil rights movement, passing along critical information about people and plans within the movement. For more information, read the Freedom of Information Act reports and a multipart exposé in the Memphis *Commercial Appeal* at http://www.commercialappeal.com/withers -exposed/. Despite this damning information to the legacy of Ernest Withers, his camera beautifully captured iconic moments of the civil rights movement and the Memphis music scene for three-fifths of a century. Withers inspired several generations of music photographers. The high quality of his work set the standard for all music photography that followed.

As with other blues photography/coffee table books, *The Memphis Blues Again* is not cheap. The book can be obtained for anywhere between fifty dollars and two hundred dollars.

More of Ernest Withers's music photography can be seen in:

> *Beale Street: Crossroads of America's Music* by William S. Worley and featuring the photography of Ernest Withers and Gary Carson. Lenexa, KS: Addax Publishing, 1998.
> *Pictures Tell the Story: Ernest C. Withers Reflections in History* by Ernest Withers. Norfolk, VA: Chrysler Museum of Art, 2000.

—*GJ*

67. Blues Lyrics for the Eyes as well as for the Ears

The Blues Line: A Collection of Blues Lyrics. Compiled by Eric Sackheim, with illustrations by Jonathan Shahn. New York: Grossman, 1969. Reprint, New York: Schirmer, 1975; Hopewell, NJ: Ecco Press, 1993; New York: Thunder's Mouth Press, 2004. ISBN 1-56025-567-6, $19.95

Why have printed transcriptions of blues lyrics? Translations of them would be useful for international lovers of the blues, certainly. But why have transcriptions from recordings of American blues musicians singing in English that are prepared for English-speaking fans? Would not the listeners understand immediately and directly the words being sung? One would think so, but that may not be. For one thing, the classic prewar blues records are now seventy years old or older, and the protorock blues records are at least fifty years old; the ways of talking and singing have changed greatly over the years. For another, these same records have deteriorated either due to punishing use by the original purchasers or due to the effects of age on the materials used to press the discs. Finally, many catchphrases and proper names understood by the singer and his or her immediate audience may be forgotten and liable to mishearing by today's listeners who are rediscovering the performances on their own.

For some years now, Chris Smith has presented in *Blues and Rhythm: The Gospel Truth* magazine his lyric transcriptions of individual blues. Older blues fans may still have issues of Bob Groom's *Blues World* periodical in which blues lyrics were printed. Jeff Todd Titon's survey, *Early Downhome Blues* (no. 30), was a source of transcriptions for many pre-1942 blues. In 1983, Michael Taft published through Garland Press *Blues Lyric Poetry: An Anthology*, a volume of prewar blues lyrics, to which a massive three-volume concordance (*Blues Lyric Poetry: A Concordance* [New York: Garland, 1984]) was prepared to facilitate the identification of the same word or phrase in two or more songs. (Taft revised the *Blues Lyric Poetry* anthology in 2005 for Routledge Press as *Talkin' to Myself: Blues Lyrics 1920–1942*.) Special mention should be made of R. R. Macleod's self-published (Edinburgh: PAT Publications, 1988–2004) thirteen volumes of prewar lyrics transcribed from Yazoo and Document reissues. As these volumes were sold only directly by Macleod from his home in Scotland and he had died in 2009, they may be very hard to find among blues collectors and libraries. But they are indispensable for Macleod's bibliographies of previously published transcriptions of the various songs in each volume.

Post–World War II and contemporary blues lyrics are transcribed and published less often, mostly due to reasons of copyright. One exception is Jeff Todd Titon's 1981 collection *Downhome Blues Lyrics: An Anthology from the Post–World War II Era* (its second edition appeared in 1990). Another is *Squeeze My Lemon: A Collection of Classic Blues Lyrics* edited by Randy Poe (Milwaukee: Hal Leonard, 2003).

The most visually attractive volume of blues lyrics continues to be *The Blues Line* compiled by Eric Sackheim. At first glance, the reader is entranced by the spatial arrangements of the typeset lyrics and the portrait sketches of blues singers from photographs. A careful examination will yield some quirks, perhaps some apparent flaws. No indexes are provided for artists' names, song titles, or song first lines. The songs, for the most part, are organized by the geographical base of each singer: there is an eastward swoop from Texas through Louisiana and Mississippi, a short stop in Memphis, then northward from Alabama and Georgia, a glancing look at the Piedmont, and landing in Chicago. In the "Various Voices" survey of transcribed spoken testimonials, there is little folklore or history to be found, but instead there are some texts from Eastern cultures, and the publication sources for the quotes are sketchily cited on the "Acknowledgments" page at the back of the book. There is no discography for the transcribed songs. While the book is not historical or anthropological in function, neither is it poetic in intent, as Sackheim claims that the transcribed lyrics are typeset to convey "breath, pause, break; spacing, weight" (ii). So this is an enigmatic book. Some professional blues researchers may deem the selection and transcription of some lyrics to be outdated. For example, Geechie Wiley is represented by "Eagles on a Half" but not by her haunting "Last Kind Words Blues" that became well known in 1996 by its inclusion on the soundtrack of Terry Zwighoff's documentary film *Crumb*. Robert Johnson is represented by ten blues, but "Cross Road Blues" is omitted. The rich prewar Piedmont blues legacy is allotted only three songs. As Sackheim admits in his introduction, transcription was hampered by worn 78s and their muddy transfers to tape for LP reissue. So what we know now as Louise Johnson's reference in "On the Wall" to "Jim Kinnane's" Monarch Saloon in Memphis was heard by Sackheim as the Ohio city "Cincinnat'" (in all fairness, Taft in *Blues Lyric Poetry* heard that line in the same way).

Toward a better understanding of *The Blues Line*, it may help to learn a bit about Eric Sackheim. He was from New York City, studied Japanese at Harvard in the late 1950s, and played a major role in the folk music revival in the Boston area (much of my information on him comes from the book *Baby Let Me Follow You Down* by Eric von Schmidt). Later he moved to Japan, from where he arranged publication of *The Blues Line* with illustrations by Jonathan Shahn, another participant in the early Boston folk music scene.

Sackheim came to the blues when little information was printed, certainly before the first blues magazines and about the same time as the first books by Charters and Oliver. In his introduction, Sackheim claims to have heard and considered approximately six thousand blues, which would have filled up 375 LPs or, today, 240 CDs (about 40 percent of the Document prewar reissue series); obviously, for the 1960s, he would have had to listen to and transcribe from 78s in addition to those relatively few reissue LPs that were then available. Altogether, about 270 songs are included, which would fill eleven CDs today. Furthermore, if he was living in Japan in the 1960s while rock was adopting prewar blues, he would have been less influenced by the choice of Delta repertory by British rock stars in 1964–1969. Finally, it seems that Sackheim was trying to present blues as having a potential for crossing from Western culture to Eastern culture, since "a man who makes a song has accomplished something of consequence." From his inclusion of Eastern thinkers in his "voices" survey, it seems that Sackheim was seeking and accepting universal authorities—not just English speakers—to validate singing the blues as a confrontation of the singer's "universe" (1). If that is indeed what Sackheim was seeking, it is in contrast to the specialization of blues studies today, such as the historical, the anthropological, the musicological, the sociological, and so on.

The open-minded blues reader should seek a copy of *The Blues Line,* ideally in the original 1969 Grossman/Mushinsha clothbound edition in 8¼" × 12" size, as its cloth covers and large pages are a luxurious joy to handle. Subsequent reprints since then, including the current one, have been in paperback with smaller pages, making it a handy volume to index and annotate. —*EK*

68. A Warning to African Americans to Remember the Blues

Blues People: Negro Music in White America. By LeRoi Jones [Imamu Amiri Baraka]. New York: William Morrow, 1963. Reprint, New York: HarperPerennial, 1999. ISBN 0-688-18474-X (paperback), $13.99

African American poet, writer, playwright, editor, and activist, for over fifty years Imamu Amiri Baraka has elicited strong reactions with his statements. His questions, however, are more provocative.

His early book, *Blues People,* was published under his birth name, LeRoi Jones; later editions would bear his Muslim name. It was published in 1963, when the "blues rediscovery" period was just beginning, jazz had more social and critical importance than blues, the civil rights movement led by Martin Luther King Jr. held its march on Washington, and John F. Kennedy was president. Within five years, many things changed beyond even what Baraka could have expected reasonably: the baby boom generation's preference in music was shifting from jazz to blues-based rock and soul, and Martin Luther King Jr. and John F. Kennedy were killed. Still, and somehow, *Blues People* endured as a cultural text, but not in ways most readers expect.

His initial thesis is stated plainly (ix): "The Negro as slave is one thing. The Negro as American is quite another. But the *path* the slave took to 'citizenship' is what I want to look at. And I make my analogy through the slave citizen's music—through the music that is most closely associated with him: blues and a later, but parallel development, jazz. And it seems to me that if the Negro represents or is symbolic of, something in and about the nature of American culture, this certainly should be revealed by his characteristic music." He elaborates further (x): "I am proposing that the weight of the blues for the slave, the completely disfranchised individual, differs radically from the weight of the same music in the psyches of most contemporary American Negroes. . . . The one peculiar referent to the drastic change in the Negro from slavery to 'citizenship' is his music." What exactly does Baraka mean by "most contemporary Negroes"? This is a question worth pondering at length here, because many writers on the blues (including some of those in the Blues 100) make no distinction of class among African Americans who have listened to or performed this music.

Baraka presents this distinction at length midway in *Blues People,* at the chapter titled "Enter the Middle Class" (122):

> Instead of the fabled existential, happy, carefree Negroes, there were now some black people who were interested in what was around them and how to get to it. (The people who wanted the white man's God had made these same separations in the old society—"I am bound for the Promised Land"—but they had long been losing ground, in the new cities.) Negroes appeared whose Promised Land was where they were now, if only they could "save a little money, send the kid to school,

get a decent place to live. . . ." The further "movement" *into* America. And this movement, this growing feeling that developed among Negroes, was led and fattened by a growing black middle class.

Baraka himself grew up in a black middle-class family, so it is with a little worry for himself that he explores the history and music of his culture from slave to citizen. That exploration is more exposition than narrative and at times more personal than historical. The reader should bear in mind that when he wrote this book, there were few books on jazz and even fewer ones on blues. Virtually all of them (including those Baraka cites as sources) were written by white authors like Marshall Stearns, Samuel Charters, Len Kunstadt, and Andre Hodeir. Moreover, Baraka seems to follow more jazz than blues, and so the titular "blues people" seems to be taken for granted rather than discussed. Therefore, today's well-read blues reader should allow the author his perspectives, facts, and arguments. His main objectives are to trace the development and eventual separation of the middle class from the labor class and likewise the development and eventual separation of jazz from the protean postbellum African American music that he identifies as "blues." As his logical conclusion, Baraka identifies blues with the labor class and jazz with the middle class.

Unstated but implicit in Baraka's text, though, are the contrasting views in the early twentieth century for how African American leaders expected freedmen and their children to work and fit in society. Booker T. Washington stressed assimilation by taking up a skilled trade or professional position, with social accommodation with whites. On the other hand, W. E. B. Du Bois advocated positive racial affirmation through higher education and political activism toward civil rights. From Baraka's characterization of the black middle class, one is tempted to equate the middle class and its jazz with Washington's assimilation and the labor class with its blues with Du Bois's demands to be recognized as a black man. For an overview of black music that explicitly is based on the Washington-Du Bois debate, Nelson George's *The Death of Rhythm and Blues* (New York: Plume, 1989) should be read.

Also unstated by Baraka are the musical distinctions of process and improvisation between blues and jazz. I offer my formulations here to develop further some points of Baraka's arguments. Whereas the unchanging basis of blues during improvisation is the melody, that of jazz is the harmonic chord progression. The more jazz developed its craft of improvising new melodies on a given chord progression, the more that music reflected the education and higher class of its listeners. What Baraka seems to want in the last chapter of *Blues People* is for jazz to readopt *melody* as the unchanging basis of jazz improvisation. Possible, yes; feasible, yes; desirable, well, not many jazz musicians wanted to give up the economic security that their musical achievements brought them. But a few of them took that chance and developed what came to be called "free jazz," and for a brief time through 1967, three of its leading practitioners were Ornette Coleman, John Coltrane, and Albert Ayler. Free jazz was a trend that seemed predictable and desirable in *Blues People*. That in a few years middle-class white kids would adopt not the jazz of the black middle class but the blues of the black labor class was certainly not expected by Baraka or any other jazz critic.

Blues People is an exceedingly important book to read, not merely because it is one of the first books written by one who would become a well-known public intellectual or because it is one of the few blues books written by an African American. It acknowledges the presence of a black middle class, and it admits that not every African American did (and does not) listen to the blues. It also warns African Americans that however much the blues may remind them of a hard past, forgetting and discarding that music may risk a harder future. —*EK*

69. The Blues at Fever Pitch

President Johnson's Blues: African-American Blues and Gospel Songs on LBJ, Martin Luther King, Robert Kennedy and Vietnam, 1963–1968. By Guido van Rijn. Overveen, Netherlands: Agram Blues Books, 2009. ISBN 978-90-814715-1-0 (paperback), €30.00. (Inquire and order direct from Guido van Rijn at the Agram website, http://home.tiscali.nl/guido/order.htm, accessed September 4, 2012.)

Guido van Rijn's remarkable series on blues and gospel songs about American presidents runs to six books, from the first about Franklin D. Roosevelt (see *Roosevelt's Blues*, no. 42) to the last covering the presidents from Jimmy Carter to Barack Obama.

As a group, they relate the African American efforts at regaining civil rights and voting rights and the renewals of those rights by Presidents Nixon and Ford. *Roosevelt's Blues* is a classic as much for establishing its methods of critiquing history and music together as for presenting the Roosevelt era from the African American blue-collar perspective. Picking one more book from this series, I recommend *President Johnson's Blues* for its documentation of the long-due restoration of civil rights to black Americans through contemporary reportage, political cartoons, and song.

Upon John F. Kennedy's assassination in Dallas on November 22, 1963, Lyndon Johnson was sworn in as the thirty-sixth president. Among the unpassed bills was that for civil rights, which Kennedy had pledged earlier that June. Previously, while senator and vice president, Johnson used to advantage his knowledge of the skills and flaws of his legislative colleagues, and he exercised it again toward having the Civil Rights Act passed into law in July 1964. The violence and killings in the southern states that summer over voter registration demonstrated the need for a Voting Rights Act, which was duly formulated and approved in August 1965. Meanwhile, the American role in Vietnam was increasing from "advisor" to soldier, for which many young men were drafted into racially integrated units. It may be said that the frustration over the lack of clear progress in subduing Communist North Vietnam was a leading factor behind Johnson's decision not to seek a second elected term in 1968.

Throughout the book, Martin Luther King Jr. stands as a counterweight to Johnson. King never served in public office, but he led the Southern Christian Leadership Conference as its president. In contrast to his violent white supremacist opponents, King used nonviolent means toward asserting human rights and calling for changes in civil rights. During the successful legislations in 1964–1965 for civil rights and voter rights, Johnson and King stayed in frequent contact. But when young men, including African Americans, were being drafted in increasing numbers for Vietnam, King felt that such violence inflicted abroad was at odds with his nonviolent mission at home. His April 1967 sermon, "Why I Oppose the War in Vietnam," led to an irreparable break between King and Johnson. Nonetheless, King persevered with his activism until April 4, 1968, when he was assassinated in Memphis. Van Rijn's careful and detailed interweaving of facts about King's death with blues and gospel song lyrics is the crowning feature of *President*

Johnson's Blues and one of the most accomplished chapters in the whole White House blues series. Here van Rijn arranges the order of lyrics transcriptions according to the chief aspect of each song emphasized by each singer, and then he examines the political content in each set of lyrics and checks it back to the known facts about the King assassination.

In the body of the book, van Rijn presents transcribed lyrics and sermons for 191 recorded performances. Forty-five of them are gathered on two companion CDs on van Rijn's Agram label, *President Johnson's Blues* (Agram 2020) and *Martin Luther King's Blues* (Agram 2021). They are necessary to acquire because blues and gospel on records were evolving quickly from 1963 to 1968, and several of these selections are considerably rare in their vinyl pressings. The "Johnson" disc contains twenty-four songs dealing with civil rights activism and Vietnam, including two late masterpieces by J. B. Lenoir and a previously unissued blues performance about Vietnam by Robert Pete Williams. The "King" CD has twenty-one of the songs woven into that tour-de-force chapter about the King assassination. Both discs contain a variety of recordings: studio recordings in stereo as well as in mono, on-location tapes, electrically amplified blues recorded in the United States, acoustic blues recorded abroad, contemporary soul music, and adaptations of older sacred tunes.

Collectors should be aware that *President Johnson's Blues* has appeared only in paperback in the author's Agram Books edition. This is a good place to advise collecting the whole six-book series. The first and third books (*Roosevelt's Blues* [1997] and *Kennedy's Blues* [2007]) were published by the University Press of Mississippi. The second installment, *The Truman and Eisenhower Blues*, appeared in 2004 from Continuum Books. The remaining three volumes—this Johnson book (2009), *The Nixon and Ford Blues* (2011), and a final volume for Carter through Obama (2012)—have been self-published by van Rijn. In addition, on van Rijn's Agram label, there are single-CD companions for the Roosevelt, Truman/Eisenhower, and Kennedy books, and two CDs each for Johnson, Nixon/Ford, and Carter/Obama. For these CDs, van Rijn excludes the chaff—let's face it, many topical recordings in general can be pretty bad—and selects much marvelous music to enjoy. The last three books and all of the CDs can be ordered only from van Rijn's Agram website, http://home .tiscali.nl/guido/ (accessed September 4, 2012). —*EK*

70. A Cautionary Tale of Musician Management

Mississippi John Hurt: His Life, His Times, His Blues.
By Philip R. Ratcliffe. Jackson: University Press of
Mississippi, 2011. 308 pp. ISBN 978-1-61703-008-6, $35.00

"Mississippi" John Hurt was one of the most beloved performers
during the 1960s folk music boom. He was sought and "rediscovered" on the basis of his 1928 recordings of ballads, sacred music,
and early blues for the Okeh record label. In those performances,
his guitar playing was deft and sometimes intricate, but it always
served to accompany his singing. His voice sounded genial, even
while relating tales of violence and murder.

In hindsight, it was fortunate that when Hurt was located in
the small town of Avalon, Mississippi, in 1963, he turned out to
be a kind man, for not every "rediscovered" bluesman and elder
folk musician found afterward would turn out to be so. Upon his
"rediscovery," Hurt was beset with greater performing opportunities than he had previously imagined: LP recordings, network
television appearances, and more live dates than can be wished
for. Hurt fulfilled them all with equanimity and uncommon grace.
Few of his aged contemporaries would have been as patient with
the high demands of Hurt's fame could they ever have attained
it. The workload alone would have killed some of those men, and
the constant travel to far-flung places and resulting culture shock
would have turned others crazy. Only the most ambitious musicians, like Skip James, would have been willing to try developing
their revived careers on Hurt's level. But James was not as charis-
matic as Hurt, and from the basis of his last surviving live recordings (1968–1969), after four years on the road, it seems that James
was only just beginning to perform for full evenings without making them seem like long evenings. For his own part, Hurt may
never have had to make such an adjustment. By being himself, he
was instantly appealing to all audiences.

One of the chief services that Philip Ratcliffe provides is
untangling the Hurt family genealogy. The question of which
family members were born to which adults has challenged alike
folk music researchers and representatives for Hurt's estate.
John Hurt was born in 1893 to parents Isom Hurt and Mary Jane
McCain, one of the few straightforward facts about his blood ties
to his family. In 1916 he married Gertrude Hoskins, having two
children with her before leaving her in 1922. Within five years

he met and eventually, in 1927, married Jessie Lee Cole; according to Ratcliffe, Hurt and Jessie raised his children from his first wife for a few years, and they would have one son of their own. The relations of Hurt's brothers would be more complicated. For example, one of his older brothers, Cleveland, was married three times, his first wife Lillie later marrying another of John's older brothers, Hennis. With his second marriage, Cleveland would have three children, who would later be brought up by a Hurt sister, Ella, with her husband Ned Moore. Place everyone in the extended Hurt family in a small village like Avalon, and the interrelations become clustered. As it turned out, John Hurt may have left his first wife, but formally speaking they were not divorced, a status that would affect Hurt's estate.

The other service that Ratcliffe provides is to tell unflinchingly the ugly tale of the management for Hurt's 1960s career. The man who located Hurt, Thomas "Tom" Hoskins, was well meaning, and he loved Hurt as a person as well as a musician. But Hoskins had a way of infuriating people with his unreliability, even those who loved him, and that would affect his management of Hurt. The most serious break came in 1965 between Hoskins and Dick and Louisa Spottswood, his friends and husband-and-wife partners in Music Research Inc. The documents and interviews from all sides of the partnership do not make for easy reading and careful weighing of statements. This is a cautionary case example for anyone thinking about entering the music business, especially in performer management. At the beginning of 1966, Hurt and Hoskins effectively found themselves having to start over, and Hurt desired to return to Mississippi from Washington, DC, where he had been living for the previous two and a half years. What helped them in their rebuilding efforts was that Hurt was still a top draw on the folk music circuit, a blessing to be sure. But it was also a curse in that at age seventy-three, Hurt was too old to fulfill the new obligations and thus overcome the previous turmoils. His death in November 1966 set in motion many issues with his estate that would not be settled for thirty-eight years, involving at various times record labels and his two wives. With all these things that did happen in Hurt's case, do you still want to be a manager for a music legend? Such a commitment may be demanded of you, as it did of Hoskins. —*EK*

71. The Blues Legend Who Lived Upstairs

Preachin' the Blues: The Life and Times of Son House. By
Daniel Beaumont. Oxford: Oxford University Press, 2011.
ISBN 978-0-19-539557-0 (hardcover), $25.00

What would it be like to have a bluesman for a neighbor? Not
merely a famous bluesman, but one legendary enough that white
people would come to visit?

Joe Beard found that out for himself shortly after moving
to an apartment building on Grieg Street in the black section of
Rochester, New York, in the spring of 1964. Beard played blues on
weekends. One evening while practicing his guitar on the building's front steps, one of his neighbors stopped to chat. It turned
out the neighbor had played blues while living in Mississippi. Beard
was born in northern Mississippi, where he tagged along with aged
singer Nathan Beauregard, and while living in Memphis he met
blues stars through his friend Matt "Guitar" Murphy. So he thought
he knew the names. But the older neighbor spoke of Charlie
Patton, Willie Brown, Robert Johnson. Who? Those musicians were
from older generations. But they were the contemporaries of Son
House, the man talking with Beard. A few months later, that June,
a red Volkswagen Beetle pulled up, from which three young white
men emerged to meet House. Not long afterward, articles about
the old man were appearing not only in the local newspaper and
little blues periodicals but amazingly in national magazines like
Newsweek and the *National Observer*.

Eddie "Son" House (1902–1988) was born in the Mississippi
Delta, and he spent his formative years there and in Louisiana.
His blues reputation rests on the records he made in 1930 for
Paramount Records, to whose Wisconsin studio he had been
brought by Charlie Patton. His 78 rpm releases didn't sell due to
the Depression, but the few copies saved by collectors presented a
forceful singer with a majestic baritone voice and a ringing bottle-
neck slide tone on the guitar. To work-song phrasing, he boomed
out sacred and secular lyrics, sometimes with a little sarcasm. He
spent the 1930s working on farms and playing weekends, but his
weekend performances made influential impressions on aspiring
bluesmen like Robert Johnson and Muddy Waters. Alan Lomax
and John Work sought him in 1941 to make some recordings for
the Library of Congress, and the following year Lomax found him
again. In 1943, House moved to Rochester.

Daniel Beaumont's biography fills in the twenty-one-year gap between his departure from Mississippi and the 1964 "rediscovery." It turns out that House had moved as much to follow a girlfriend as for the work opportunities, even though he was married for nine years. His wife, Evie, joined him by the end of the 1940s. For the next fifteen years, he worked some menial jobs, but by 1964 they dried up, and he was spending much time drinking. One of the men in the red Beetle, Dick Waterman, offered to manage him in a performing career, touring not southern juke joints where House had played in the 1930s but the folk festivals, clubs, and college campuses that held concerts of folk music and blues. Over the next six years, the blues magazines reported in detail House's remarkable Indian summer career, including tours of England and Europe, his 1965 Columbia LP *Father of the Folk Blues*, and the occasional performances like those at the Newport Folk Festival (1965), the Ann Arbor Festival (1969), and the festival of blues at Beloit College organized by young white blues musician Leroy Jodie Pierson (1970). Upon House's final performance in 1974 and his move with Evie to Detroit two years later, his revived career was over. Yet there are few published reports of his life in Rochester off the road except for the later reminiscences of young musicians like John Mooney.

That is where Beaumont helps again. House spent his life not just in the Delta in the 1930s but also in an area of Rochester in the 1960s that has since been torn down as a part of urban renewal. One aspect of his Rochester years, of course, is his friendship with Beard, who today is the locally acknowledged elder statesman in Rochester blues. Another facet is seen through Armand Schaubroeck, the longtime entrepreneur at the House of Guitars music store. His memories of House are clear and tough, such as the time before a local performance when Schaubroeck (who is white) had to fetch House from a bar that served only African Americans. It may seem romantic to know a bluesman. Although Schaubroeck described with respect and understanding House as "he was who he was," his, Waterman's, and Beard's stories help the reader think again about life with a blues legend. —*EK*

72. Access to Stunning and Powerful Sights

Between Midnight and Day: The Last Unpublished Blues Archive. By Dick Waterman. New York: Thunder's Mouth

Press, 2003. ISBN 1-560-25547-1. San Rafael, CA: Insight, 2004. ISBN 1-886-06975-1 (trade edition), ISBN 1-56025-547-1 (limited edition with print), $175.00

In 1964, three blues enthusiasts, Phil Spiro, Nick Perls, and Dick Waterman, found Son House, who had seemingly disappeared for over twenty years, living in Rochester, New York. This same year, Skip James was "rediscovered" by John Fahey, Bill Barth, and Henry Vestine. These two events were a major part of the blues revival. Dick Waterman was at the core of this revival as a promoter of performances featuring artists like Son House, Skip James, Mississippi John Hurt, "Bukka" White, and others.

In the 1950s, Dick Waterman studied journalism at Boston University and later served as editor of *Broadside* magazine, a Boston publication of and about topical songs supportive of civil rights and other progressive struggles in the 1960s. Following his work in "rediscovering" Son House for music fans and promoting blues and folk shows, Waterman created Avalon Productions. Through this booking agency, Waterman served as promoter, manager, agent, driver, and any number of other roles for a staggering number of blues musicians. In addition to those already mentioned, Waterman managed Mance Lipscomb, Buddy Guy, Luther Allison, Junior Wells, Arthur "Big Boy" Crudup, Otis Rush, and many more. He also befriended a young Bonnie Raitt and served as her manager for almost twenty years. Through it all, Dick Waterman always had a camera handy.

This book is a presentation of Waterman's black-and-white photographs complemented by his stories and anecdotes of time lovingly spent with the artists. The subjects of the book are towering blues figures, such as Mississippi John Hurt, Son House, Skip James, Mississippi Fred McDowell, Big Mama Thornton, Bobby Bland, and Lightnin' Hopkins, as well as less popular but no less important artists like Will Shade, Junior Kimbrough, and Robert Pete Williams. Though overwhelmingly centered on blues artists, *Between Midnight and Day* also features Bob Dylan, Joan Baez, and Janis Joplin. In all, Waterman includes entries for forty-nine musicians, though other artists appear alongside them in some photographs.

The quality of the photographic reproductions is excellent. The photos are crisp and all the compositional elements are good, but the aspect that sets these apart from so many other blues photographs is their intimacy. As Dick Waterman said in a 2003 interview

on National Public Radio, "[These photos are] like my children.
. . . I hope my book will help to humanize some of the men and
women who made this great music." As a manager and promoter,
Dick Waterman developed strong friendships with many artists, getting to know them as people, not just performers. As Chris Murray
states in the foreword, "access was key" to setting Waterman's photographs apart from shots taken by many others. Candid shots of
musicians joking backstage capture smiles and camaraderie not
often experienced in front of a crowd. His manager position also
allowed for close physical proximity during performances, resulting
in stunning close-up shots of powerful moments on stage as well as
audience responses to these moments.

The stories that accompany the photographs are a joy to read.
Unlike so many of the books on blues history, these are stories of
people's lives, not just their onstage personas. Waterman gives us a
better sense of who these musicians were outside the limelight and
away from their instruments. Waterman doesn't just point out the
good times and exalt the positive qualities of the subjects in this
book; the chapter on Big Mama Thornton, for instance, shows how
difficult she could make someone's life. Readers will get a sense of
the joys and frustrations of being a music manager.

Because of his close connection with so many blues musicians
and his spirit of fighting injustice, Dick Waterman helped fight
many legal battles to ensure musicians and/or their estates would
receive financial compensation for royalties that, in many cases,
weren't properly paid. The chapter on Arthur Crudup details part
of the legal battle to get him paid a fraction of what he was owed.

The book was published in conjunction with a Govinda
Gallery, Washington, DC, exhibition titled "Between Midnight
and Day: The Photographs of Dick Waterman." The 2003 printing
was published by Thunder's Mouth Press, an imprint of Avalon
Publishing Group and produced by Insight Editions. The 2004
printing lists only Insight Editions as the publisher. The foreword
was written by Govinda Gallery owner Chris Murray, Bonnie Raitt
provides a preface, and the introduction is by Peter Guralnick.

Originally the book sold for $29.95. It now lists for $175,
though new copies can be found for as low as $60. While this isn't
an inexpensive book, the photographs and stories make this a valuable addition to any personal library. It is hoped that the subtitle is
just a hook and that there are more unpublished photographs and
stories forthcoming.

(Dick Waterman worked with B. B. King to create the book *The B. B. King Treasures: Photos, Mementos, & Music from B. B. King's Collection* [New York: Bulfinch, 2005].) —*GJ*

73. Images of Chicago Blues Long Past

Chicago Blues as Seen from the Inside: The Photographs of Raeburn Flerlage. By Raeburn Flerlage. Toronto: ECW Press, 2000. ISBN 1-55022-400-X (paperback), $22.95

Through his photography, Raeburn Flerlage documented the Chicago blues scene from 1959 through the early 1970s. Flerlage had been involved with music since 1939, writing articles and columns on music, penning concert reviews, doing promotions for record stores, lecturing on music, and more. He moved from Cincinnati to Chicago in 1944, where he would become immersed in music. In 1946 he became Midwest executive secretary and began promoting concerts for People's Songs, a New York–based organization to "create, promote, and distribute songs of labor and the American people." In 1955 he became a sales representative for Folkways Records' wholesale distributor. During this time, Flerlage began studying photography at the Art Institute of Chicago. He received his first professional photographic work in 1959 when Moses Asch of Folkways hired him to take the cover shot for a Memphis Slim album. Many of the iconic 1960s Chicago blues album covers for Folkways, Delmark, Chess, Testament, Prestige, Bluesville, and others were taken by Flerlage. His work appeared in *Rhythm & Blues, Down Beat*, and other music magazines of the day.

Flerlage had planned a book of his photography as early as 1965, but the group of friends (Pete Welding, Mike Bloomfield, and Willie Hopkins) helping to organize the book project got busy with various engagements. Over three decades later, film editor Lisa Day discovered some of his photographs while researching images for a documentary. Her persistence that these images get published in book form was the catalyst Flerlage needed to finally get the book done. Day served as editor for what ultimately became *Chicago Blues as Seen from the Inside.* The book documents Muddy Waters, Howlin' Wolf, Little Walter, Willie Dixon, and many other 1960s Chicago blues stars. Perhaps even more important, Flerlage photographed many lesser-known artists—figures such as Maxwell Street Jimmy, Jazz Gillum, Arvella Grey, St. Louis Jimmy,

Blind Jim Brewer, and so many more. There are incredible shots of blues sidemen like bassist Ransom Knowling, drummer Fred Below, and saxophonist Eddie Shaw. Other photos capture non-Chicagoans performing in the Windy City: Son House playing at the University of Chicago in 1964, Mississippi Fred McDowell in 1966, and Mississippi John Hurt in 1965. Flerlage also captures the essence of Chicago's South Side and other neighborhoods. Many of the performances featured in these photographs were in Chicago's larger venues, such as the Regal Theater or the Trianon Ballroom, but many others were in the city's various nightclubs—Sylvio's, Pepper's, Smitty's, and others.

Raeburn Flerlage had a good eye for photography and a spirit that set people at ease, allowing him to freeze a vast array of emotions for posterity. These photos show the pensiveness of Memphis Slim, the powerful joy of Howlin' Wolf, the smoothness of Muddy Waters, and the intensity of Freddie King. There is an immediacy to these shots that really dissolves the concept of time between viewers and subjects.

In the introduction, Flerlage gives many interesting insights into issues of race in Chicago, from his perspective as a white man living in Chicago's predominantly black South Side. Raeburn Flerlage passed away two years after the book was published.

Though mostly focusing on white folk music, some more of Flerlage's blues photographs can be seen in *Chicago Folk Images of the Sixties Music Scene: The Photographs of Raeburn Flerlage* (Toronto: ECW Press, 2009), compiled by Ronald Cohen and Bob Riesman. Charles K. Cowdery's *Blues Legends* (Salt Lake City: Gibbs Smith Publisher, 1995) features almost sixty of Flerlage's photographs. A number of Raeburn Flerlage's photos can also be seen in Charles Keil's *Urban Blues* (no. 76). *Down at Theresa's . . . Chicago Blues: The Photographs of Marc PoKempner* (Munich: Prestel, 2000) is an excellent addition to Flerlage's book. PoKempner snapped incredible shots of locals enjoying themselves at blues shows at Theresa's Lounge and other clubs in Chicago during the 1970s. A section on Chicago in Paul Trynka's *Portrait of the Blues* (New York: Da Capo, 1996) features some excellent photography by Val Wilmer. —*GJ*

74. Play the Harmonica Fast and Live Faster

Blues with a Feeling: The Little Walter Story. By Tony Glover, Scott Dirks, and Ward Gaines. New York: Routledge,

2002. ISBN 0-415-93710-8 (hardcover), $115.00, ISBN 0-415-93711-6 (paperback), $42.00.

Little Walter (1930–1968) was the one who developed the "boss" amplified harmonica sound that is now associated with Chicago blues. His other innovations were adopting the chromatic harmonica, exploring the uses of third and fourth positions on the diatonic harmonica, and formulating new techniques of improvisation. For over sixty years, his hit record "Juke" has been an audition piece for blues harmonica players to prove their instrumental mastery. His fans can't get enough of his recorded performances: a five-CD reissue of Little Walter's collected master recordings (with some alternate takes) for Chess Records (Hip-O-Select, released in 2009) sold out within three years.

His music is enough cause for a biography to be written. His life makes that project a challenge. For Little Walter died young, and he spoke little about himself during the few interviews he granted. He performed mostly for black audiences; by the early 1960s when he came to the attention of white listeners, his peak creativity and his best health were behind him. Much of the challenge is going beyond the memories of his last flawed performances to recover the early achievements and innovations.

Working as a team, Tony Glover, Scott Dirks, and Ward Gaines met the challenge to produce this accomplished biography. Older blues readers will remember Tony Glover as a member of the 1960s group Koerner, Ray & Glover and as an author of many music publications, including the instructional book *Blues Harp* (New York: Oak, 1965). A program director for a Chicago radio station, Scott Dirks is also a prolific researcher on Chicago blues, writing for magazines, CD labels, and reference books. Ward Gaines may be the least known of the authors to blues readers; Ford's blues bibliography lists him as author only for this biography. The irony of the three authors sharing information about Little Walter among themselves is that the musician seemed to keep his friends, family, and acquaintances apart from each other, never letting each person know much about who else he knew.

Born Marion Walter Jacobs, Little Walter lived a fast life. He first came to Chicago in 1945 at age fifteen, began making records at seventeen, hit with "Juke" at twenty-two, was a has-been by thirty-three, and was dead at thirty-seven. If he had not died shortly after a street beating, his alcoholism would have finished him off within a year or so. The last photographs taken of him seem to be of someone twice his age: heavy-lidded eyes, facial scars, and crippled posture. He consumed everything quickly, including alcohol, cars, women, and money. By the time British and European fans brought him to their countries in 1964 and 1967, seemingly he had little music left in him. The task for any biographer is to show that Walter was among the most musical of bluesmen and that he had every right to bristle whenever someone compared him to a "folk-blues" musician like Sonny Terry.

In his prime, he laid his talent down on records, and Glover, Dirks, and Gaines decipher them toward a musical portrait of this dynamic artist. His Chess label sessions from 1950 through 1960 for himself, Muddy Waters, and guitarist Jimmy Rogers are painstakingly re-created from the master releases and the alternate takes available to the authors. For many songs, they discern the models on which Little Walter, Muddy Waters, and bassist/composer Willie Dixon drew from. With those precedents identified, Walter's contributions can be better heard. The most obvious of them is the tone that he got from playing his harmonica through a microphone and amplifier. The authors bemoan rightly that in the late 1950s Chess made Walter play into the recording microphone without the power of the amplifier, thus weakening his sound. For some Muddy Waters recordings whose personnel have not been fully accounted for by discographers, arguments for Walter's presence on them are made on musical bases. Most valuable for musician readers are the identifications of harmonica types and techniques that Walter used on individual takes. But in addition to his innovations, the authors recognize that he retained his knowledge of the harmonica styles with which he began his performing career, especially that of John Lee Williamson (Sonny Boy I).

Both the hardcover and paperback editions are available, with no differences aside from covers and prices. To understand fully the musical content, readers should buy Glover's book *Blues Harp* for the full presentation of harmonica types and the demonstrations of the four positions toward scales on the diatonic harmonica. Those who have access to a music library should also look up Richard Hunter's "An Appreciation of Little Walter" in the *Journal of Jazz Studies* 5, no. 1 (1978): 108–115, an early scholarly gem that may be helpful. —*EK*

75. Snoots! Snoots!

Me and Big Joe. By Michael Bloomfield. With S. Summerville. San Francisco: Re/Search Publications, 1980. ISBN 1-889307-05-X. German translation published as *Unterwegs mit Big Joe.* Frankfurt am Main: Juergen-A.- Schmitt-Publ., 1982. ISBN 3-923396-01-5

Young musicians learn from their elders. For the blues since the 1960s, many of the young have been white. I am afraid that in today's pop culture, the romantic story of the old black bluesman teaching the young white mannish-boy is told too often. Call it the "Crossroads" syndrome, after the 1986 movie starring Ralph Macchio and Joe Seneca. But it may also be read in novels, in biographies, even between the lines in folklore fieldwork. The younger man comes away enriched, even richer, from the experience, but the older man remains the same as before. The more I read or hear such heartwarming tales—which always involve a bluesman, never a blues woman—the less I wonder why old blues musicians are so grumpy. As an antidote, Dick Waterman's *Between Midnight and Day* (no. 72) is effective. To dispel any lingering romance, I reach for Michael Bloomfield's *Me and Big Joe.*

Michael Bloomfield (1943–1981) may not be well known to many younger readers. In the 1960s, he was one of the most promising of American blues/rock guitarists. Living in Chicago, he heard many African American bluesmen in neighborhood bars, and during the daytime he sought them out. He came to national fame as a member of the Paul Butterfield Blues Band, playing on its first two albums. He went on to record as a member of the Electric Flag and with Al Kooper. His performances and albums in the 1970s were hampered by an addiction to heroin, of which he died from an overdose in 1981. Nonetheless, his classic early work, such as the two Butterfield Band albums and his contributions to Bob Dylan's *Highway 61 Revisited* (1965) have remained available. Not so his little memoir, *Me and Big Joe.* Its publisher, Re/Search Publications, admits on its website, http://www.researchpubs .com, that it is out of print. It should be reprinted, whether as a monograph or as a long blues magazine article.

Big Joe Williams (1903–1982) was born in Crawford, on the east side of the state of Mississippi. By the time he met Bloomfield in the early 1960s, Williams had logged over forty years of playing in the Mississippi Delta, St. Louis, Chicago, and many places in between. Before World War II he was a frequent recording artist for RCA Victor, for whom he made his initial versions of "Baby Please Don't Go" and "Crawlin' King Snake." In 1958, his Delmark album *Piney Woods Blues* made him better known to white record buyers, especially to those who bought jazz and folk music. Before long, he was playing as often at folk music venues and festivals as in the blues bars.

Williams was always nomadic, but when in Chicago, he stayed in the basement of the Jazz Record Mart. It was there where Bloomfield first visited Williams at the latter's invitation. Through him, Bloomfield met Tampa Red, Kokomo Arnold, Tommy McClennan, and Jazz Gillum. To say the least, they were not informative visits. Tampa Red shook too much to play guitar, Arnold and McClennan were in hospitals, and Gillum was distrustful enough of Bloomfield to border on paranoia. Far more enjoyable were the "jaunts" the two made to hear in club settings Aleck Miller "Sonny Boy Williamson II," J. B. Lenoir, and Lightnin' Hopkins. Dating when Bloomfield and Williams heard these men is uncertain, but it is likely they heard Williamson in 1963, before the latter traveled to Europe and England.

"In early July"—as Bloomfield recalled vaguely, possibly 1964—Williams decided to travel to St. Louis. As owner of Delmark Records and the Jazz Record Mart, and as Williams's landlord, Bob Koester—not Kaercher, as misspelled in the book—took the opportunity to ask Big Joe to scout talent for Delmark, lending him a tape recorder. Bloomfield agreed to go along, but he asked George Mitchell (see no. 79) to join them. The trip turned out to be the worst combination of a long-distance jaunt with bad visits. There was the hangover resulting from drinking with Big Joe in one evening "gin and Schnapps and beer and wine." There was waking up to see Williams hovering a barbecued pig's snout over Bloomfield's face and saying, "Snoots! Snoots!" The Ralph Macchio character in *Crossroads* never got stabbed in the hand by his blues guide, but Bloomfield was. Finally, Big Joe took Bloomfield and Mitchell to an apartment building to record an aged fiddler. Bloomfield was revulsed not by the old man playing an instrument with two strings but by a "twelve or thirteen-year-old girl who weighed at least 400 pounds" in the adjacent room. "She was mumbling and drooling, and her face was smeared with grease. On a table in front of her was a plate of rib bones, and beside the plate was a jar of mayonnaise that looked like zinc ointment left too long in the sun. What the girl would do was take a bone and dip it in the mayonnaise, then run it back and forth through a gap in the front teeth to get the meat off." On the verge of vomiting, Bloomfield asked where the bathroom was, to which he was shown a hole in a closet floor from where the waste dropped to the apartment below.

"You don't like my people!" accused Big Joe, referring to the fiddler, the girl, and the woman living with them. By replying that they were "just not my scene," Bloomfield admitted to his guide that the accusation was correct. By bringing the two young white men to that apartment, Big Joe introduced them to people for whom the blues was unavoidable and beyond any means of dealing with, coping with, or singing away. "I had thought I could be part of his culture and live out on the street with him, but I couldn't," Bloomfield tells us. He is depleted, not enriched, by the St. Louis road trip. We, too, should feel drained by this account he left us. —*EK*

76. A First Look at the Urban Bluesman

Urban Blues. By Charles Keil. Chicago: University of Chicago Press, 1966. Reprint with a new afterword, Chicago: University of Chicago Press, 1992. ISBN 978-0-226-42960-1 (paperback), $22.50. (Japanese editions published in Tokyo in 1968 and 2000.)

Urban Blues began as Keil's impressive 1964 master's thesis in anthropology at the University of Chicago. Two years later, it was published by the University of Chicago Press, and in 1968 it appeared in Japan through the Tokyo publishing firm Ongakunotomosha. From 1970 to 2000, Keil taught American studies at the State University of New York at Buffalo. Upon the beginning of the 1990s blues boom, *Urban Blues* was reprinted in paperback with an afterword added by Keil. It has not gone out of print since. Since 2000, Keil has resided in Connecticut.

At the time when *Urban Blues* was being written and published, civil rights legislation was being passed and enacted in the United States. With the long-prevailing obstacles for African Americans being lifted, social expectations for public behavior were changing. In particular, white Americans were wondering what to expect of African Americans, especially African American males in the labor economic classes. As Keil states on the first page of the book, his "primary concern" in his study is the "expressive male role within urban lower-class Negro culture—that of the contemporary bluesman." The reader has to be careful to break down Keil's statement into two parts. One is to learn what has been the social role of the "blue-collar" black man. By "social," we should understand not so much the legal standing or the financial earning status but more the personal interaction as man to woman, as man to fellow man, and as resident to local neighborhood. By asserting positively that indeed "Negroes have a culture" (4), Keil seems to acknowledge that the prevailing mainstream American view of black men had been as outcasts with no function within society. Furthermore, these men had been perceived as shiftless, irresponsible, and— especially to women—"no good." To readers "outside the culture," so to speak, Keil calls for a positive embrace of the "no-good" man as an abiding and positive figure in lower-class urban African American culture. For middle-class and upper-class Americans, finding some value in the "no-good" man is very difficult; perhaps it is quite distasteful, even, to attempt.

The other part of Keil's opening statement, about bluesmen, requires an understanding of what "contemporary bluesman" meant in the mid-1960s. To be sure, the author cites as exemplars B. B. King, Bobby "Blue" Bland, and Junior Parker. King and Bland remain today as the most famous elder statesmen of blues and soul. But in 1965, these three musicians were performing mostly (if not only) to urban African American audiences, and King was least half as old and much skinnier than he is today. For a proper understanding of Keil's depictions of them, we need to put aside the richly deserved lionization they now enjoy, and we should seek the ways in which they were emblematic to their audiences of the "no-good" men fifty years ago.

For Keil, during the previous forty years, the bluesman had undergone two transformations to his relation to his culture. Before World War II, the self-accompanied "rural" bluesman played acoustic instruments and sang in a very personal style to small audiences. Then rural bluesmen were transformed into what Keil calls "city" bluesmen, performing with electrically amplified instruments but nonetheless singing of "vulnerable" feelings and "crying of hurts" resulting from the adjustment to urban life; Muddy Waters, Howlin' Wolf, and John Lee Hooker are cited by Keil as examples of "city bluesmen." The second transformation leading to the "urban bluesmen"—namely King, Bland, and Parker—is brought about by one's "coming to grips" with urban life, with none of the artful complaints that Keil associates with the 1940s/1950s postwar city musicians. The urban bluesmen may sing with less personal expression than their "rural" and "city" predecessors, but they have to present themselves in such general ways in order to appeal to large audiences. Furthermore, to reach and communicate to all of their considerably large audiences, urban bluesmen need to use the recording labels and media.

As an aside, I advise readers to avoid getting the impression from Keil's distinctions of "rural," "city," and "urban" bluesmen that the smaller a bluesman's audience is, the more personal and hence more "pure" is the bluesman's style. Some writers who have touted inept pickers as great unrecognized bluesmen seem to have made that mistake in thinking. I don't think Keil makes that error, because he makes his three distinctions of bluesman with corresponding audience size, not as an aesthetic end in itself but as a means of recognizing the efforts that urban bluesmen have made to make their acts very appealing. Furthermore, Keil argues, the urban bluesmen are not merely entertainers but also agents of accepting socially those who had been mistaken as outcasts.

In the later chapters of *Urban Blues,* Keil focuses intently on a few mid-1960s performances of King and Bland to urban African American audiences in order to point out and discuss the aspects of mellowness, role and response, and soul and solidarity. To the casual listener, these musicians seem to be cathartic in order to purge hurts and frustrations, but to Keil, they proceed past cathar- sis to the subsequent state of "mellowness," which then enables a bonding among audience members. Note that such "mellowness," especially toward what we would now call "male bonding," stands in stark contrast to the 1920s blues women "going public" on their erring men, as described by Daphne Harrison in *Black Pearls* (no. 17). For Keil, Bland's performance at the Ashland Auditorium in Chicago is a textbook example of the urban bluesman as a secular preacher exhorting and enjoining his listeners into the state of mellowness. To that purpose, then, there are no "good" or "bad" blues and songs but instead what are valid or ineffectual during a performance. What exactly is "mellowness" is pursued through the notions of "soul" and "solidarity." Now what Keil meant in 1964– 1966 by "soul" does not necessarily mean "soul music" as we in the 2010s now call it, because that use of the term was not yet widely seen in the record marketplace. Rather, in the context of this book and in the mid-1960s culture of urban African Americans, "soul" meant a commonly felt unity—a "solidarity"—among persons on their own understandings and acceptances of who they are. When someone like B. B. King or Bobby Bland sings the positive virtues inherent in the seeming "no-good" men and speaks of "soul brothers," he points out the value of such men and the desirability of keeping them in the urban African American culture.

As I pointed out previously, Keil wrote the thesis version of *Urban Blues* nearly fifty years ago. Obviously, the blues, Chicago, and African American cultures have changed much, and Bland died in 2013. What transformations should be noted? Have the urban bluesmen been transformed into soul men or into rap masters? Has the introduction of crack corrupted the idea of the "no-good" man, or has it intensified it? Is the 2010s version of the "no-good man" acceptable to today's musicians? If the answer to the last question is no, then apparently, a breakdown in urban African American culture has occurred. —*EK*

77. Collecting, Not Making, History

Burn, Baby! Burn! The Autobiography of Magnificent Montague. By Magnificent Montague with Bob Baker. Urbana: University of Illinois Press, 2003. ISBN 978-0-252-02873-1 (hardcover), ISBN 978-0-252-07684-8 (paperback), $19.95

The disc jockey Magnificent Montague may be remembered in history for his radio on-air phrase "Burn, baby, burn!" which was adopted and shouted as a password by the African American culture during the Watts, California, riots in 1965. Watts was the first catastrophic race riot, foreshadowing the widespread violence that devastated many American cities upon the assassination of Dr. Martin Luther King Jr. in 1968. Up until Watts, Montague had been saying the phrase while a good record was playing in order to help its music raise the emotions of his listeners. However dismayed he was to see that phrase appropriated for a different and destructive use, he never regretted or apologized for coining it. Nor was he, nor has he been, interested in making history. Rather, he was more concerned with saving history, collecting the printed and written records of African Americans.

Montague was born Nathaniel Montague in 1928 in New Jersey. He grew up middle class—his father gave him not a guitar, but an accordion—but at age sixteen, near the end of World War II, he joined the Merchant Marine. In 1949, he began his radio career, in which he recognized immediately that company sponsorship of on-air time was the "straight hustle" business of radio. For the next quarter century, he worked at various radio stations between the coasts. Despite the fast pace of each job, two early experiences shaped him. One was hearing Paul Robeson speak in 1951; although Robeson was famous as a singer and actor, he exhorted his audience to recognize that African Americans past and present were contributing to mainstream American culture and to be proud of their contributions. The other was being made all too aware of being African American in then-segregated Texas and Louisiana, where he worked in the mid-1950s. Despite the blunt force, verbal and physical, used by whites in those years to keep him "in his place," it was in the South where Montague said he found his "soul" as an African American. In Chicago he began fitting together his newfound cultural soul and his racial pride by collecting books by and about black Americans. The coalescing element to his life and studies was brought about while studying Judaism with a St. Louis rabbi. Montague realized that blacks didn't have a racial religion to bind themselves as a people like the Jews have had, but he saw that music—"the Gift of song"—was inherent in black lives and that music's uses and purposes should be recognized, saved, and celebrated. From there, Montague's mission in life was set.

Through the mid-1960s, Montague was busy as disk jockey, collector, writer, and family man. His radio work was the most public of these activities. Surviving tapes (excerpts may be heard on Montague's website, "MagnificentMontague.com," http://www.magnificentmontague.com, accessed May 27, 2013) preserve his smooth baritone speaking voice that he would intone at an intimate speaking level. It was little wonder that he was popular with female listeners during the days, while the men were working. But he also wrote a narrative about a boy named Henry J. who wended his way through the echoes of African American history. Yet Montague seized and included the present, too, and his chapters about Malcolm X and Sam Cooke are among the most indelible in this book. Then, in 1964, Malcolm X and Cooke were killed, and in 1965, Watts burned to the recurring invocation of Montague's radio phrase. He was thirty-seven at the time, still young but old enough to recognize that he may have to reprioritize his activities.

In 1976, Montague began working toward getting a bigger piece of the radio business by building his own station. The official process toward getting a frequency from the Federal Communications Commission was cutthroat, pitting him against competing entrepreneurs who desired a frequency. There were also the myriad regulations to learn and follow. There were a lot of hoops to be jumped through, yes, but they were American hoops from which no one was excused by the FCC. Getting the approval for the radio frequency may have been the most unconditional American process that Montague underwent. He succeeded in winning the frequency and its call letters, and then he built the station itself, maintaining it to 1985.

All the while and afterward, Montague continued his collecting of African Americana, from colonial-era slave documents to contemporary art. Eventually, the collection took on a life of its own within the lives of Montague and his wife. They became the conduits through whom the past continued to live. In his final chapter, Montague lets an original Fisk Jubilee Singer, a compiler of an African American biographical directory, a chronicler of the Underground Railroad, a blind musical prodigy, and several other historical personages speak from their writings and relics through him to our present.

As of the time of this writing (2013), Montague at age eighty-five is very much alive. But the early 2010s recession and an overextended loan forced him to place his collection of eight thousand rarities on auction in 2012. It was purchased complete by the financial services consultant Clinton F. Byrd. Plans for promoting the collection, including a website (http://www.montaguecollection .com, accessed May 27, 2013) are in progress. If carried through, such an online guide to the collection will be a supplement to the book *Burn, Baby! Burn!* toward rediscovering the African American voices of the past. —*EK*

78. The Blues Folk Who Stayed

Blues from the Delta. By William Ferris. New York: Anchor Doubleday, 1978. Reprint with a new introduction by Billy Taylor, New York: Da Capo, 1984. ISBN 0-306-80327-5 (paperback), $16.50

For about fifteen years, from the mid-1960s through the late 1970s, William Ferris spoke with, recorded, and filmed a small group of African American artisans and musicians in the southern half of the Mississippi Delta. He was captivated especially by the group of blues musicians who played regularly in Leland at a small juke joint owned by Shelby "Poppa Jazz" Brown. At the time, all of them were obscure, and most would remain so. The one exception was singer/guitarist James "Son" Thomas, who had come of musical age during the 1940s and 1950s. Through Ferris's books and films, Thomas became better known outside Mississippi, eventually making some performing tours of Europe.

Blues from the Delta is very much a folklore book, giving its information in the present tense, regardless of when the sources were recorded. It is as much about its author as it is about the music's creative culture. Ferris's education culminated in a PhD in folklore (University of Pennsylvania, 1969), for which the dissertation "Black Folklore from the Mississippi Delta" was written. He pursued an academic career at Jackson (Mississippi) State University (1970–1972), Yale (1972–1979), the University of Mississippi (1979–1997), where he directed its Center for the Study of Southern Culture, and the University of North Carolina at Chapel Hill (2002–present), along with a term as chair of the National Endowment for the Humanities (1997–2001).

The version of *Blues from the Delta* kept in print by Da Capo Books is the second, expanded edition prepared for Anchor Doubleday in 1978. It is a rustic yet warm book, populated with faces along with their names and sayings. The lyrics aspect of the blues craft is emphasized, with transcriptions of the words to songs captured on Ferris's tapes as well as the interviews with performers about what the words mean and why they choose to sing them. The final chapter is a transcription of a small "house party" in Clarksdale, where a local pianist traded one-line quips with a select group of local listeners. The social and cultural contexts of the Mississippi Delta in 1965–1975 have helped introduce the place and times to many readers. Lacking, though, are the historical explanations of how and why the contexts of the 1960s became so, but for a compatible narrative, see James C. Cobb's *The Most Southern Place on Earth: The Mississippi Delta and Its Roots of Regional Identity* (New York: Oxford University Press, 1992), whose chapter on delta blues is strongly influenced by Ferris's work. When the impact of the Great Migration from the Delta is taken into account, one realizes in historical hindsight that Ferris's book isn't so much about the blues coming from the Delta as it is about the blues that stayed behind in the Delta through the 1960s.

The first version of *Blues from the Delta* was published by Studio Vista in England in 1971 as part of The Blues, a book series edited by Paul Oliver with Tony Russell. It did not stay in print for long, but nonetheless any copy in hardcover or paperback is worth seeking out. Having been drawn from his dissertation, the chapters are quite academic in tone—Ferris exhorts researchers to include vocal responses, attitudes, and customs of blues audiences in descriptions of the blues creativity process—and they emphasize more the racial and political aspects of late-1960s Delta blues culture, mentions of which were toned down for the later edition. In 1972, a companion LP was issued in England, *Blues from the Delta*, on Saydisc/Matchbox Records (SDM 226), of musical performances selected from Ferris's tapes, including some of the earliest recordings of Son Thomas.

If one wants to read, see, and hear more of the Leland group, one should buy Ferris's *Give My Poor Heart Ease: Voices of the Mississippi Blues* (Chapel Hill: University of North Carolina Press, 2009). Many photos from *Blues from the Delta* are reproduced with vivid clarity, and the interview transcripts are presented with little or no anthropological framework. If for some reason you have to buy a used copy, make sure that the CD and the DVD are both in the double pocket in the back of the book. The CD has several tracks from that now-rare *Blues from the Delta* Saydisc album and two other LPs. The DVD contains seven short films made by Ferris. The earliest of them, *Black Delta, Part 1* (1968), serves as a video illustration for both editions of *Blues from the Delta*, depicting Louis Dotson setting up and playing a one-string instrument on the side of his Delta shack, Wade Walton, Son Thomas, and portions of the Clarksdale "house party." —*EK*

79. East of the Delta

Blow My Blues Away. By George Mitchell. Baton Rouge: Louisiana State University Press, 1971. ISBN 0-8071-0416-7. Reprint, New York: Da Capo Press, 1983, 1984. ISBN 0-3067-6173-4 (paperback)

While the Delta is the part of Mississippi that has long fired blues imaginations, the "hill country" to the east has had a distinctive blues legacy of its own. Mostly in Tate, Panola, Marshall, and Lafayette Counties, the hill country has long been home to African American farmers and laborers. The core style of music is fife-and-drum music, where drummers pound out polyrhythmic drone patterns while a fifer is riffing and repeating short melodies and motifs. By the 1950s, fife-and-drum music would have an influence on the blues played in the hill country, especially by Fred McDowell, R. L. Burnside, and Junior Kimbrough. Early efforts at documenting hill country music may have been scant, but they were serious. In 1942, Alan Lomax recorded Sid Hemphill and Lucius Smith for the Library of Congress collection. On a later visit, in 1959, he made the first recordings of Fred McDowell. David Evans made the first of his important field studies in the region in the mid-1960s. It was through Evans that George Mitchell learned of the hill country and the kinds of music not heard in the adjacent Delta.

Although *Blow My Blues Away* was written in the present tense about the culture, over the years it has taken on a historical importance as the first in-depth treatment of blues in the hill country. With a foreword by Dr. Robert Coles and a preface and introduction by Mitchell, there are eleven chapters of content. The interview with fifer Othar Turner is framed by the description of the local and social settings of the hill country and an account of a fife-and-drum performance at a picnic. The interviews with three women—Rosa Lee Hill, Jessie Mae Brooks, and Ada Mae Anderson—are followed by the chapter about a service at a Baptist church where many women come to pray and celebrate on Sundays. The book is rounded out with three more interviews, with men living outside the hill country who speak with their masculine grit and honor, and with a selection of blues lyrics.

The book is notable for early encounters with musicians who became well known in the 1990s. Othar Turner (whose first name Mitchell spelled here as "Other") was nearing sixty at the time of his interview, but despite his many years of hard work as a farmer, in his remarks and in the book's photographs he appears as a strong man who knows how to support his family with the "enough to get by on" that he earns. Jessie Mae Brooks will become better known as Jessie Mae Hemphill, working as a domestic, but in the little off-time she had, she was already performing blues with guitar and assisting in fife-and-drum music. There is a mention in the picnic chapter (and what appears to be a blurred glimpse in a photograph) of R. L. Burnside, who during Mitchell's visit made his first recordings.

But the other interviewees and the people they mention merit attention, too. Rosa Lee Hill was the aunt of Jessie Mae Hemphill, and Mitchell managed to speak with her before her 1968 death. She speaks at length of her father, Sid Hemphill, the legendary early hill country musician recorded by Alan Lomax. She also testifies about practical sacred needs—not merely in a broad spiritual way, but practically, in terms of keeping a roof over her head despite fires and tornadoes. For Robert Johnson, I wonder how many times since 1990 readers have turned to his chapter with the expectation of reading about the creator of "Cross Road Blues." This Robert Johnson is different, living in a Delta settlement named Skene, chopping cotton during the week, playing knife-slide guitar on the side. Robert Diggs also lived in the Delta, at Friar's Point, and he tells a gritty, uncompromising account involving guns, murder, trouble, and blues. William "Do-Boy" Diamond lived in Canton, near Jackson, south of the delta and the hill country, driving a tractor and sharing the operation of a cotton gin. He speaks of his blues life without apology, having had his fun but quitting when playing the dances became tiresome and annoying.

What is most remarkable about this book is the feeling of hope shared by several of the people interviewed during that summer of 1967. Noticing the recent advances made in civil rights and in opportunities in education and labor, Anderson, Johnson, Diamond, and Diggs allowed themselves to speak of a little optimism, for their children and grandchildren if not for themselves. Turner and Hemphill spoke of thinking about leaving Mississippi, but to the end of each of their lives, neither left. In April 1968, Martin Luther King Jr. was assassinated in Memphis. To his credit, Mitchell let stand in the transcripts the hopeful comments from the previous year; they glimmer still.

Blow My Blues Away appeared twice, both editions now out of print. The original 1971 edition from Louisiana University Press was in hardcover, the 1984 Da Capo reprint in paperback. A new presentation of Mitchell's blues and fife-and-drum photographs was published in 2013 as *Mississippi Hill Country Blues 1967* (University Press of Mississippi), with greater attention to Turner, Hemphill, and Burnside, yet giving lesser space to the other remarkable people featured in the 1971 book. Over the years, Mitchell released a number of performances on various record labels. In 1969, Arhoolie released *Mississippi Delta Blues*, volumes 1 and 2 (Arhoolie ST 1041 and 1042), which were superseded on CD in 1994 by *Mississippi Delta Blues: Blow My Blues Away*, volumes 1 and 2 (Arhoolie CD 401 and CD 402). Additional Mitchell recordings appeared on *Masters of Modern Blues*, volume 4 (Testament LP T-2215, 1969, reissued on CD in 1994 as *Robert Nighthawk with Johnny Young* et al., Testament TCD 5010). In recent years, Fat Possum Records has held the Mitchell tapes, and it has issued a seven-CD comprehensive set, *The George Mitchell Collection* (Fat Possum GMBOX-2, 2008) and a number of single-artist CDs devoted to Burnside, Fred McDowell, Callicott, Rosa Lee Hill, and Diamond. —*EK*

80. Portraits by an Author as a Young Man

Feel Like Going Home: Portraits in Blues and Rock 'n' Roll. By Peter Guralnick. New York: Outerbridge and Dienstfrey, 1971. London: Omnibus, 1978. New York: Vintage, 1981. New York: Dutton, 1971. New York: HarperCollins, 1989. London: Penguin, 1992. Cambridge, MA: HarperPerennial, 1994. Edinburgh: Canongate, 2003. Boston: Little, Brown, 1999. ISBN 0-316-33272-0 (paperback), $19.00. French translation by Nicholas Guichard, Paris: Payot et Rivages, 2009. ISBN 2-7436-1998-8. Japanese translation by Kayoko Takahashi and Ryuji Nazuka, Tokyo: DAI-X. ISBN 4-88682-595-8

The inclusion of *Feel Like Going Home* among the Blues 100 may seem very obvious. This may well be one of the few—or perhaps the only—book that every fan has already read. Appearing before Greil Marcus's *Mystery Train* (1975) and Robert Palmer's *Deep Blues* (1981, no. 46), *Feel Like Going Home* was the first book published by a writer who came to the blues by way of rock and roll. With his sensibilities and literary flair, Guralnick succeeds in presenting the blues to rock fans and not merely to white record collectors of blues, jazz, and folk music, to whom the blues books published in the 1960s were addressed.

As Guralnick explains in his preface, he intended to show something of the progress from blues to rock. After two overviews of rock and blues, he proceeds with a series of portraits. Most of them are of bluesmen: Muddy Waters, Johnny Shines, Skip James,

Robert Pete Williams, and Howlin' Wolf. After a transitional chapter focusing on Sun Records, Guralnick looks quickly at rock (Jerry Lee Lewis) and country (Charlie Rich). He then closes with an unflinching look at Chess Records circa 1970 and a brief epilogue. To keep the history simple for his rock readers, Guralnick states (1999 edition, 46) that the blues went up the river from Mississippi through Memphis to Chicago, hence the seeming historical leap from Mississippi Delta blues through Elvis Presley to the Rolling Stones.

Despite the book's simple historical context, the portraits it contains are timely and invaluable since they were written at the time when the 1960s "blues revival" was beginning to ebb. Guralnick wrote of a visit with Muddy Waters while the latter was recovering from injuries inflicted by a crippling car accident. His chapter on Johnny Shines has datable references to 1968, when the musician was still seeking rediscovery recognition in his own right rather than as Robert Johnson's traveling companion. Howlin' Wolf is seen initially in a hospital bed, recuperating from an operation; Guralnick proceeds to follow him to his first rehearsals toward a return to the stage. Flitting throughout these chapters is the name of Robert Johnson, who remains phantomlike due to having no chapter of his own. In some ways, Guralnick's 1989 book *Searching for Robert Johnson* (no. 34) may be read as a new chapter of *Feel Like Going Home.*

Two other profiles present singular men outside the mainstream, even for blues. Nehemiah "Skip" James is depicted sympathetically as someone who knew he was a genius, whatever the word "genius" meant to those around him. Robert Pete Williams had no such pretensions about himself, and his unusual "air-music" blues is presented as the product of continual musical work for over twenty-five years, despite his years of labor and, for nine years, prison and parole.

A short look at Sam Phillips and his Sun record labels leads to chapters about two Sun pianists, Jerry Lee Lewis and Charlie Rich. For two years, 1957–1958, Lewis challenged Elvis Presley and Little Richard simultaneously for their claims to rock and roll kingship. Instead, his 1958 marriage to his underage cousin led to public outrage, especially in England, where he was about to tour. Around 1969–1970, Guralnick visited Lewis at his mansion home in northern Mississippi, when the musician had achieved a comeback of sorts through country music. Rich was not as popular a Sun artist as

Lewis. In fact, his first substantial record successes came a little later with Smash Records. Guralnick observes him seemingly in limbo at a Memphis-area nightspot, not quite country but not quite jazz or pop, not quite neglected but not yet popular. He would achieve unqualified national fame in 1973 with two hit records, "Behind Closed Doors" and "The Most Beautiful Girl."

The book's epilogue is titled "A Fan's Notes," which invites comparison with Frederick Exley's 1968 "fictional memoir" of the same title. In his book, Exley wrote of himself as someone relegated like a football fan to the sidelines of life, who does not possess the achievements, power, and charm of the most accomplished people, such as pro football running back Frank Gifford. Likewise, at the blues performances he attends, Guralnick looks on with yearning at the sharing of friendship and mutual recognition among African Americans and their interactions with the blues musicians. He feels because of his race and culture he is relegated to the walls of blues performing venues, from where he can only observe the participants. That feeling is foreshadowed by young Marshall Chess in the preceding chapter about the last days of Chess Records in Chicago. Marshall Chess protests (218) to sharing an interview with his uncle Phil Chess, explaining, "He was a participant and I was like an observer, you know what I mean? And there's a big difference." On a musical level, when rock was becoming mainstream US popular music, was blues becoming a "benchwarmer?" There is something odd, perhaps frivolous, about making notes as a marginalized fan of an outcast style of music. Yet Guralnick makes it seem adventurous and romantic, too, and since 1971 he has influenced many writers about popular music.

Feel Like Going Home has stayed in print for over forty years, and it has been translated into French and Japanese. To my knowledge, the only hardcover edition is the 1971 first edition published by Outerbridge and Dienstfrey. Later editions have some update additions in the bibliography, discography, and some text passages. —*EK*

81. The Evolution of Soul from Rhythm and Blues

Sweet Soul Music: Rhythm and Blues and the Southern Dream of Freedom. By Peter Guralnick. New York: Harper and Row, 1986. ISBN 0-06-015514-0 (hardcover), ISBN 0-06-096049-3 (paperback). German translation by Harriet

Fricke, Berlin: Bosworth, 2009. Reprint, Boston: Little, Brown/Back Bay Books, 2009. ISBN 0-31-633273-9 (paperback), $19.00

A reader may think at first of *Sweet Soul Music* as yet another book about music as it was experienced by the record labels, not by the musicians. But perhaps alone of the authors of the Blues 100, Guralnick explains the necessity of viewing soul music at least from the record industry's position (6): "that soul music, far from taking place in a vacuum or developing an aesthetic in splendid isolation from other more corrupt and hybridized strains, was in fact developing in tandem with rock 'n' roll and country music, was competing, really, for the same dollar, could never give up the hope of transcending its parochial origins and breaking into the pop marketplace." This is very much in accord with what Keil stated in folklore terms in *Urban Blues* (1966, no. 76), that "urban bluesmen" like B. B. King and Bobby Bland have had to present themselves in general ways in order to appeal to large audiences, and the recording labels and media were among their means of publicity and presentation. As Atlantic producer Jerry Wexler told Guralnick (4), soul music was simply an evolved style of rhythm and blues. Blues purists may ignore *Sweet Soul Music* if they wish, but in so doing they may deprive themselves of a valuable reason for reading about the business of blues records.

Guralnick tells a tale of two record labels, Atlantic Records in New York and Stax Records in Memphis. Musically, it was the best of times, but culturally, it was the worst of times. Atlantic was run by the Ertegun brothers, Ahmet and Neshui, and Jerry Wexler. It had stumbled upon soul in 1954 when Ray Charles sang "I Got a Woman" with a gospel feel. The resulting single was as successful commercially as it was artistically. When Charles left Atlantic for ABC-Paramount in 1959, Wexler sought a new singer of gospel-inflected R & B, and he eventually found one in Solomon Burke. Meanwhile, after leaving the Soul Stirrers for pop music, Sam Cooke was carving a large niche for himself at Keen and RCA Victor Records. The possibilities in the South for recording soul music were many. Stax Records was a brother-and-sister label that began realizing those possibilities with its first hit singles with Rufus Thomas and his daughter Carla.

From 1960 to 1968, Stax and Atlantic worked closely yet sometimes at odds, depending on whether and to what extent Jerry

Wexler was involved. Stax had made a deal with Atlantic involving the rights to the recordings, thereby establishing national distribution; that deal would come back to haunt Stax and benefit Atlantic in 1968. In the meantime, there were stars, records, and reputations to be made. Stax nurtured Booker T. & the M.G.'s, Carla Thomas, Isaac Hayes and David Porter, Sam and Dave, and Otis Redding. Atlantic had Wilson Pickett, Joe Tex, Solomon Burke, Arthur Conley, and Aretha Franklin. The making of the records was all-consuming; Stax artists had no idea of how popular they and their records were until they toured England and Europe in 1967. Not long afterward, Otis Redding and most of the Bar-Kays were killed in an airplane crash. If that loss wasn't enough to stagger the Memphis label, the news that Atlantic had the rights to recordings by all Stax artists, not just Rufus and Carla Thomas, and that the northern label was retaining them when it was being purchased by Warner Brothers, meant that Stax had to start over.

Likewise, the civil rights movement was staggered by the assassination in Memphis of Martin Luther King Jr. While many American cities burned in the subsequent rioting, Boston was spared, largely thanks to the televising of a concert by James Brown, "Soul Brother No. 1." Brown recorded not for Stax or Atlantic but for King Records, whose owner, Syd Nathan, had died in March 1968. With King, Stax, and Atlantic sold to other companies that year, the recording outlets for soul narrowed considerably. Under the leadership of Al Bell, Stax persisted into the mid-1970s; the story of the label's later years is told in detail by Rob Bowman in *Soulsville*, but Guralnick spares nothing in his closing chapter, too.

In the book's introduction, Peter Guralnick says he intended *Sweet Soul Music* to complete a trilogy begun by *Feel Like Going Home* (no. 80) and *Lost Highway*, thereby covering blues, rockabilly and country, and soul. The two predecessors were mostly of individual profiles, with a contextual overview occasionally inserted. This one is opposite, containing mostly historical narrative with the few biographical profiles embedded at appropriate points. Moreover, as Guralnick states in the epilogue, while writing *Sweet Soul Music* he matured as a writer, capable now of comparing and contrasting multiple viewpoints toward "an objective synthesis." With this new-found skill, he would proceed to write authoritative biographies of Elvis Presley and Sam Cooke.

If the means of writing this book is one of professional growth, the framework on which the subject matter hangs is similarly about the author's personal growth from teenager to man. Two-thirds of the way through the book, Guralnick revives the feeling of cultural exclusion that he had brought up previously in *Feel Like Going Home*. In both books, he wrote of looking on at the sharing of friendship and recognition among African Americans and their interactive appreciation of the blues musicians. In 1971, he felt himself excluded by race from this cultural camaraderie, thinking of himself as only a sideline observer, much like Frederick Exley's hapless narrator in the novel *A Fan's Notes*. In 1986, he mentions this feeling again, as something he observed while attending a 1964 soul revue in Boston. For some reason, the bill was shortened when Rufus Thomas and Joe Tex failed to show up. At the time, it seemed odd to Guralnick that no one in the African American audience seemed to care about those absences. In hindsight, he came to understand that for the audience, the concert was a convenient occasion for gathering and that two of the featured performers were not going to sing that night was not going to lessen the communal fun. This bit of wisdom may be worth keeping now, despite the current attitude of "the customer is always right." —*EK*

82. Natural-Born Eastmen

Sweet as the Showers of Rain. By Samuel Charters. New York: Oak Publications, 1977. ISBN 978-0-8256-0178-1 (paperback)

Also known as *The Bluesmen,* Volume II, *Sweet as the Showers of Rain* is the conclusion of what Samuel Charters initially intended in 1967 as a three-volume work looking at "the men who made the blues." While *The Bluesmen* (no. 29) was limited to Alabama, Mississippi, and Texas, *Sweet as the Showers of Rain* centers on the Carolinas, Georgia, and Tennessee.

The first half of the book focuses on Tennessee, primarily Memphis. After an introductory overview chapter on Memphis, Charters dedicates chapters to the Memphis Jug Band, Cannon's Jug Stompers, Furry Lewis, Frank Stokes, Sleepy John Estes, and Memphis Minnie. The chapter "Other Memphis Singers" looks at Jim Jackson and Jack Kelly. "Some Singers outside of Memphis" briefly acknowledges Allen Shaw and Noah Lewis and then mentions the names of several other musicians in one paragraph, but it doesn't go into any real detail. Charters acknowledges that much of the information on musicians in and around Memphis came from Bengt Olsson's book *Memphis Blues and Jug Bands* (no. 18), though he does expand on that biographical information.

The next five chapters look at the Atlanta and surrounding music scenes, with chapters on "Peg Leg Howell," "The Hicks Brothers—Barbecue Bob and Laughing Charley," "Willie McTell," and briefly describing the rest in a three-page chapter, "Some Other Atlanta Singers." The research of George Mitchell forms the core of much of the information on Atlanta.

"The Atlantic Coast and the Carolinas" are covered in the following four chapters, with Blind Blake, Buddy Moss, Blind Boy Fuller, and Gary Davis receiving the most attention. Charters drew upon the work of Bruce Bastin, particularly *Crying for the Carolines* (no. 28), for this section.

The final chapter, "To the End of the Thirties," summarizes the social, political, and technological changes of this time and sets the stage for the coming war and postwar blues years.

A two-page appendix, "A Note on Some Available Recordings," gives a summary of some of the reissues on Yazoo, Herwin, Biograph, and other labels.

Sweet as the Showers of Rain is less romantic in style than *The Country Blues* (no. 63) and *The Bluesmen* except for the title, which Charters says, in the introduction to *The Blues Makers*, "was chosen to make it clear that this was a different book from the first." A devout progressive, Charters was deeply upset with the direction the United States was taking with Vietnam and continued civil rights abuses. After his earlier social optimism faded and the killings at Kent State occurred, he moved to Sweden in 1970. This tone influenced his newer writing.

Like *The Bluesmen, Sweet as the Showers of Rain* is beautifully written but contains some errors and odd arguments. As in the first book, this one could have used more editing. There are a number of small errors that could have easily been fixed. For example, Charters refers to Bastin's book as *Crying for the Carolinas* instead of the "Carolines." Charters looks to the origins of Piedmont fingerpicking techniques and sound in the West African kora, which influenced the banjo and later the guitar. This may ultimately be true, but Charters doesn't give much attention to more recent and perhaps obvious influences of ragtime piano. In this same section discussing the influence of the kora, Charters confuses the argument by stating that Gary Davis developed his technique "by listening to local piano players." Though devoting a separate section to Atlanta makes sense based on the number of musicians there, Charters's description of an Atlanta sound that is significantly different from the greater Piedmont region isn't firmly convincing.

The work contains several black-and-white illustrations, less than half the number in the earlier work *The Bluesmen*. The cover oddly features "Bukka" White, though he receives only two passing mentions in the book, and he was a major subject in *The Bluesmen*. There is also an index.

A lot of the information in *Sweet as the Showers of Rain* wasn't new knowledge at the date of publication, but having it published in a single source was useful.

Sweet as the Showers of Rain and *The Bluesmen* were republished together as *The Blues Makers* (1991). (Note: See entry no. 29 on *The Bluesmen* for more information about *The Blues Makers*.) The appendix of available recordings is not included in *The Blues Makers*, but the rest of the text is included with no changes.

Though out of print, used copies can be found for an average price of twelve dollars. While *The Blues Makers* is also out of print, used copies run about the same price, making it a better buy. —*GJ*

83. Freedoms and Recognition Previously Not Dreamed Of

I Say Me for a Parable: The Oral Autobiography of Mance Lipscomb, Texas Bluesman. As told to and compiled by Glen Alyn. New York: Norton, 1993. ISBN 0-393-03500-X (hardcover), ISBN 0-393-33327-2 (paperback), $28.00

The title phrase is initially puzzling. When it is read in the context of this "oral autobiography" (488), it seems to mean "take me, for example." Glen Alyn knew Mance Lipscomb for about eight years, and of him Alyn wrote (474), "Mance saw himself as a farmer, a guitar player and songster, a spinner of stories, a husband, the foundation of his family, and a teacher for a younger generation that offered him freedoms and recognition he had never dreamed of in his youth and middle age." As Lipscomb told Alyn in the tapes that are the basis of this book, he didn't so much leave his church as the church left him. Nonetheless, he led an ethical life, thinking that what goes around comes back around.

Mance Lipscomb (1895–1976) is valued most as a singer and guitarist from the songster and blues eras. As a singer, he knew the lyrics to several thousand songs, and for some of those songs, he sang over two dozen stanzas. As a guitarist, he could make the bass strings rumble and the treble strings ring forth brilliantly. It is no wonder that during his middle age, playing outdoors on Saturday nights, he could be heard for several miles. From 1960 through the middle 1970s, he was among the most attractive draws on the folk revival and acoustic blues circuits. Moreover, he may have been the most healthy among the bluesmen he traveled with. Unlike his fellow elder bluesmen, Lipscomb did not make records before World War II. He wasn't "rediscovered," he was simply discovered. His reputation was made nearly solely from his first album for Arhoolie Records and his festival debut at Berkeley, California, in 1961, when he was sixty-six.

Lipscomb thought of himself as an east Texan farmer who played music only on weekends. Still, he took every opportunity to hear live music, to observe other guitarists, and to learn songs. His musical memories span the circus and sideshow bands of the late 1900s, hearing blues for the first time in the 1910s, attending street performances by Blind Lemon Jefferson and Blind Willie Johnson shortly afterward, meeting Lightnin' Hopkins in 1938, and acquiring his first electric guitar in the late 1940s. Through the 1950s, he performed dance music, rags, and blues on Saturdays at parties and suppers in and around Navasota, Texas. One contribution to blues literature that Lipscomb and Alyn make is explaining what were "Saturday night suppers." They were not little communal "bring a dish to pass" meals. They were full-blown affairs attracting hundreds of people to whom food was available at a price. The host of a Saturday night supper stood to make a lot of money. By hiring a musician, the chances of a supper outdrawing any rival supper were increased. Lipscomb was one of the few musicians in the Navasota area and very likely the best one of them. For some time, Lipscomb and his wife held suppers as a way of earning livable income during the years when the farming earnings looked to be lean or none.

Many of Lipscomb's memories are of racially charged events, whether of discrimination, systematic cheating by landowners, imprisonment, or violence, including lynching. The word portraits Lipscomb gives of two white men stand out remarkably in contrast. One was Walter Mobley, an employer during the 1930s who provided Lipscomb a team of mules so as to move him from 50 percent sharecropping to 25 percent cotton rent-farming, thus giving him a good chance of making some sort of profit at each harvest. The other was Frank Hamer, the legendary Texas Ranger. Today Hamer is best known for having killed the gangsters Bonnie Parker and Clyde Barrow in 1934. But from 1908 through 1911, he served as the city marshal in Navasota, where the teenage Lipscomb came to know him. For his unwavering if unusual fairness to blacks, Hamer is described by Lipscomb not merely as a do-gooder but as a righteous agent, settling disputes as they should be settled, not compromising them to the prevailing white man's benefit.

About 80 percent of the book is devoted to Lipscomb's life as a farmer and weekend guitarist. Through reading that much, one becomes ingrained in the times and culture of rural Texas. The 1960 recording visit by Mack McCormick and Chris Strachwitz and the ensuing trip the following year to Berkeley, California, is as much a surprise to the reader as it was to Lipscomb. Astounding, then, is the photograph (417) of him performing to 41,000 attendees—nearly all of them white—at the 1961 Berkeley Folk Festival, because until then the greatest number of people he had played to was perhaps two hundred or three hundred people in his front yard. His popularity on the folk circuit was high enough that he had to worry about his clothes and his body being torn by admirers for touches and souvenirs—and kisses. Having seen friends lynched in Texas for kissing white women, he was understandably worried by white fans who insisted on kissing him. Such was how topsy-turvy his life became when he left farming for what he called "the music business."

Because Lipscomb told on tape his whole life story and his core beliefs, this transcribed autobiography is among the treasures of blues literature. At about five hundred pages, its physical bulk is imposing. Alyn's transcription into phonetic spellings may be off-putting to some readers; some sentences do have to be read aloud in order to be intelligible (for example, from page 230: "I heard tell a people could go ta Looziana an git a Mojo Hand an do myaculls wit it" = "I heard tale[s] of people could go to Louisiana and get a 'mojo hand' and do miracles with it"). But the effort to read the book is rewarding, and by its end, one wishes there were more stories. —*EK*

84. Succumbing to the Blues

How Britain Got the Blues: The Transmission and Reception of American Blues Style in the United Kingdom. By Roberta

Freund Schwartz. Aldershot, England: Ashgate, 2007.
ISBN 978-0-7546-5580-0

Europeans have always loved the blues. At the very least, they have loved what blues they could hear. Not every bluesman and not all of their records have crossed the Atlantic Ocean to the United Kingdom and Europe. In the 1950s and 1960s, some artists had to be selected first, and some record labels took greater initiative to import their discs than other firms. As a result, some styles of blues had greater influence on young white musicians overseas than others.

Roberta Freund Schwartz, an American professor of musicology at the University of Kansas, wrote *How Britain Got the Blues*, a history of England's early obsession with this music through 1970. It was published by Ashgate, an academic publisher whose books can be quite expensive. Furthermore, it has appeared only in hardcover, not in paperback, but in recent years an electronic version for Kindle has been available through Amazon.

For all intents and purposes, the British collectors before 1940 of American jazz on records were the first on that island to notice the blues. Initially, they thought of it as a historical antecedent to jazz. Their recognition of blues as a style in its own right eventually came by the end of the 1950s, with Paul Oliver's *Blues Fell This Morning* (no. 64) as a landmark book. Meanwhile, the performances of Big Bill Broonzy in England during the 1950s did much to establish Mississippi blues as a primal tradition in English minds, an impression reinforced by the tour of England by Muddy Waters in 1958 and those of the American Folk Blues Festival revues during the 1960s.

Some British teenagers were attempting to play some of this music that seemed so exotic to them, if not weird. The first style they took up was skiffle, which for them was exemplified by Lonnie Donegan's "Rock Island Line," a 1956 rendition of a Leadbelly song. Skiffle wasn't merely a London fad; it was also played up north in Liverpool, which had several amateur skiffle groups, including the Quarrymen, led by John Lennon. While skiffle didn't last through 1957 as a musical trend, it set the conditions for the young musicians to discover the blues as a whole.

Eventually, momentum in England toward "getting" the blues—in terms of understanding it or simply succumbing to it—would build through the studies and performances by musicians, writers, radio broadcast officials, record store owners, and theater managers. Freund Schwartz makes this book worth reading for the way she juggles the perspectives of these kinds of participants, showing how one group's activities informed another's. For example, London performances led to written critical notices, which were written or read by present and future historians of the blues, who then ordered the records through the best stores (like Dobell's), whose dealers sold them to writers and musicians, the latter imitating the music in performance, which led again to new written reviews, and so on. I hope someday that the entire run of the pioneering British blues magazine *Blues Unlimited* (1963–1988) may be reprinted with its editorials and ads, as they would exhibit this very circular process that Freund Schwartz describes.

I had always thought that the British blues revival was one long era. Freund Schwartz advises that we should see there were two phases. The first one, she says, was from 1963 to early 1965, when many white blues bands were imitating the music imported by the labels Chess and Excello. Authenticity was a prime concern for fans and musicians; now as I think about it, the concern for authenticity may be said to have shaped the performances on the first two LPs that the Rolling Stones issued through the British firm Decca. The second phase began in 1965, in which authenticity became less of a concern. If so, then the Rolling Stones' single "Satisfaction" could be heard as a herald of this change in attitude. If American blues was indeed becoming less trendy in England in 1965, the author argues that British musicians were beginning to move from imitation to improvisation. The results were long guitar solos, the most extended of which could last as long as an African American blues legend's whole set.

British musicians and writers have long accused Americans of being ignorant of bluesmen and blues women. Yet there have been Anglo misunderstandings of the blues that African American writers have recently been addressing. Is the music merely for listening? The blues is to be respected, yes, but need it be adored? Schwartz relays the reports and reviews of the place and period despite their historical flaws, documenting each one in footnotes if a reader wants to read it whole. Despite the book's high price, it is worth reading in order to avoid the creative and critical digressions made by a few well-meaning blues lovers "across the pond" fifty years ago. —*EK*

85. Blues Traveler

Lightnin' Hopkins: His Life and Blues. By Alan Govenar.
Chicago: Chicago Review Press, 2010. ISBN 978-1-55652-
962-7, $28.95

One fact about Sam "Lightnin'" Hopkins (1912–1982) to be admitted even by his most diehard fans is that he made a ton of records. The discography of recorded performances by Andrew Brown and Alan Balfour in the back of Alan Govenar's *Lightnin' Hopkins: His Life and Blues* occupies forty-six printed pages, spanning from 1946 to 1981. To be sure, some records are of live concert performances, but the vast majority comes from studio sessions through the early 1970s. Some of the individual performances are electrically amplified guitar boogie instrumentals, but the rest were vocal blues, often to Hopkins's own acoustic guitar accompaniment. Does Hopkins's discography constitute an "Autobiography in Blues," to quote the title of one of his LP albums?

Alan Govenar has been an authority on Texas blues for over thirty-five years; his book *Meeting the Blues: The Rise of the Texas Sound* is also worth the effort to seek and read. In this biography, he resists this temptation to interpret Hopkins's blues life as a work of blues, and in so doing he uncovers a life that possibly could not be contained in a twelve-measure AAB blues lyric. One basic guiding rule for blues biographers is to seek surviving family members and spouses. The woman long known as Hopkins's wife, Antoinette Charles, lived for many years after the musician's death. As he tells us in this book, Govenar had tried many times to schedule an interview with her. Only after her death did he learn why she avoided him. For nearly thirty-five years until Hopkins died, she led a double life, as the musician's lover in Houston, Texas, and as a wife and mother raising a family with her formally married husband in another part of town. While it is understandable why Charles remained silent to researchers, at her death she took a lot of memories of Hopkins and postwar Texas blues with her to the grave. However, other friends and associates agreed to speak for this biography. The most important of them were Chris Strachwitz, owner of Arhoolie Records, who reissued Hopkins's early 78s on Gold Star and recorded many of the musician's later blues; and David Benson, who served as a road manager through the 1970s. A good view of Hopkins in the 1960s is provided by J. J. Phillips, with whom he had an affair. She fiction-alized aspects of her relationship with Hopkins in her 1966 novel *Mojo Hand: An Orphic Tale* (Trident/Simon and Schuster), which is worth seeking; through the years it has been reprinted several times, and it was translated into German.

Lightnin' Hopkins received his nickname in 1946 from a record producer who was pairing him with a musician known as "Thunder." Until then, he had spent most of his life in northeast Texas, but he moved to Houston during World War II. He had come of musical age in the 1930s, as suggested by a few melodies he sang on records through the early 1950s, and he did spend a few years performing with legendary blues singer Texas Alexander. From 1946, when his blues "Katie May" became a hit for the Aladdin label, through the 1970s, he accepted seemingly every paying opportunity to make records. They were made in a bewildering variety of settings: professional recording studios, cut-rate studios, beer joints, coffeehouses, concert halls, and festivals. His total legacy may be less an autobiography and more a travel journal in blues.

During the 1950s and 1960s, Hopkins was seen as the archetypal bluesman. He was depicted as such by Samuel Charters in the opening chapter of his pioneering book *The Country Blues* (no. 63). That may surprise those today who think of Robert Johnson at the dusty crossroads as the archetype. But blues fans were different back then, especially the white fans who were beginning to discover the music. Words were more important than guitar solos, and Hopkins sang lots of words. He fit the romantic mold of the nomadic bard playing an acoustic guitar. By wearing sunglasses, he appealed to the cool among the whites, yet his engaging smile on- and offstage drew the curious into becoming new fans. Yet he sometimes confounded this image by playing instrumental boogies, by playing an electric guitar, and by performing with a rhythm section. If Johnson continues to occupy what many people hold as the archetype of the bluesman, then Govenar affirms the dynamism of a bluesman by presenting and embracing as many of Hopkins's seeming contradictions. —*EK*

86. The Blues at the End of the Rediscovery Era

Listen to the Blues. By Bruce Cook. New York: Charles Scribner's Sons, 1973. SBN 684-13376-8. Reprint, New York: Da Capo Press, 1995; ISBN 978-0-306-80648-3

Bruce Cook may be an unfamiliar name now. Some readers of the Beat authors will know his 1971 book, *The Beat Generation*. He also wrote biographies of Bertolt Brecht and Dalton Trumbo and some fiction. He wrote for some periodicals, but not for the blues magazines like *Blues Unlimited* and *Living Blues*. But around 1970, he embarked on an odyssey across the United States, with a short trip to Paris, to reacquaint himself with the blues, which he had first heard while growing up in Chicago in the late 1940s. At the time of his travels, there were few books about the blues available, so Cook often had to conduct some research for context. Yet in each chapter, he gives up trying to write context, and he goes abruptly to listen firsthand to someone who can testify about the blues in present-day terms. The result of his conversations with blues people is this remarkable depiction of where the blues stood at the end of the 1960s revival.

The first three chapters are attempts at orientation, definition, and origins. Cook's seeming lack of success at them allows him to listen with an open mind. His blues journey begins properly in Chicago at Pepper's, where he listens to Hound Dog Taylor and talks with the underrecorded guitarist Lefty Dizz, then to Theresa's, where he talks with Junior Wells, Louis Myers, and Fred Below. Cook cannot find the words to say what the blues is, but he points toward the blues when he presents Robert Pete Williams, a natural at modal blues poetry if there was ever one. During the 1950s, Williams was incarcerated for murder in self-defense, and his parole was facilitated with the help of Dr. Harry Oster, the folklorist conducting research for his book *Living Country Blues* (no. 65). When Cook visited him, Williams's parole was completed, and he was continuing his blues craft unencumbered by his previous legal and social confinements. The origins of the blues were not any more clear in 1970 than they are now, but Cook has the good sense to seek the musical contexts through a songster. To be sure, Henry Thomas was long dead, and so was John Hurt, but John Jackson performed a variety of the ballads, dances, and pre-1942 popular songs he knew with the blues, "like pieces of the same long song," as Cook thought while listening to Jackson play them.

With the next six chapters, Cook burrows through the heart of the music. His first stop is Mississippi, the whole of which he mistakenly characterizes as the Delta (in all fairness, so did other writers at the time). He writes of Robert Johnson and Johnny Shines, who had criss-crossed the delta in the 1930s, but also of Nehemiah

"Skip" James and Fred McDowell, who lived on its fringes. James was from Bentonia on the southeastern rim of the Delta, but in the early 1930s through Johnny Temple he exerted an influence on Johnson. James died in 1969, but Cook spoke with Dick Waterman, who booked many of his last performances. James was a genius, "a natural genius" as Waterman termed him, but James's haughty behavior often stemmed largely from his living up to his conception of genius. More congenial than James as a person was Fred McDowell of Como, on the northeastern edge of the Delta, who granted Cook one of his last interviews before dying of cancer. McDowell refers to his changed times, playing more often at college campuses than juke joints and fish fries.

In New Orleans, Cook talks with Lars Edegran, a Swede who moved there in 1966 to play Dixieland. Cook depicts the young Edegran as a sympathetic guide to other kinds of southern music, as I learned for myself in 2000 while assisting Edegran on a transfer of delta blues 78 rpm records owned by a mutual friend. The Texas chapter is dominated by Mance Lipscomb, another great songster active during the 1960s, who tells plenty of stories to Cook (and many more to Glen Alyn that would become the basis of his posthumous autobiography *I Say for Me a Parable*, no. 83). For Tennessee, Cook meets with Furry Lewis and "Bukka" White, but also he affirms positively the popularization of blues in the 1910s by W. C. Handy, in contrast to the other writers who have discussed grudgingly Handy's contributions in the music industry. The Chicago chapter leads from Big Bill Broonzy through Sunnyland Slim but not to Muddy Waters—who shows up later in the book—but instead to J. B. Hutto, whose death from cancer at age fifty-seven in 1983 robbed us of one of the most vibrant postwar slide guitarists. Finally, there is the profile of Memphis Slim, a pianist in a blues world of guitarists, living not in Chicago or Mississippi but in Paris, France, explaining and defending the United States to Europeans.

The next set of chapters assesses blues in country music, rock, jazz, and gospel. Of the artists featured in these four chapters, only Charley Pride in the country chapter is securely accepted by audiences. For rock, Cook looks at Muddy Waters, who would be more at home in the Mississippi chapter, and for jazz he interviews B. B. King, who would be better placed after his cousin "Bukka" White in the Tennessee chapter. Waters has always been viewed as a forerunner by rock fans and historians but never emphatically hailed as a rock musician. Cook's placement of King in the jazz chapter may seem to us today as odd and wrong, but in 1973 that may be where King's future seemed to lie. Gospel culture may have been the toughest for Cook to accept and assess because of its firm if arbitrary standards of accepting musicians into its fold. His profile of Roebuck Staples and the Staple Singers is uncompromising, telling of the impossibly high demands that religious participants put on those singers who have ventured into popular music and of the damning faint applause conceded when those singers meet such performance demands.

Talk is cheap, though. Blues musicians have to perform if they are to eat today, never mind tomorrow. The last two chapters deal with artist management. The first of them is a portrait of Dick Waterman, relating while they were happening the kinds of activities for managing older blues artists that Waterman would later tell as his past in his book *Between Midnight and Day* (no. 72). The second is about their finances, presenting as case studies Sleepy John Estes with Hammie Nixon, and Arthur "Big Boy" Crudup. Getting the payments and royalties as artists is one thing, but getting those as composers is quite another. The Crudup story was still in progress when Cook wrote about it; Waterman tells its bitter conclusion in *Between Midnight and Day*.

Listen to the Blues enjoyed a trade issue from Scribner's in 1973, but by 1990 it had been largely forgotten. Possibly due to its out-of-print and forgotten status, Austin Sonnier used the portions of the Mississippi chapter without due credit for his 1994 book *A Guide to the Blues: History, Who's Who, Research Sources* (Westport, CT: Greenwood Press). This was discovered by Peter Aschoff when he was reviewing the Sonnier book shortly after reading the 1995 Da Capo reprint of *Listen to the Blues*. Certainly Aschoff's review stirred blues fans' interest in rediscovering Cook. The book is worth finding in either the original Scribner's issue or the Da Capo reprint because it captures a time when our elders were young and the legends were alive. —*EK*

87. Blues and the Triumphant Dream

Blues and the Poetic Spirit. By Paul Garon. London: Eddison Press, 1975. ISBN 0-85649-018-0 (hardcover). Reprint, New York: Da Capo, 1978. ISBN 0-30677-542-5 (hardcover). Republished with new material, San

Francisco: City Lights Books, 1996. ISBN 0-87286-315-8
(paperback)

Readers taking up this title for the first time may want to read the
end of the book first. Doing so is as appropriately subversive as surrealism. Seriously, though, if you have the 1996 City Lights edition
or its reprints since then, you really should read the end of the
book first, as its closing chapter, "Tough Times," and appendix,
"Surrealism and Music," provide many explanations that are not as
clearly given in the opening chapters.

The thesis is most clearly stated in the "Tough Times" chapter
(198): "The principal thesis of *Blues and the Poetic Spirit* is that the
blues is a music that signifies the rebellion of the spirit, a body of
song that achieves poetry by its insistent revolt and demand for
liberation." By "blues," Garon means indeed the "body of song"
and not the more wide-ranging "culture-since-slavery" definition
that later African American writers like Houston Baker (no. 93),
Julio Finn (no. 94), and Jon Michael Spencer (no. 98) would use.
But what does Garon mean by "achieves poetry"? Early in the book
he takes issue with Peter Guralnick's assertion in *Feel Like Going
Home* (no. 80) that blues is not poetry. If Guralnick was concerned
with poetry as a "craft of literature," Garon (in 1975 and in 1996)
differed by declaring that the "true essence of poetry" is "revolt
and desire." It seems, then, that Garon takes a dynamic view of
poetry, and it may help some readers to substitute "poetry" with
"poetic act," "poetical acting," or "poetic spirit" whenever that word
appears in Garon's text.

Reactivating the purpose of the blues—and not merely its
meaning—has to be done by every student of the music. But if
one is not from the blues culture, how can one who loves the
blues reaffirm and reactivate it? That was Garon's challenge while
writing *Blues and the Poetic Spirit* during the early 1970s. Back then,
the key writings of Baker and Finn about the blues had yet to
appear. His suggestion to borrow the attitudes and methods of
the surrealist artistic movement is intriguing. What the artists and
poets associated with surrealism did, as Garon says in the second
chapter, was to regard African artifacts as "primitive," that is, as
"primal" and hence undiluted in their power. The conventional
use of the word "primitive" in Western art cultures is often to note
an artifact as crude, less developed, and hence of little more interest than exoticism to the Western mind. If I understand Garon

and the surrealists correctly, perhaps the word "primitive" should be pronounced "prime-i-tive," and any object called such should be examined for its power to communicate its purpose directly and without inhibition.

Garon cautions, however, that the blues often deals with unpleasant topics. If the blues is regarded as "prime-i-tive," its direct and uninhibited communication may be too strong to allow its enjoyment. What can facilitate that enjoyment, he says, are "identification" and "aesthetic illusion." Identification would be the blues fan listening sympathetically, adopting the bluesman's feelings during the course of the music's performance. What would then keep the blues fan from panicking over the situation described in the poetic blues, or even from killing himself or herself in despair? Garon says such listeners—all of us, really—need as a protective device the "aesthetic illusion." I am not sure what exactly is meant by that phrase, but by breaking down its component words, I think it may mean a blues listener has to recognize that a blues song can pose a situation that could happen to the listener, but not every song poses something that has happened or will happen in the listener's real life. Perhaps a translation of this phrase in 2010s terms may be "vicarious pleasure," or maybe "fictional situation." So, in sum, appropriate listening to the blues demands simultaneously an attraction through identification and a detachment through recognizing that the blues is a performance.

How do these principles operate in the blues, then? Garon spends the rest of the book applying them to blues lyrics about love and eros, aggression, humor, travel, alcohol and drugs, male supremacy and female liberation, night, animals, work, the police, African American Christian churches, crime, magic, and the workings of the mind. What blues and the poetic spirit all boil down to are dreams, in which the dreamer reorganizes his or her circumstances either consciously in daydreams and art or unconsciously in nighttime dreams. Indications of free, unrepressed thoughts are the dream's "images of a capacity for fantasy that has not been crushed." As Garon states conclusively in the chapter titled "The Dream," the ultimate result of such dreaming is "the transformation of everyday life as it encumbers us today, the unfolding and eventual triumph of the marvelous."

Garon's text is not easy to understand unless the reader has taken a college course in psychology or another one in modern literature, or both. While the original 1975 edition and its 1978

Da Capo reprint were important in their time, readers should seek the editions since 1996, for which Garon removed one chapter and added new explanatory material using everyday words. Even if one cannot accept Garon's means and conclusions—some of his critics have had a hard enough time understanding them—one has to admit that he pointed toward a truly primal appreciation of the blues that is worth attaining through one method or another. —*EK*

88. The Soul Projects

Chicago Soul. By Robert Pruter. Urbana: University of Illinois Press, 1991. ISBN 0-252-01676-9 (hardcover), ISBN 0-252-06259-0 (paperback), $35.00

Lovers of southern blues recognize that contemporary southern audiences have embraced artists in the soul and "soul-blues" styles, among them Bobby Rush and Denise LaSalle. These singers and their younger imitators may be heard at today's southern blues festivals. Their musical styles were developed during the 1960s and 1970s through the soul styles of Chicago. Robert Pruter, a longtime editor of the rhythm-and-blues for the record collectors' publication *Goldmine*, published his account in 1991 through the University of Illinois Press, which has kept it in print as a paperback.

At first glance, the book seems to be organized by record label, and its foreword suggests that record producer Calvin Carter and singer Jerry Butler will be present throughout the history. In truth, it is producer Carl Davis and composer/performer Curtis Mayfield who shape the trends, if not the styles, of Chicago soul, and the order in which Pruter presents the recording firms is in accord with the arrivals of Davis and Mayfield to each one.

At the beginning of the 1960s, the postwar styles of blues and gospel music were what Chicago African Americans were listening and dancing to. In the introductory chapter, Pruter lays out the neighborhoods in the city's South Side and West Side, and he enumerates the projects and the nearby high schools. The expansion of radio programming for blacks comes upon the Chess brothers' purchase of a radio station and rechristening it as WVON. The Regal Theater was a central showcase for black talent (and where B. B. King would record his classic 1964 live album, *Live at the Regal*). Vee Jay Records and Chess Records had established themselves by recording and selling records by blues artists. However, younger artists like Dee Clark and Etta James at these firms were combining the emotional singing of gospel music with the forms and instruments associated with blues and rhythm and blues. The result was what we now call soul music, although it was different from that engendered by Sam Cooke and Ray Charles because it was grounded very much in Chicago music—and dance. In a keystone chapter, Pruter insists on taking into account the Chicago teenage black dances of the 1960s, not only toward reclaiming much recorded music that may now sound trite and insipid, but also to provide a key toward appreciating a social culture that has been gone for over thirty-five years.

Much of that culture came from the projects, especially the Cabrini-Green projects north of the Chicago Loop; the map of black Chicago at the book's beginning helps the reader's understanding of local distinctions among neighborhoods. As Pruter writes (76): "Aside from Jerry Butler, Cabrini-Green gave rise to Curtis Mayfield, Major Lance, Otis Leavill, Billy Butler and the Chanters, and through the Lance connection the West Side group, the Artistics." Nearly all of these names were acts associated in some way with Carl Davis, who produced R & B and soul records for the Columbia Records subsidiary Okeh from 1962 through 1966. Jerry Butler and Curtis Mayfield, as members of the Impressions and later as solo artists, were two of the longer-abiding artists in Chicago soul. Mayfield cemented his triple-threat standing within the record industry as songwriter, producer, and performer when he signed in 1961 with ABC-Paramount.

Meanwhile, through the mid-1960s, there were many local hustlers who succeeded as small entrepreneurs by identifying young men and women who were looking for their first breaks as singers, musicians, and composers. Some of these small operators led labels with colorful names like Formal, Nike, Satellite, Crash, Ole', and Lock. A few Chicago labels were nurturing a substyle of soul called "hard soul," which emphasized more the blues manner of singing, much like what Etta James was already recording for Chess. One such firm was One-derful, led by George Leaner, whose singers included Otis Clay and Tyrone Davis, each of whom was beginning a long performing career. Another hard-soul label was Twinight, which issued many classics of the substyle by Syl Johnson.

When Carl Davis left Okeh for Brunswick in 1966, Chicago soul was in full swing. Brunswick was known then for being the label of the dynamic performer Jackie Wilson, and Davis's arrival as producer would result in several more years of classic hits for Wilson, including "Higher and Higher." Davis set up the Dakar subsidiary, and through 1976 he oversaw the production of records by Barbara Acklin, Tyrone Davis, and the Chi-Lites. Meanwhile, Mercury tried developing new repertory, going so far as to work with Jerry Butler in maintaining a workshop for young soul composers in the early 1970s. A few artists were starting out independently, among them Denise LaSalle, who had begun singing in Chicago, yet when the time came for her to record soul, she opted to do so at Willie Mitchell's recording studio in Memphis.

From 1968 through the end of the 1970s, Curtis Mayfield worked through his Curtom operation, producing and performing on singles, albums, and film soundtracks. He also took on recording veterans like Major Lance and the Staple Singers, and with the singer Linda Clifford he ventured into disco music. But as Mayfield later admitted, he was spreading his activities quite thin, and over time he wasn't producing the hits necessary to keep his brand of Chicago soul on the radio and in the stores. Meanwhile, during the 1970s, the record industry was using less the hustlers and entrepreneurs who in the previous decade were middlemen in sales and record distribution, preferring more the national labels' "branch offices" to move the vinyl. As one result, the homogenous sound of black popular music, including disco, on national labels was crowding the local styles off the retail shelves and airwaves. For another, the national labels seemed to not bother promoting outside of Chicago the music made in Chicago. In 1980 Mayfield shifted his working base from Chicago to Atlanta. At that same time, Carl Davis was making what turned out to be a final effort for Chicago soul with the Chi-Sound label, but that flickered out in January 1984.

What makes Pruter's book outstanding is his attention to detail (for many years, he worked for the *New Standard Encyclopedia*). Rather than merely recite names and song titles, he describes dance steps, geographic features of Chicago, cultural slang, and methods of record sales and promotion. He also loves the records, whether they are Davis and Mayfield productions or the small-time 45 rpm discs featuring promising singers making the best they can of uninspiring songs. Also, the four sections of photographs show how young everyone was during the era of Chicago soul. —*EK*

89. You Don't Know My Mind

Black Culture and Black Consciousness: Afro-American Folk Thought from Slavery to Freedom. By Lawrence W. Levine. New York: Oxford University Press, 1977. ISBN 0-19-502088-X (hardcover), ISBN 0-19-502374-9 (paperback). Thirtieth anniversary edition (2007), ISBN 0-19-530569-8 (hardcover), $65.00, ISBN 0-19-530568-X (paperback), $18.95

African American writers have said repeatedly that the blues came from slavery. How, then, should a blues lover learn about slavery? If one is African American, one may learn about it from family members. If one is not, then either one should talk to an African American or, at the very least, read about it. For the context toward understanding early blues, *Black Culture and Black Consciousness* by Lawrence Levine (1933–2006) provides the necessary historical information and many relevant examples drawn from folklore.

Levine's premise is simple (ix): "What were the contours of slave folk thought on the eve of emancipation and what were the effects of freedom upon that thought?" Levine himself wasn't African American; rather, he was Jewish Eastern European American. As he recounts in the preface to the 2007 anniversary edition, he had come to the topic during the mid-1960s through his friendships and activist associations with African Americans. Early in his research, he realized he needed to read not the accounts by the cultural leaders but instead those by slaves, ex-slaves, and their descendants. Since many of them were illiterate, their testimonies were written down or recorded by folklorists over the course of 120 years and more. Levine himself was not a folk-lorist but a historian whose eye for change led him to write (5), "Culture is not a fixed condition but a process: the product of inter-action between the past and the present." Obviously, emancipation upon the end of the American Civil War was the signal historical event for African Americans, but the changes within their culture would serve as the events in their internal history. It is that internal history that Levine seeks.

The first two of the book's six lengthy chapters treat slavery with an emphasis on music. Levine reports that nineteenth-century witnesses thought that the slaves' spirituals were more impres-sive than their secular music and dances. Perhaps so, but Levine emphasizes more that slave music in itself was a cultural form—in spite of many white assertions then and later that blacks had no culture—and that such music was performed communally. Spirituals constituted a "quest for certainty," that is, they were the musical means for African-born slaves and their children to survive in the face of a slave-owning system for which music was enjoyed only on the side, so to speak. Two other means of survival were religion, for which the slaves adopted elements of the Christian Old Testament that matched their traditional theology and folk beliefs, which slaves exercised to retain a personal sense of assertive well-being and, Levine argues, health and sanity. Through their cultivations of music, religion, and folk beliefs, the slaves prevented their legal slavery from becoming spiritual slavery. In the second chapter, Levine presents slave tales, especially the trickster tales that were later collected by Joel Chandler Harris for his Uncle Remus books. In these stories, Br'er Rabbit and not Legba was often the trickster. The overall purpose of these tales, Levine says, was to "[identify] the forces which shaped their lives and [to give] prescriptions for overcoming or at least surviving them." Sometimes Br'er Rabbit overcame his foes, sometimes he survived them, but as often as not he was eaten by them.

The remaining four chapters deal with emancipation, freedom, and the changes they wrought. The sacred world changed greatly, becoming less important when African Americans traveled longer distances than before and when they migrated to cities for industrial jobs. Oddly, despite the seeming weakening of sacred life, sacred singing was infused with retentions of African musical characteristics and new secular music to produce sanctified music and gospel music. The purpose of humor is explored, not only as a social safety valve through which frustrations may be vented but also as a proving ground, through "the dozens," among young African American men on which they could toughen themselves for the racial insults they would surely hear from whites later in life. The final chapter is about heroes, whether ex-slave survivors, bad men, folk heroes, or boxing heroes. It is one thing for a man of Jewish Eastern European descent to present a history of African American culture, quite another (and possibly presumptuous) for him to try to discuss African American consciousness as revealed through spoken or written thought. As blues woman Virginia Liston once sang, "You don't know my mind." But how else other than through changes in consciousness can Levine demonstrate that the new heroes through their achievements were replacing the cautionary examples of animal and human tricksters?

Black Culture and Black Consciousness is essential reading for blues fans, especially to those born outside the African American culture. Ironically enough, the one flawed chapter is "The Rise of Secular Song," which presents the blues. Levine had shown previously that spirituals and trickster tales were retained through many generations from slavery times through the twentieth century. He made a mistake, however, by believing the blues was also retained in oral culture since at least 1850 until its initial publications in print and on record but failing to show its presence in slave culture and early freedom throughout that time, as he had done for sacred music and secular tales. As a result, his presentation of the blues comes off as vague, even similar to some presentations of folklore, and so this chapter reads very differently from the histories given in the rest of the book. Furthermore, he placed the chapter early among the four "freedom" chapters, in order to emphasize the manner of work-song singing in the blues over that music's improvisational process and its compositional forms. To be fair to Levine, he had begun research on this book in 1965, five years before the publication of Paul Oliver's *Story of the Blues* (no. 2), and the blues specialists of the time had thought work songs and field hollers were direct antecedents of the blues. Despite this mistake, Levine saves the chapter at its end by asserting plausibly that blues and jazz were the postemancipation replacements for spirituals, religion, and folk beliefs for well-being, health, and sanity. That assertion may be read as a thesis for a few later Blues 100 books, including those by African American authors Houston Baker (no. 93), Julio Finn (no. 94), and Jon Michael Spencer (no. 98). —*EK*

90. B. B. King as Boss Man

The Arrival of B. B. King: The Authorized Biography. By Charles Sawyer. Garden City, NY: Doubleday, 1980. ISBN 0-385-15929-3 (hardcover). Reprint, New York: Da Capo, 1982. ISBN 0-306-80169-8 (paperback)

There are currently available a number of books about B. B. King, the most widely recognized ambassador of the blues. There is the autobiography, *Blues All around Me*, written with assistance from

David Ritz (New York: Avon, 1996) and also the remarkable *The B. B. King Treasures: Photos, Mementos & Music from B. B. King's Collection* (New York: Bulfinch, 2005) compiled by Dick Waterman and Charles Sawyer. To study King's guitar style and playing technique, guitarists have various method books and notated transcriptions to choose from. Oddly, Sawyer's *The Arrival of B. B. King* is out of print. It was the first trade book biography of him and, considering how few books about the blues there were in 1980, it set a new standard for blues biographies.

The Arrival of B. B. King was written and published at an interesting time in King's career. From the 1940s through 1968, King played mostly for African American audiences. Then in 1969 and early 1970, his single "The Thrill Is Gone" became his biggest hit, reaching number 15 on the Billboard Hot 100 sales chart. Around the same time, he began to be noticed by white rock fans, and he was being booked to play rock venues instead of the chitlin' circuit. Throughout the 1970s he attracted both black and white listeners, although his potential for becoming the face of the blues was still unrealized. In 1981, his album *There Must Be a Better World Somewhere* was released, whose title track is often the latest song by King that many southern blues radio shows play with some regularity, along with his 1950s and 1960s hits, of course. If his record releases for the rest of the 1980s seemed ho-hum, the recognition of him as a blues icon soared. The recent lionization of him has been well deserved, but memories of his prime creative years through 1981 are fading.

In 1966, Charles Keil included a sociological depiction of King in *Urban Blues* (no. 76). Toward the end of the following decade, when Sawyer was writing his biography, the musician was in his early fifties and—amazingly enough after more than thirty years of touring—still ambitious and hungry. The opening chapter, "Living by the Odometer," is a remarkable portrait of the bluesman when he was still being booked regularly to play in African American venues. The pressure on King to arrive on time for a performance never lets up, and it is carried over into every performance and intermissions, too, when he poses for photographs with fans.

The pressure was always there. In seven chapters, Sawyer presents King's life from his birth in 1925 through the late 1970s. Likening him to fictional lowly-youth-made-good Horatio Alger, Sawyer retraces King's steps from teenage sharecropper to blues star. Through all his life's events, how has King kept himself sane and in front of his audiences? Sawyer tries to seek answers by taking side looks at the lives of Johnny Ace, who showed signs of mental wear from touring, and Leslie "Greasy" Simmons, who may have had more natural talent than King but had left music for a day job in Chicago. What King may have possessed that Ace and Simmons did not, Sawyer suggests, are physical and mental staminas and a demanding evaluation of self that comes close to doubt. He also had retained Sid Seidenberg as his manager, who was a key factor in King's success from the 1960s into the 2000s.

Rather than Horatio Alger, the patrician "boss man" seems more what King appeared to be in the late 1970s. Sawyer admits as much, especially in the opening chapter when describing King's relationship to his touring musicians. This isn't the only instance of the term "boss man" being applied to a blues musician. James Rooney had given the title *Bossmen* to his double portrait of Muddy Waters and bluegrass icon Bill Monroe (New York: Dial, 1971). But King by name, demeanor, and example fulfills the role of boss man, looking after his band and his touring assistants, hiring them, paying them, giving them extra money when necessary, and ordering them when and where he wants to see them next. Certainly he may have learned something about being a boss man from the white landowners he farmed for in the 1930s and 1940s, and Sawyer says that King had worked for some unusually fair ones. As certainly, he would have known of the many boss men who kept their tenant farmers in economic bondage. It would have been very easy for King to bind his employees in like fashion. But he didn't, and so he broke the trend of this abusive supervisory practice. In his book's introduction, Sawyer states that recording the end of the "Jim Crow" treatment of white bosses to their employees was one reason why he wrote *The Arrival of B. B. King*. If so, then the achievement of B. B. King was avoiding such "Jim Crow" treatment of his own employees, however firm he has had to be with them. —EK

91. Soft Murmurs of Conversation

The Voice of the Blues: Classic Interviews from "Living Blues Magazine." Edited by Jim O'Neal and Amy van Singel. New York: Routledge, 2002. ISBN 0-415-93654-3 (paperback), $39.95

Since its humble beginnings from a typewriter in a Chicago apartment, *Living Blues* has become one of the world's most important blues periodicals, generating over twenty thousand pages of content since its first issue. *Living Blues* was founded by four blues enthusiasts, Jim O'Neal, Amy van Singel, Paul Garon, and Bruce Iglauer, in 1970. The magazine moved its center of publication to the University of Mississippi in 1983. Unlike the focus on historical performers and 78 rpm recordings in British magazines *Blues Unlimited* and *Blues World*, the founders of *Living Blues* (the name was suggested by Iglauer) wanted the magazine to feature living practitioners of the blues. In the magazine's first issue, the editors write, "Blues speaks for itself. We do not intend to explain, define, or confine the blues. We believe that the blues is a living tradition, and we hope to present some insights into this tradition."

At the heart of every issue of *Living Blues* are the interviews. These tend to be much longer than ones published in other music magazines and provide a wealth of information directly from the mouths of blues performers. These interviews provide the basis for *The Voice of the Blues: Classic Interviews from "Living Blues Magazine."* The previously married Jim O'Neal and Amy van Singel selected and edited interviews with thirteen bluesmen and one blues woman that had previously appeared in *Living Blues* before 1985. Most of the interviews were conducted in the early 1970s by O'Neal and van Singel. Other interviewers include Kip Lornell, Bill Lindemann, Tim Schuller, Bruce Iglauer, Hans Shweitz, Janne Rosenqvist, Linn Summers, and Bob Scheir. The introduction states, "We present these interviews in the spirit in which they were shared with us—to help us understand not only the music but also the life experiences that created the blues." In the foreword, Peter Guralnick notes that the *Living Blues* interviewers had a way of setting interview subjects at ease, allowing them to give more open answers in ways many other interviewers don't. He adds, "Carefully edited and conscientiously presented less as conclusions than as loosely guided journeys, these interviews can read sometimes like elegant memoirs, gently supported by the soft murmur of conversation." The words of interviewees are kept intact, though the editors clarify ambiguities and complete dates and names to provide a more user-friendly read.

Along with giving the date, location, and original publication information, contextual remarks about each musician are provided at the beginning of each interview. Several of the interviews are expanded from the earlier printings in the magazine, including portions of the interviews that weren't originally printed. O'Neal's interview with Houston Stackhouse is almost seventy pages long.

The interviews in *Voice of the Blues* provide a rich source of information about the lives and careers of famous blues musicians like Muddy Waters, John Lee Hooker, T-Bone Walker, Jimmy Reed, and Freddie King, but the book also highlights less popular but no less important figures like Louis Myers, Esther Phillips, and Hammie Nixon.

The interviews give many interesting insights into the music-making process and making money through music. Freddie King discusses anything from his two-finger technique to his guitar tone to how names were chosen for instrumentals. Eddie Boyd talks about the various trials and tribulations of the record industry as well as touring in the 1950s. Some of the gigs required more performers than Boyd had in the band, "So those cats who the union would send to fill in my band and make it the minimum number of men, some of them were those bebop boys and some of them were so antique, he hadn't had a job in 20 years. But he'd just come there and sit on the bandstand and hold his horn." Esther Phillips bemoans so many talented young musicians ignoring the basics: "You know you just can't jump on a Coltrane level when you can't even play a 12-bar blues." Hammie Nixon relates stories of hoboing when times were tough. "Money was very scarce, times were hard, they had soup lines everywhere. . . . Somehow or another, those guys would get money from somewhere. . . . I carried [a] gallon jug back then, had it full of money."

There are also plenty of stories about life that show these musicians as people. Jimmy Reed talks about getting German measles at boot camp. T-Bone Walker describes the effects of stomach surgery on trying to work. Little Walter and Louis Myers reminisce about being stopped by the police for driving all over town in a Lincoln Zephyr with all the doors removed. Houston Stackhouse remembers getting in big trouble with his parents for drinking canned heat with Tommy Johnson: "Mama and them was mad with Tommy for a long time. I was a minor, you see." John Lee Hooker even expresses his annoyance with a lot of interviewers, explaining, "The first thing they want to know, how old you is, how long you been in the world. I say, 'Is that gonna do you any good? Is that gonna make you feel any better? Or is that gonna put any money in your pocket.'"

In addition to a well-done index, *Voice of the Blues* includes a number of good black-and-white photographs interspersed throughout the book. The book was inducted into the Blues Foundation Hall of Fame in 2012 and received an ASCAP Deems Taylor Award of Special Recognition in 2003.

Readers who enjoy these interviews may also like Steve Cushing's *Blues before Sunrise: The Radio Interviews* (University of Illinois Press, 2010), which features twelve interviews from Chicago Public Radio's (WBEZ) "Blues before Sunrise" radio show. Barry Lee Pearson's *Jook Right On: Blues Stories and Blues Storytellers* (Knoxville: University of Tennessee Press, 2005) includes snippets from almost one hundred interviews conducted over thirty-five years. Also, see the entry (no. 92) for Pearson's *"Sounds So Good to Me": The Bluesman's Story* (University of Pennsylvania Press, 1984). —*GJ*

92. You Know What You're Going to Get Now? Interviews!

"Sounds So Good to Me": The Bluesman's Story. By Barry Lee Pearson. Philadelphia: University of Pennsylvania Press, 1984. ISBN 978-0-8122-1171-9 (paperback), $13.99

Many books about blues examine the music and life of musicians through historical, sociological, musicological, and literary lenses. Regardless of academic approach, most of these works primarily present ideas and information from the researcher. Barry Lee Pearson, in *"Sounds So Good to Me,"* prefers to let the actual words of bluesmen drive the text, reserving his own words to help frame the discussions and arguments.

In the preface, Pearson writes, "I wanted to know what blues musicians generally say about themselves, what that means in relation to the blues tradition, and, to a certain degree, why they say what they say." He noticed similar themes and topics cropping up in interviews with blues musicians he had been conducting for years: "their first instrument, their parents' response to their music, how they learned to play, who inspired them, first jobs, work-related experiences with alcohol, violence, and rips-offs, their relationship with other musicians, and their vision of the future." In *"Sounds So Good to Me,"* Pearson certainly finds much useful information from the stories bluesmen tell, but he examines "the blues artist's story . . . as a creative document in its own right."

Pearson was most interested in the "public figure" of his interview subjects. He wanted to hear how these musicians "present themselves to the public." He uses the first two chapters as good examples of bluesmen's stories, through interviews with David "Honeyboy" Edwards and Johnny Young. In chapter 3, "You Know What You're Going to Get Now? Interviews!," Pearson examines the relationship between interviewer and interviewee and the complex combination of factors that "conspire to make interviews rather formalized exchanges between the bluesman and the outside world." Bluesmen's insights into being interviewed are one of the most interesting sections of the book. They are often asked the same questions and usually develop stock answers and/or respond with what they think the interviewer or audience wants to hear (e.g., stories about Robert Johnson). Pearson also asks veteran blues interviewers Jim O'Neal and Amy van Singel (then O'Neal) about the interview process. In the next five chapters, Pearson looks at the topics or themes that so often appear in blues interviews. Chapter 4, "I'm Gonna Get Me a Guitar If It's the Last Thing I Do," examines stories of musicians' first instruments. Pearson has interesting observations about blues musicians talking among themselves about the qualities of various commercial interests but saving talk of homemade musical instruments for the interviewer. Chapter 5, "They Used to Say It Was the Devil's Music," looks at what musicians have to say about community and family views on blues, especially discussing the blues as the "devil's music." In chapter 6, musicians talk about why they learned blues in the first place and what sustains them as musicians. In chapter 7, "The Wages of Sinful Music," bluesmen talk about the practical nature of playing the blues—making a living. The stresses of playing all night, drinking too much, and getting ripped off by various club owners and record labels are the subjects of chapter 8, "Wasn't Only My Songs, They Got My Music Too." In chapter 9, "Well, That's It, That's My Life Story," Pearson revisits the ideas presented in the third chapter but focuses on the bluesman persona that many musicians put on for the public. He looks at stereotypes perpetuated by white culture but often reinforced by musicians. "I've Had Hard Luck, but It Will Change Some Day," the book's final chapter, relates the many ways bluesmen define the blues and give the value of blues and how this all relates to their life stories, now and what they see for the future.

Portions of interviews with many musicians such as Sam Chatmon, Fred McDowell, Yank Rachel, Johnny Shines, Roosevelt

Sykes, Big Joe Williams, John Cephas, and Otis Rush appear in *"Sounds So Good to Me."* Big Mama Thornton is the only blues woman interviewed by Pearson, and these were only "off-the-cuff remarks" in a conversation with several people. Pearson does, however, include fourteen blues women in his later book *Jook Right On: Blues Stories and Blues Storytellers* (University of Tennessee Press, 2005).

In addition to the cover photo, there are twenty-one black-and-white photographs. Pearson includes extensive endnotes, a bibliography, and an index. The index is missing some key information; for instance, there is no mention of Big Mama Thornton.

While the stories in *"Sounds So Good to Me"* are fascinating in their own right, this book should be essential reading for anyone preparing interviews with musicians, blues or otherwise. Pearson's training as a folklorist and years of interviewing musicians have given him some wonderful insights into the interview process, the influence of previous interviews on both the interviewee and interviewer, and the influence of a tape recorder on what is said.

Barry Lee Pearson is a professor of folklore in the Department of English at the University of Maryland. Portions from more than one hundred interviews can be read in his later book *Jook Right On: Blues Stories and Blues Storytellers.* Pearson is also the author of *Virginia Piedmont Blues: The Lives and Art of Two Virginia Bluesmen* (University of Pennsylvania Press, 1990). For more interviews, see *Voice of the Blues: Classic Interviews from "Living Blues Magazine"* (no. 91). For another book containing shorter interview segments with a large number of musicians, see Paul Oliver's *Conversation with the Blues* (1965; second edition, Cambridge University Press, 1997). Studying *"Sounds So Good to Me"* will provide some interesting insights that may prove beneficial before reading other collections of blues interviews. —*GJ*

93. The Blues Book Most Corrective

Blues, Ideology, and Afro-American Literature: A Vernacular Theory. By Houston A. Baker Jr. Chicago: University of Chicago Press, 1984. ISBN 0-226-03536-0 (hardcover), ISBN 0-226-03538-7 (paperback), $25.00

Houston Baker's *Blues, Ideology, and Afro-American Literature* may contain the most difficult vocabulary among the Blues 100 books for most fans to read. Its sentences are laden with academic jargon and precise philosophical terms. Some words are stubbornly retained, even if they seem unintentionally funny to general readers. One example is "trope," which in plain English may mean "figure of speech" or "metaphor." Baker develops his use of the word "trope" to "tropological" and "tropical," the last term in its context meaning "metaphorical" instead of "sunny and hot." Likewise, a few of his statements use long words in place of short wit. One such sentence occurs in chapter 1 (56): "The commercial, subtextual contours of eighteenth- and nineteenth-century black narratives find their twentieth-century instantiations in works that are frequently called 'classic' but that are seldom decoded in the ideological terms of a traditional discourse." In other words, as Mark Twain had quipped years before, "'Classic'—a book which people praise and don't read."

Once the first thirty pages are read, the rest of the two-hundred-page book becomes easier to understand. Indeed, *Blues, Ideology, and Afro-American Literature* may be the most comprehensive study of African American art, applicable not only to literature but also to oral traditions, games, visual arts, blues music, and other kinds of African American popular music. Since its publication in 1984, its importance has been acknowledged by blues writers like Jon Michael Spencer and Paul Garon and by the many professors who have cited the book in footnotes and bibliographies. However, it is one thing to be told how important a book is; it is another to read its message firsthand. But its academic style will be an obstacle for many readers. To aid them, I offer the following outline in the most plain English I can muster.

The three parts of the book's title correspond to the introduction and the first two chapters. By "blues," Baker means in the introduction (5) not merely the music, but also work songs, sacred music, folk wisdom, political observations, humor, and laments—the overall mind-set of African Americans since their transports to the Americas. By using the optical illusion that may be viewed either as a vase or as two faces looking at each other, Baker shows that the white and Christian perspectives on one hand and the black and African perspectives on the other may be discerned from the same sight. For example, the white/Christian view may yield the form of a vase, but of the same picture the black/African view would recognize two faces in opposing profiles. So also in American history, Baker argues. If the African slaves and their American descendants had been regarded by the white establishment as having no culture and therefore needing Christian indoctrination, the captives and their children saw themselves not as poor but as rich, yet in danger of losing their African domain of culture and ideas. The blues in Baker's large sense is the remembrance and exercise in the Americas of that African domain.

The "ideology" is the way that the African American earns freedom. In the first chapter, Baker shows that the earning is not spiritual, but financial, using as exemplars the published slave narratives by Oladuah Equiano (Gustavus Vassa), Frederick Douglass, and Harriet Jacobs. The way these three slaves became free was not by following Anglo-Christian doctrines but by using a crass American way, that is, by raising enough money to literally pay their prices for freedom with money or bartering leverage. By buying back their freedoms, they could then (48) "enter the kind of relationship disrupted, or foreclosed, by the economics of slavery." Likewise for the emancipated slaves and their present-day African American descendants, who may include musicians, entrepreneurs, hustlers, players—and writers. How they all achieved their self-reliant, self-sufficient freedom as Americans of African descent is through economics, drawing from their retentions of African domain to supply the needs and greeds of American mainstream society. The life of the jazz saxophonist Charlie "Bird" Parker (1920–1955) is a great example of this. From the "vase" perspective of mainstream history, Parker achieved his jazz innovations much too early in his short life, and he died as a discarded, drug-ridden, diseased pauper. But from the "two profiles" view of African Americans, Parker was a hero who used his jazz talents profitably enough to remain unbeholden to the white men who oversaw the entertainment industry; in short, he used the prevailing establishment just like any white man could, and it did not use him. The same may be said of African American bluesmen, too.

The "Afro-American Literature" part of the title is treated in the second chapter. The reader may think "Afro-American" is simply a generic term for the culture, especially in 1984 when this book was published. But it also refers to a 1979 anthology of essays, *Afro-American Literature: The Reconstruction of Instruction*, edited by Dexter Fisher and Robert B. Stepto, to which Baker gives a lengthy critique. This chapter may be of greater interest to literary scholars than to music fans, but its last page should be read for Baker's affirmation that an understanding of the blues in Baker's large sense can lead to unconditional participation in a United States where there is no discrimination. This isn't a matter of whether the vase is half empty or half full but of whether the vase is really two people facing each other. Let's hope the people are doing so in order to talk.

The remaining third chapter is a grand demonstration of that affirmation in the works of the African American authors Paul Lawrence Dunbar, Richard Wright, and Ralph Ellison. In recent years, book critics have spoken with desire of the (perhaps unattainable) "Great American Novel," usually suggesting novels by white writers. True to his vision, Baker resists that label, using instead "The Blues Book Most Excellent," whose criteria are various aspects of the African domain saved in African American cultures. Blues readers should have handy a copy of Ellison's *Invisible Man* (1951; we thought about including it as one of the Blues 100) to follow Baker's masterful interpretation of the sharecropper's dream episode in the novel.

What relevance does *Blues, Ideology, and Afro-American Literature* have for the study of blues as music? For one thing, Baker posits a new picture of the crossroads, not as the intersection of two dusty roads outside town but as the intersection of a road with a railroad track on which the blues travels. It is as if to say that blues culture is more durable than is often acknowledged, and it can lead to (in)sights that may be new to the observer. For another, Baker's example of the vase/profiles optical illusion leads me to think anew of blues melody. African ways of speaking include rising and falling pitches that can alter the meaning of a word. If I understand Baker correctly, this mode of communication among Africans was heard superficially as a kind of music by whites and Christians and transcribed as such in Western musical notation. For many years, the harmonic chords were presented as the consonant standard, to which the "blue notes" in the melody were compared as dissonant and exotic. Recently, though, Gerhard Kubik in *Africa and the Blues* (no. 7) explained that when a native African hears an African American blues, he thinks the chords are dissonant, yet he finds the melodic blue notes consonant with the scales he is accustomed to hearing. If that is the case, then a new history would have to be written on the premise that it is the harmonic chords that sound "wrong" and exotic, not the melodies. The result would be very different from the narratives of Oliver (no. 2), Cohn and his writers (no. 1), and Oakley (no. 4). But in accordance with Baker, we should not view such a new history as revolutionary but rather as corrective. —*EK*

94. Rolling Stones Are Hard to Swallow

The Bluesman: The Musical Heritage of Black Men and Women in the Americas. By Julio Finn. London: Quartet Books, 1986. ISBN 0-704325-23-3. Reprint, Brooklyn: Interlink, 1991. ISBN 0-940793-91-1 (hardcover), ISBN 0-940793-93-8 (paperback). Reprint, 1998. ISBN 0-940793-98-9 (hardcover), ISBN 0-940793-91-1 (paperback)

What should have been asked about the blues, says author Julio Finn in his introduction to *The Bluesman,* were its psychology and spirituality, not its history and sociology. We should have been "looking into their *souls,*" he opines. But what of the autobiographies of many blues musicians that have been published? Had they not spoken from their souls? Finn would say that these books are flawed because of the writers who assisted in writing them. As he says further in the introduction, "Both black and white authors have failed in these attempts to discover the roots of the blues, their mistake being to seek this precious source in the *history* of black Americans."

For his part, Finn is an African American bluesman. He was born Jerome Arnold in 1936; harmonica master Billy Boy Arnold is his brother. Through 1972, he played bass in the bands led by Howlin' Wolf and Paul Butterfield. Since around 1978, his name has been Julio Finn, under which his books are published. Being a bluesman who has performed with Chicago blues legends, Finn should at least be able to look into his own soul. Hence he gives us not a method but a subjective report about "the true nature of the blues and its roots." History-minded blues fans may find that Finn may play with some of the historical facts a little too fast and loose for their liking. Still, they should continue reading for the sake of Finn's overall message.

"The precious source" of the blues, Finn asserts, is voodoo and its related form, hoodoo, the latter which he calls "the secret religion of the Afro-American." For that reason, he begins the book with depictions of blacks living as slaves in colonial Haiti, Jamaica, Cuba, and Brazil. These early chapters are not merely context, but rather they establish an assertive bearing for many of the Africans transported to the New World. By comparison, those in the United States became subdued and deprived of African culture, with the exception of those in New Orleans. Even so, some hoodoo traits were retained and passed down, including the uses of music, dance, charms and fetishes, and rituals and ceremonies. What may seem like an African American Christian celebration, Finn suggests, may be in truth a hoodoo function. So may also be an African American musical performance, particularly the blues performance.

But why single out the blues as hoodoo—why not jazz, too? This question leads to some of the provocative statements in this book. In addition to being hospitable to hoodoo, New Orleans in the Louisiana bayou was the earliest jazz center. Yet being mostly instrumental, jazz repertory contains few lyrics at all, never mind any containing references to hoodoo. But Finn reminds us that "hoodoo tells of supernatural agencies invading reality," and, moreover, hoodoo remembers its origins in the African jungles. It would be a bit much for us to think that hoodoo and blues demand trips to Africa. But if I understand Finn correctly, I think it may be more appropriate for us to regard the African home-lands as the spiritual origins for hoodoo, like the Garden of Eden is for Judaism and Christianity. There are no jungles in the United States, but the nearest type of terrain would be the Louisiana bayou and the Mississippi Delta. It is to those swampy areas that Finn looks for the least diluted forms of hoodoo and for the lyric sources of the blues. The final section, "The Initiations," is confusing to me because I am not sure whether the bayous and the delta are posited as the actual homes of hoodoo and blues or as mythical reminders of the spirituality of hoodoo and blues. That is to say, should I think that Finn believes literally in his depiction of Robert Johnson and the devil at the crossroads as having happened "in the bayous," or instead that he believes spiritually (but not necessarily literally) toward a mystical truth that is not tied to one location? Regardless of which answer to that question is true, at the very least Finn looks to the African American music most associated with the bayous and the Delta, and to his mind, that would be the blues with its hoodoo lyrics, not jazz.

Finn writes with strong feelings, by turns celebratory, solemn, mocking, weepy, angry, and pleading. He has bile for the white slaveowners of the past and for the prevailing white powers in the United States. But he spits a burning venom on the African Americans who since Emancipation have tried to assimilate into the American mainstream (122). "They sought to show the whites that they could be just as 'white' as Europeans! Piteous folly!" he shrieks. Many black readers about the blues may find this denunciation hard to take. But like what Amiri Baraka had advised for the blues in *Blues People* (no. 68), forgetting altogether hoodoo wisdom may be lamentable.

The chief value of Finn's *The Bluesman* is that he reaffirms hoodoo as having a living and abiding relevance to the blues, and in so doing he snatches the religion from the hands of the folklorists who had written abstractly about it. His emotional style may be off-putting to many readers, yet we should remember from him that emotion in hoodoo, not reason, brings the individual into communication with the gods. On the whole, the book's content may be hard for some readers to accept. But in the Cuba chapter, Finn may have anticipated that difficulty. There, he describes "rolling stones," the sacred stones that Africans swallowed and transported in their stomachs during their transport west to the Caribbean and North America. As Finn explains, the swallowers were risking death by choking or stomach ruptures. When a carrier died, his stomach was cut open for the stone, which would then be swallowed by another man. Upon the first such death after landing in the New World, the stone would be saved but this time hidden for slave group use. Likewise, maybe Finn's hoodoo messages in *The Bluesman* are meant to be indigestible to many African Americans and unassimilable to sympathetic whites. Nonetheless, they should be retained. —*EK*

95. And the Blues Was Willie Dixon

I Am the Blues. By Willie Dixon with Don Snowden. New York: Da Capo, 1989. ISBN 978-0-306-80415-1 (paperback), $16.95

I Am the Blues offers readers a look into the rise of Chicago blues from arguably the most important figure in postwar blues history. While well known to blues fans, Willie Dixon is an unfamiliar name to many others. Though he led several bands and played bass with countless musicians, Dixon's songs have become the signature pieces for many of the top blues singers. "Hootchie Cootchie Man," "Wang Dang Doodle," "Spoonful," "Back Door Man," "I Ain't Superstitious," "I Just Want to Make Love to You," "Little Red Rooster," and "My Babe" are just a small sampling of the more than five hundred songs penned by Dixon. Some of the most well-known songs of Muddy Waters, Koko Taylor, Howlin' Wolf, and Little Walter were written by Willie Dixon and later covered by rock bands like Led Zeppelin, the Rolling Stones, the Doors, Elvis Presley, and even Megadeth.

I Am the Blues chronicles all but the last few years of Willie Dixon's life (he died three years after the book was published). According to Dixon, "They've got blues books out there that tell a little bit about everybody—his name and what songs he sang—but they don't have none of the actual blues experience involved." This book does delve into that "blues experience," beginning with Dixon's childhood in and around Vicksburg, Mississippi. His excellent memory brings many of his early memories to light.

His mother's love of poetry inspired Dixon to start writing poems at a young age. The long life span of his songs and the number of bands covering his music is a testament to Dixon's lyrical craftsmanship. But it isn't just clever lyrics that have helped his songs stand the test of time. He also got to hear Little Brother Montgomery play around Vicksburg. This established a firm sense of the blues sound into Dixon. As a young man, Dixon began singing in Leo Phelps's Jubilee Singers. This gave him a good grasp of harmony, allowing for more elaborate arrangements of his later songs.

Dixon grew up relatively poor but saw true poverty in the county outside of Vicksburg, where he worked making charcoal after briefly running away from home for what he thought was a better life. At age twelve, Dixon was arrested for stealing plumbing from an abandoned house. He was later arrested for hoboing, but he escaped from the prison farm and set out traveling all over the country. His work on the prison farm and for the Civilian Conservation Corps, combined with his natural girth, built Dixon into an incredibly strong man. He made his way to Chicago and had a brief but successful boxing career that would have continued had he not gotten into a fight with his manager about money.

Luckily, Dixon had met "Baby Doo" Caston, who encouraged him to pursue music seriously. The two would go on to found the Five Breezes. The piano/vocal group performed until World War II. Dixon was once again sent to jail, this time as a conscientious objector. After the war, Dixon and Caston reunited and, together with Bernardo Dennis (later replaced by Ollie Crawford), formed the Ink Spots–inspired group the Big Three Trio.

Dixon gives a detailed insider's perspective of Chess Records and the Chicago record industry of the 1940s–1950s. In addition to being a studio bass player for Chess, Dixon served as a talent scout, songwriter, engineer, arranger, and just about everything else essential to the operations of making a record.

Chess really established the electric Chicago blues sound and set the stage for rock and roll by recording Muddy Waters, Howlin' Wolf, Little Walter, Lowell Fulson, Chuck Berry, Bo Diddley, and many other seminal artists. While much credit should be given to company owners Leonard and Phil Chess for their role in shaping the history of modern music, they were also known for not paying their artists what they were owed. Indeed, arguments over money make up a significant portion of *I Am the Blues*. Willie Dixon, unlike a number of other blues musicians, was quite financially savvy. He was aware of how he was being ripped off and saw the mechanisms used by the Chess brothers and others in the industry to take advantage of artists. Despite his understanding, Dixon continued working for Chess for more than a decade, needing the money for his family. Frustration with Chess led him to work with Cobra Records and later to run his own label—Yambo.

The bulk of each chapter is told in Willie Dixon's own words. These are supplemented with the words of those who knew and worked with him—people like Leonard "Baby Doo" Caston, Bob Koester, Jimmy Rogers, Buddy Guy, various family members, Marshall Chess, engineers at Chess Records, and many others. Each chapter begins with a historical overview, penned by Don Snowden, of events that will be discussed by Dixon and his associates.

Included are an index, discography, a list of Willie Dixon's labels and releases, a list of Dixon's song titles and bands who covered them, a list of song titles for which Dixon played bass, a list of print resources on Dixon, and a list of film and television segments featuring Willie Dixon. Forty-four black-and-white photo reproductions are included in the center of the book.

I Am the Blues is an enjoyable read. Willie Dixon's stories of growing up in Mississippi, tales of working with all the Chicago blues greats, and his unique perspective of the music industry provide a wealth of fascinating material. The book is much broader than simple autobiography, as Willie Dixon was so integral to the lives of the top Chicago blues artists and had such a profound impact on the sound of postwar blues. His influence was so great that it isn't too much of an exaggeration to say that Willie Dixon was indeed "the blues." —*GJ*

96. No Dope Smoking or Cussing Allowed in Here

Juke Joint. By Birney Imes. Jackson: University Press of Mississippi, 1990. ISBN 0-87805-437-5 (hardcover), ISBN 0-87805-846-X (paperback). Reprint, 2012. ISBN 1-617-03692-7 (hardcover), $45.00

Juke joints (alternately called jook joints, jukes, jooks, or barrel-houses) are generally temporary buildings or rooms that serve as gathering spots for socializing, drinking, gambling, and music primarily by African Americans. In times when black men and women were barred from white clubs and bars and/or Prohibition prevented the sale of alcohol, juke joints provided outlets for socializing and winding down after a workweek. Some jukes were operated legally, while others had no license and operated until shut down by the law. Some were structures dedicated solely to the operation of the juke, while others served one purpose during the work week and transformed on the weekend. There was often a transient nature to juke joints, though some, like Poor Monkey's Lounge in Merigold, Mississippi, have operated for over fifty years. In more recent years, with the end of state-sanctioned segregation and Prohibition, juke joints have largely been replaced with more permanent bars and clubs. A number of bars try to capture the visual aesthetics of juke joints, often incorporating "outsider art" (real or faux). The term "juke joint" seems to have expanded to mean any establishment designed with a "down-home" southern feel that primarily serves up beer and blues.

Photographer Birney Imes's book *Juke Joint* explores the world of jukes through fifty-eight color photographs. Covering Mississippi, Imes takes us into the Evening Star Lounge in Falcon, Bell's Place in Yazoo City, the Pink Pony Café in Darling, Shorty's Place in Artesia, the Skin Man Place in Belzoni, and many more. Many of these jukes no longer exist.

While black-and-white photography offers a certain richness, depth, intimacy, and seriousness often lacking in color photography, the color images in *Juke Joint* are stunning. In a way, they are like the first viewing of the Farm Security Administration/Office of War Information photographs of the Great Depression in color after having seen only black-and-white images of this time period (the Library of Congress made these public in the 2006 exhibition "Bound for Glory: America in Color" and placed digital copies online in 2010—http://www.loc.gov/pictures/collection/fsac/).

But unlike the dissolution of the sense of time between modern viewers and the 1930s and 1940s in those Library of Congress photographs, Birney Imes's color images from the 1980s create an almost otherworldly feeling. Many of the shots are the result of a long exposure time, which results in extreme clarity of structures, but moving people appear blurry, almost ghostlike.

In the introductory essay, Pulitzer Prize–winning author Richard Ford writes, "So appealing in Birney Imes's photographs is the sensation they create in us that here we are being shown, are even intruding on things—expressions of face, dispositions of furniture in rooms, eventful effects of light—that have not been shown before and that seem secret, even forbidden, exotic to us, even though we may have stood in these very rooms and roads ourselves, or believe we know what lies outside each frame."

These images don't focus on the music; indeed, other than several shots of jukeboxes, the only photograph alluding to music simply shows several amps and a drum kit sitting alone on a stage at Booba Barnes's (Imes misspells it "Burns") place in Greenville. These are images capturing the essence of place and those who frequent jukes. They show the visual expressiveness of the same culture that birthed the blues. The photos show hand-drawn signs banning the smoking of dope, warning of the dangers of crack, and asking people to refrain from bad language. These are photos of decaying structures at the heart of poverty and the many colorful ways owners have decorated and painted them. Imes captured mostly interior shots. Only eight photos are exterior shots of juke joints.

Other than the introductory essay and photo captions, the only other text in *Juke Joint* is Birney Imes's afterword, where Imes explains his photographic process.

Juke Joint was reprinted in hardcover in 2012. The newer printing lists for forty-five dollars. The more collectable 1990 printing can be found new for seventy dollars and up or used for less.

Ken Murphy and Scott Barretta's book *Mississippi: State of Blues* (Jackson, MS: Proteus Publications, 2010) features excellent color photography of twenty-first-century juke joints and blues festivals. Photographer Bill Steber has taken some incredible black-and-white shots of juke joints over the past twenty years. His work is regularly featured in *Living Blues* magazine. His photos for Barry Lee Pearson's article "Jook Women" (*Living Blues* 169, 2003) are particularly noteworthy. —*GJ*

97. Talking about Lucille and Other Battle-Axes

Blues Guitar: The Men Who Made the Music. By Jas Obrecht. San Francisco: GPI Books, 1990. Expanded and updated second edition, 1993. ISBN 0-87930-188-0. Second edition, ISBN 0-87930-292-5

While W. C. Handy wrote about hearing a guitarist playing what can be described as blues as early as 1903, it would be almost twenty years before blues guitar would be recorded. The earliest blues recordings featured female singers like Alberta Hunter, Ethel Waters, Lucille Hegamin, and the unrelated "Smiths"—Mamie, Bessie, Clara, and Trixie. These singers came out of vaudeville, cabaret, and minstrel-show traditions, which featured solo singers backed by small jazzlike ensembles of piano, trumpet, trombone, clarinet, saxophones, and other instrumentation. Guitar wasn't featured in blues recordings until Sylvester Weaver's "Guitar Blues" was recorded in 1923. His guitar can also be heard accompanying a Sara Martin recording that same year. The recording of country blues (what Jeff Todd Titon calls "downhome blues") artists wasn't until 1924, when Atlanta guitarist Ed Andrews was recorded for Okeh. The earliest fairly well-known rural songster/bluesman to record was Papa Charlie Jackson, who also recorded in 1924, though he mostly played banjo guitar, a six-string banjo tuned like a guitar. The most influential of the early blues guitarists were recorded in the latter half of the 1920s. The first recordings of Blind Lemon Jefferson and Blind Blake were cut in 1926. Tommy Johnson, Bo Carter, Scrapper Blackwell, and Tampa Red's first sides appeared in 1928. First recorded in 1925, Lonnie Johnson would influence countless blues, jazz, and rock guitarists. His playing helped pave the way to the development of the guitar solo within a song. Known as the "father of the Delta blues," Charlie Patton first recorded in 1929. Patton's sound would greatly influence the development of the blues. The 1930s saw the first recordings of Son House, Skip James, and Robert Johnson. These and other guitarists recorded in the 1920s and 1930s would have a profound influence on later blues guitarists like Muddy Waters, Robert Nighthawk, Elmore James, and Buddy Guy, as well as rock guitarists like Jimmy Page, Keith Richards, and Jimi Hendrix.

Blues Guitar is a wonderful tribute to a number of key blues guitarists from the 1920s to today. The chapters are all articles written by Jas Obrecht that first appeared in *Guitar Player* magazine.

Obrecht has devoted his life to writing about the guitar as well as blues and rock guitarists. He served as editor of *Guitar Player* for twenty years and is the author of several guitar-based books, including *Rollin' and Tumblin': The Postwar Blues Guitarists* (San Francisco: Miller Freeman Books, 2000). *Blues Guitar* is divided into two sections: "Country Roots" and "Prime Movers." The first section is a tribute to the prewar blues guitarists who paved the way for everyone else. Here, Obrecht focuses not only on prewar guitarists like Robert Johnson and Skip James but on the next several generations of blues guitarists who followed in their country blues tradition, musicians like Robert Junior Lockwood, Mississippi Fred McDowell, Mance Lipscomb, Son Thomas, R. L. Burnside, and others. In the second half of the book, Obrecht gives attention to postwar electric blues performers and the generations of blues guitarists they inspired. Some artists featured here are Muddy Waters, John Lee Hooker, B. B. King, Clarence "Gatemouth" Brown, Albert King, Otis Rush, Freddie King, Little Milton, Albert Collins, and more. The majority of chapters in *Blues Guitar* are interviews (not all conducted by Obrecht) with the musicians. While most of the questions obviously relate to guitar (technique, influences, sound, tunings, gear, etc.), they also give wonderful insights into the lives and personalities of the musicians and even offer advice for life. "Gatemouth" Brown, when asked what keeps him growing, stated, "Positive thinking, positive living, treating you like I wished to be treated. . . . We're all people. We need each other. If we don't have each other, what the hell we got?" B. B. King, in responding to an oft-asked question of what he would do differently with his life if given another chance, says, "I would finish high school and go to college and try to learn more about the music, and I wouldn't marry until after 40!" With the exception of the first chapter on Robert Johnson, each chapter concludes with a brief selected discography of the artist's work on solo albums, anthologies, recordings of others, soundtracks, and film.

The second edition adds chapters on Elmore and Homesick James, "Gatemouth" Brown, Little Milton, Robert Junior Lockwood, John Hammond, and Johnny Winter. Obrecht adds to the previous chapters on B. B. King, Albert Collins, Otis Rush, John Lee Hooker, Buddy Guy, Robert Johnson, and Muddy Waters. He also completely replaces the earlier Johnny Shines interview with a different one. There is also a new interview between B. B. King and John Lee Hooker. A really interesting update to the second edition is an assignment Obrecht had for *Blues Revue Quarterly*, where Obrecht met with John Lee Hooker to play records of musicians like T-Bone Walker, Albert King, Blind Blake, Lucille Bogan, Robert Johnson, and others. After and during the playing of select songs, Hooker would comment on the songs, discussing anything from musical characteristics, to describing "The Dirty Dozens," to reminiscing about musicians he knew. Obrecht also updates all of the discographies in the 1993 edition.

The book is true to its subtitle in that it covers only bluesmen; no female blues performers are covered, even in the second edition. Obrecht doesn't just focus on black blues guitarists, though; the book features chapters on white guitarists John Hammond, Michael Bloomfield, and Johnny Winter.

The book makes an important contribution to our understanding of key blues guitarists. While any aspiring blues guitarist will want a copy of *Blues Guitar*, it has broader appeal to any general blues fan.

Used copies of both editions can be purchased for as low as $3.94 or found in numerous libraries. —*GJ*

98. I Want Somebody to Tell Me What "Lord Have Mercy" Means

Blues and Evil. By Jon Michael Spencer. Knoxville: University of Tennessee Press, 1993. ISBN 0-87049-782-0 (hardcover), ISBN 0-87049-783-9 (paperback), $19.95

For many years, it was thought by blues scholars that blues and religion did not mix. In 1986, in his book *The Bluesman* (no. 94), Julio Finn pointed out it was blues and Christianity in particular that did not mix; nonetheless, he added, blues and some African American religions did mix, especially hoodoo. While Finn had shown many readers how to think about the blues in ways new to them, new questions arose. One was why and to what purpose did blues and some black Christian music share some melodies in common? Another question came up in the wake of the success of the 1990 CD reissue of Robert Johnson's complete recordings. White fans especially were asking, "Did Robert Johnson really sell his soul to the devil?" But the deeper issue within that question was about the nature of the devil. Was the devil a red-skinned agent of evil who rewarded his followers with eternal torments? Or was he simply an eight-foot man who tuned guitars for free? The writings about Robert Johnson published during the 1990s that tried to answer those questions often failed and verged on the ludicrous.

In 1993, much sense was provided by Jon Michael Spencer through his book *Blues and Evil*. Today his name is Yahya Jongintaba (by which I will refer to him in the rest of this entry), and he now lives in East Africa. In the early 1990s, for Duke University Press he edited the journal *Black Sacred Music: A Journal of Theomusicology*. Some of its book-length issues were written entirely by him, bringing to bear everything he had learned to date about music and theology. In the midst of this productive activity, he wrote *Blues and Evil* to expound to blues readers the religious nature of the blues. This timely corrective has held up remarkably well through the years because of its deeply informed answers. Because it was written for an academic press, general readers will have to be patient with some of its terms and specialized jargon.

Jongintaba presents first the "mythologies" and "theologies" contained in the blues. The chapter on mythology is rooted in conventional Christianity and two myths derived from the Bible. One myth is the fall of Adam, a manifestation of which is the prodigal son who returns to civility after living in rampant sin. The other is the "tragic hero" who is presumed guilty, even when he has committed no crime or faults. The bluesman may be viewed as both, as a prodigal son by Christians and as a tragic hero by black society. In black folklore, there is the trickster personage called Legba, who is often described as having magical conjuring powers. Jongintaba advises that we should not be so hasty in attributing magic to Legba, rather that he should be recognized for embodying non-magical qualities like trickiness, capriciousness, lawlessness, and sexuality. For those qualities, Legba should be regarded not as a malice who gums up social works and ruins personal efforts but as a liberating force who (to quote Jongintaba) "enlarge[s] the scope of the human." Hence, the shift from trickster Legba to bad man to bluesman is recorded in the surviving lore from the 1880s through the 1920s. So why go to a crossroads to meet the devil? Jongintaba answers by saying, foremost, that the devil is "not the terror that he was in early modern European religious belief and lore." Rather, he represents the deepest font of hoodooism and, by inference of his location at the crossroads outside of town, a kind of "back to nature" attitude.

For all its affirmation of hoodoo values, the blues is nonetheless positive about Christian expressions, to the extent of referring to the Lord and occasionally using sacred music melodies. Jongintaba goes so far as to demonstrate a theology from the blues perspective in which bluesmen have accused in return the denunciations from preachers of indulging in food, drink, and women, as may be heard in Charlie Patton's "Elder Greene Blues." Moreover, some bluesmen have shown by example that there may be social "justifications" and "exonerations" acceptable to God that need no approval from sacred congregations. Even so, as Jongintaba suggests, there is no greater drama than the reformed bluesman preaching on the pulpit.

In addition to mythology and theology, Jongintaba explores one more area, theodicy, which is the defense of a perfect God despite an imperfect world where evil exists. In the world where blues is a social force, Jongintaba takes the perspective of a laboring African American "blues person" who doesn't view the bluesman as evil. Rather, such a laborer may use the crossroads figure as a standard to realize fully the prevailing systemic imbalances of mainstream American Christianity, business, and social rights. Jongintaba finds in theodicy through the blues not an answer but a blunt practical question per Little Hat Jones in "New Two Sixteen Blues": "I want somebody to tell me what 'Lord have mercy' means." If evil is to be associated with the blues, it isn't in the singer but in whom or what he or she is singing about.

In *The Bluesman*, Finn scolded those African Americans who had moved to the cities and forgotten the hoodoo roots of their rural lives. In his lengthy conclusion to *Blues and Evil*, Jongintaba keeps a cooler head, asking not "how dared we forget" but "how did we forget?" He seeks an answer through the history of the Great Migration of black labor and with the use of Keil's (no. 76) three-part transition of rural blues through city blues to urban blues. His inquiry assigns historically religious functions to the vocal expressions classified by Keil, so that (137) "country blues was a product of the mythological world . . . city blues was transitional religiously," and urban blues was "denatured" of the rural mythology. Keil had noted that urban bluesmen made their blues generic in order to make them appealing through the media to mass audiences. Jongintaba doesn't blame the musicians for forgetting that the devil at the crossroads was once considered kind. Instead, he blames the audiences. —*EK*

99. The Tough Times Haven't Left—
They Have Merely Changed

Chicago Blues: Portraits and Stories. By David Whiteis.
Urbana: University of Illinois Press, 2006. ISBN 0-252-
03068-0 (hardcover), ISBN 0-252-07309-0 (paperback),
$21.00

I wish the indexer for David Whiteis's *Chicago Blues: Portraits and Stories* could have included the phrase "set list from hell." So let me say that it appears on page 182. This kind of set list contains the songs so overplayed that even the musicians don't care to hear them again, never mind to play them. Whiteis lists as blues examples "Sweet Home Chicago," "Got My Mojo Workin'," and "Hoochie Coochie Man." Then again, Whiteis hasn't viewed blues as "roots music." Rather than bemoaning what Chicago blues once was, he has listened to and accepted what Chicago blues continues to be. The articles and interviews that he has published in *Living Blues* magazine are the results of finding and talking with the people. The chapters in *Chicago Blues* are more about the searches, during which the blues does not present itself initially when the places and people are found. Some of the reasons why the blues isn't readily apparent have to do with that "set list from hell." There is only so much a contemporary musician can take. Singers Sharon Lewis and Cicero Blake told Whiteis they can't bother anymore with the boogie-shuffle "lump-de-dump-de-dump music" (5) in 12/8 meter. So what now for Chicago blues?

At the outset of his "journey of discovery" (2), Whiteis chooses his "elders" carefully: Junior Wells, Sunnyland Slim, and Big Walter Horton, none of them guitar players and none with songs that became hits for rock stars. But for all of their fame, these three men stayed active in the local African American blues scene until their deaths, staying in contact with the audiences for whom the venues were as much for living as for entertainment. Then he looks at two places past, Florence's Lounge and the Maxwell Street Market, evoking their sights and sounds and celebrating the blues heard there without overrating or romanticizing his memories of them.

It is with the chapter on the current Chicago clubs that Whiteis introduces the present. Especially important is the section on Denise LaSalle's performance at the ballroom of the East of the Ryan motel. Since the 1970s, LaSalle has been the queen of soul blues and one of the chief draws on the African American music circuit. Blues purists may call her music "soul." But her fans know her hits "Drop That Zero" and "My Tu-Tu," and they often call them "blues." However one may disagree with her audience's use of the word "blues," one has to respect it—and understand it. Whiteis reinforces this lesson near the end of the book with the example of Cicero Blake, a singer who considers R. Kelly as having as much blues feeling as anyone singing twelve-measure blues. For more on what is "pure" and "authentic" in Chicago blues, one should read David Grazian's *Blue Chicago: The Search for Authenticity in Urban Blues Clubs* (Chicago: University of Chicago Press, 2003).

The remainder of *Chicago Blues* is devoted to profiles of musicians who are trying in musical and personal ways to broaden what is meant by the word "blues." Whiteis shows in the chapters on Sharon Lewis and Lurrie Bell that the tough times haven't left African Americans on the South and West Sides of Chicago; they have simply changed, which led the blues musicians to sing and play the blues according to the new situations. Billy Branch, on the other hand, tries to sustain the blues past; that means that he isn't afraid to play a song from the set list from hell if an appropriate occasion calls for it (but the occasion would have to be absolutely appropriate). Jody Williams and Bonnie Lee embody the postwar blues past from opposite extremes of recognition. During the 1950s, Williams was one of the promising young guitarists in Chicago blues, a contemporary of Bo Diddley, and one of Howlin' Wolf's most trusted sidemen. After army service in 1958–1960, Williams refrained from performing until 2000, and then only on his own terms. Bonnie Lee has similar terms for performing, but she earned them with more difficulty than Williams, as she never had that early spell of commercial recognition that Williams once enjoyed.

What does the current status of blues in Chicago amount to? Whiteis looks not to the "touristy" North Side where the "set list from hell" is played in many clubs and bars. Instead, he points to the places where the audience may contain several blues and soul stars such as Artie White or where the stage may feature someone like Little Scotty, whom the audience had seen often among them. For these singers and their communities, participation isn't enough. There are times in a performance when a responder gives the call and the caller helps to lead the response. For Whiteis, such moments make for blues heaven, and their absence can lead to blues hell. They may be found in the blues of the past and in the blues and soul in our present. Whiteis notes that Chris Thomas King has been developing rap as an extension of the blues, which may be understandable in principle if not in performance. Whiteis prudently withholds judgment on King's effort— "it is too early to tell"—but by insisting in the book's final pages on both the music and dance of the blues, he seems to expect King's rap to allow the intermixing of the caller/responder roles found in blues and soul heaven. —*EK*

100. A Living Link

When I Left Home: My Story. By Buddy Guy with David Ritz. Boston: Da Capo, 2012. ISBN 978-0-306-81957-5 (hardcover), ISBN 978-0-306-82107-3 (paperback), $15.99

Buddy Guy has been one of the most influential guitarists to several generations of blues and rock musicians, such as Eric Clapton, Jimmy Page, Stevie Ray Vaughan, Keith Richards, and even Jimi Hendrix. Buddy Guy is a recipient of the National Medal of Arts and Kennedy Center Honors, a member of the Blues, Rock and Roll, and Louisiana Halls of Fame, and a winner of multiple Grammy and W. C. Handy awards.

George "Buddy" Guy was born in Lettsworth, Louisiana, in 1936. Guy fondly remembers the day in 1949 when his family first got electricity and purchased a record player. Hearing "Boogie Chillen" profoundly impacted him: "When the man said, 'Mama told Papa, let the boy boogie woogie,' I figured that this John Lee Hooker had to be talking about me. I figured that one way or the other I had to get me a guitar." Like many other children who would go on to become blues guitarists, Buddy Guy began playing a homemade diddley bow. His father later helped set Guy on an eventual path to stardom by purchasing his first guitar. Guy's musicality progressed quickly, and he soon began playing gigs in southern Louisiana. In 1957, Buddy Guy left Louisiana to try to make it in Chicago. Breaking into an already strong blues scene proved difficult, and Guy was almost ready to go home when Otis Rush let him play guitar with him onstage at the 708 Club. Guy's incredible playing that night won over the crowd and got the attention of Muddy Waters. Through these connections, Buddy Guy began gigging all over Chicago as a sideman with Muddy

Waters and others. He also worked as a studio guitarist at Chess; his playing can be heard on recordings by Howlin' Wolf, Koko Taylor, Muddy Waters, and others. He would later get the opportunity to record his own music.

When I Left Home passionately relates Buddy Guy's life story. While remembering the good times, he doesn't gloss over the negative experiences. Numerous anecdotes describe the two sides of Junior Wells: "Sober Junior would give you the shirt off his back and the last dollar in his wallet. . . . Drunk Junior was a different deal. He could get ornery, mean, and downright evil." Like many other Chicago musicians, Buddy Guy also complains about the unfair practices of the Chess brothers, but he also is critical of Willie Dixon. While Dixon is often used as one of the most popular examples of a blues musician whose songs were ripped off by others, Guy claims that Dixon was doing the same thing, by putting his name on song credits and leaving others' names off.

Buddy Guy largely fell out of public attention until the late 1980s. As it took years for Buddy Guy to receive the international recognition he deserved, one could think this autobiography would be one of anger or jealousy. But while he is clear to set several records straight, Guy's story is optimistic and filled with praise and thanks for those, like B. B. King, who inspired him. He fondly remembers and honors those who made his career possible.

Buddy Guy is one of the most important living links between the early years of Chicago blues and blues and rock today. Not only did Guy influence the playing of numerous guitarists, his showmanship had a profound effect on many aspiring rock musicians. Learning early on that good musicianship alone wasn't enough to win over an audience, Buddy Guy became the consummate showman, playing his guitar behind his head (like Charlie Patton and others before him) or walking offstage to play a guitar solo in the middle of the audience. Guy knew when to be a showman and when to show restraint as a sideman, particularly in the studio: "Support the star. Help the star sound better. Don't worry about bringing no attention to me because the session ain't about me. Stay the hell out of the spotlight." His stories of the men and women who helped shape modern blues offer an important perspective.

Coauthor David Ritz also collaborated on autobiographies of Ray Charles, Etta James, and others. Ritz does an excellent job presenting the feel of Guy's speech patterns and phrasing. The overall effect is of Buddy Guy talking directly to the reader.

In addition to an index, there is a very brief selected discography and sixteen black-and-white photographs. Those wanting to learn more about Buddy Guy and see more photographs of him will also want to read *Damn Right I've Got the Blues: Buddy Guy and the Blues Roots of Rock-and-Roll* by Donald Wilcock with Buddy Guy (San Francisco: Woodford Press, 1993). This book features over 120 black-and-white photographs and quotes from numerous associates of Guy. There are several guitar technique books devoted to Buddy Guy's style, of which Dave Rubin's *The Best of Buddy Guy: A Step-by-Step Breakdown of His Guitar Styles and Techniques* (Hal Leonard, 2009) is particularly good. *The Buddy Guy Anthology* (Hal Leonard, 2010) contains good transcriptions of Buddy Guy songs and solos on record.

This book highlights the story of a musician inspired by the Chicago blues pioneers of the 1940s and 1950s and his influence on later generations. Those wanting to read about the lives of musicians influenced by Buddy Guy and others may enjoy Art Tipaldi's *Children of the Blues* (San Francisco: Backbeat Books, 2002). —*GJ*

THE PLAYLIST

Nothing but the Blues: The Music and the Musicians edited by Lawrence Cohn (1993)
> **Song:** "How Blue Can You Get" performed by B. B. King. *Live from the Regal.* MCA-ABC Paramount, 1964.

The Story of the Blues by Paul Oliver (1969; 2nd ed., 1997)
> **Song:** "Pratt City Blues" performed by Bertha "Chippie" Hill. Okeh, 1926.

12-Bar Blues: The Complete Guide for Guitar by Dave Rubin (1999)
> **Song:** "Good Morning Little School Girl" performed by Junior Wells and Buddy Guy. *Hoodoo Man Blues.* Delmark, 1965.

The Devil's Music: A History of the Blues by Giles Oakley (1976; 2nd ed., 1997)
> **Song:** "Devil's Got the Blues" performed by Lonnie Johnson. Decca, 1938.

Nobody Knows Where the Blues Come From: Lyrics and History edited by Robert Springer (2006)
> **Song:** "Papa's on the House Top" performed by Leroy Carr. Vocalion, 1930.

Savannah Syncopators: African Retentions in the Blues by Paul Oliver (1970)
> **Song:** "Praise Song" performed by Kunaal and Sosira (recorded in the field by Paul Oliver, 1964). *Yonder Come the Blues.* Document, 2001.

Africa and the Blues by Gerhard Kubik (1999)
> **Song:** "Mean Conductor Blues" performed by Ed Bell. Paramount, 1927.

The Spirituals and the Blues by James H. Cone (1972)
> **Song:** "Let Your Light Shine on Me" performed by Blind Willie Johnson. Columbia, 1929.

Out of Sight: The Rise of African American Popular Music 1889–1895 by Lynn Abbott and Doug Seroff (2002)
> **Song:** "Poor Mourner" performed by Cousins and DeMoss. Berliner, 1897.

Ragged but Right: Black Traveling Shows, "Coon Songs," and the Dark Pathway to Blues and Jazz by Lynn Abbott and Doug Seroff (2007)
> **Song:** "All Birds Look Like Chicken to Me" performed by Sweet Papa Stovepipe. Paramount, 1926.

Long Lost Blues: Popular Blues in America, 1850–1920 by Peter Muir (2010)
> **Song:** "Jelly Roll Blues" performed by Jelly Roll Morton. Gennett, 1924.

Father of the Blues: An Autobiography by W. C. Handy; edited by Arna Bontemps; foreword by Abbe Niles (1941)
> **Song:** "St. Louis Blues" performed by Bessie Smith with Louis Armstrong. Columbia, 1925.

Born with the Blues: Perry Bradford's Own Story; The True Story of the Pioneering Blues Singers and Musicians in the Early Days of Jazz by Perry Bradford (1965)
> **Song:** "Crazy Blues" performed by Mamie Smith. Okeh, 1920.

Big Road Blues: Tradition and Creativity in the Folk Blues by David Evans (1982)

Song: "Big Road Blues" performed by Tommy Johnson. Victor, 1928.

Mother of the Blues: A Study of Ma Rainey by Sandra Lieb (1981)
Song: "Shave 'Em Dry Blues" performed by Ma Rainey. Paramount, 1924.

Bessie by Chris Albertson (1972; revised and expanded ed., 2003)
Song: "I Need a Little Sugar in My Bowl" performed by Bessie Smith. Columbia, 1931.

Black Pearls: Blues Queens of the 1920s by Daphne Duval Harrison (1987)
Song: "Wild Women Don't Have the Blues" performed by Ida Cox. Paramount, 1924.

Memphis Blues and Jug Bands by Bengt Olsson (1970)
Song: "Cocaine Habit Blues" performed by Memphis Jug Band. Victor, 1930.

Songsters and Saints: Vocal Traditions on Race Records by Paul Oliver (1984)
Song: "The Half Ain't Never Been Told" performed by Rev. F. W. McGee. Victor, 1928.

Paramount's Rise and Fall by Alex van der Tuuk (2003; revised and expanded ed., 2012)
Song: "Got The Blues" performed by Blind Lemon Jefferson. Paramount, 1926.

78 Blues: Folksongs and Phonographs in the American South by John Minton (2008)
Song: "Special Agent (Railroad Police Blues)" performed by Sleepy John Estes. Decca, 1938.

Blues Legacies and Black Feminism: Gertrude "Ma" Rainey, Bessie Smith, and Billie Holiday by Angela Y. Davis (1998)
Song: "Strange Fruit" performed by Billie Holiday. Commodore, 1939.

Stomping the Blues by Albert Murray (1976; revised ed., 1989)
>   **Song:** "C-Jam Blues" performed by Duke Ellington. RCA-Victor, 1942.

Long Steel Rail: The Railroad in American Folksong by Norm Cohen (1981; 2nd ed., 2000)
>   **Song:** "Railroadin' Some" performed by Henry Thomas. Vocalion, 1929.

The Life and Legend of Leadbelly by Charles Wolfe and Kip Lornell (1992)
>   **Song:** "Bottle Up and Go" performed by Leadbelly. Library of Congress, 1940.

Kansas City Jazz: From Ragtime to Bebop by Frank Driggs and Chuck Haddix (2005)
>   **Song:** "Confessin' the Blues" performed by Jay McShann with Walter Brown. Decca, 1941.

Red River Blues: The Blues Tradition in the Southeast by Bruce Bastin (1986)
>   **Song:** "Statesboro Blues" performed by Blind Willie McTell. Victor, 1928.

Crying for the Carolines by Bruce Bastin (1971)
>   **Song:** "Red River Blues" performed by Buddy Moss. Vocalion, 1933.

The Bluesmen by Samuel Charters (1967)
>   **Song:** "Parchman Farm Blues" performed by "Bukka" White. Okeh, 1940.

Early Downhome Blues: A Musical and Cultural Analysis by Jeff Todd Titon (1977; 2nd ed., 1994)
>   **Song:** "M & O Blues" performed by Willie Brown. Paramount, 1930.

A Blues Life by Henry Townsend as told to Bill Greensmith (1999)
>   **Song:** "Cairo Is My Baby's Home" performed by Henry Townsend. *Tired of Bein' Mistreated.* Prestige/Bluesville, 1961.

The Devil's Son-in-Law: The Story of Peetie Wheatstraw and His Songs by Paul Garon (1971; revised and expanded ed., 2003)
> **Song:** "Devil's Son-in-Law" performed by Peetie Wheatstraw. Bluebird, 1931.

Deep South Piano: The Story of Little Brother Montgomery by Karl Gert zur Heide (1970)
> **Song:** "Vicksburg Blues" performed by Little Brother Montgomery. Paramount, 1930.

Searching for Robert Johnson by Peter Guralnick (1989)
> **Song:** "Hell Hound on My Trail" performed by Robert Johnson. Vocalion, 1937.

The Road to Robert Johnson: The Genesis and Evolution of Blues in the Delta from the Late 1800s through 1938 by Edward Komara (2007)
> **Songs:** "I Believe I'll Make a Change" performed by Leroy Carr and Scrapper Blackwell. Vocalion, 1934; and "I Believe I'll Dust My Broom" performed by Robert Johnson. Vocalion, 1936.

Escaping the Delta: Robert Johnson and the Invention of the Blues by Elijah Wald (2004)
> **Songs:** "King of Spades" performed by Peetie Wheatstraw. Vocalion, 1935; and "Little Queen of Spades" performed by Robert Johnson. Vocalion, 1937.

Hard Luck Blues: Roots Music Photographs from the Great Depression by Rich Remsberg (2010)
> **Song:** "One o'Clock Jump" performed by Count Basie. Decca, 1937.

Woman with Guitar: Memphis Minnie's Blues by Paul and Beth Garon (1992)
> **Song:** "When the Levee Breaks" performed by Memphis Minnie and Kansas Joe McCoy. Columbia, 1929.

The Rise of Gospel Blues: The Music of Thomas Andrew Dorsey in the Urban Church by Michael W. Harris (1992)
> **Song:** "If You See My Saviour" performed by Thomas Dorsey. Vocalion, 1932.

Chasin' That Devil Music: Searching for the Blues by Gayle Dean Wardlow (1998)
> **Song:** "Trouble Hearted Blues" performed by Ishmon (Ishman) Bracey. Victor, 1928.

Blues and Gospel Records, 1890–1943 compiled by Robert M. W. Dixon, John Godrich, and Howard Rye (4th ed., 1997)
> **Song:** "Phonograph Blues" performed by Robert Johnson. Vocalion, 1936.

Roosevelt's Blues: African-American Blues and Gospel Songs on FDR by Guido van Rijn (1997)
> **Song:** "President Blues (President Roosevelt Blues)" performed by Jack Kelly. Banner, 1933.

Lost Delta Found: Rediscovering the Fisk University-Library of Congress Coahoma County Study, 1941–1942 by John W. Work, Lewis Wade Jones, and Samuel C. Adams Jr.; edited by Robert Gordon and Bruce Nemerov (2005)
> **Song:** "Country Blues" performed by Muddy Waters. Library of Congress, 1941.

The Land Where the Blues Began by Alan Lomax (1993)
> **Song:** "Carrier Line" performed by Sid Hemphill. Library of Congress, 1942.

The World Don't Owe Me Nothing: The Life and Times of Delta Bluesman Honeyboy Edwards by David "Honeyboy" Edwards (1997)
> **Song:** "Gamblin' Man" performed by Honeyboy Edwards. *Old Friends, Together for the First Time.* Earwig, 1979.

Deep Blues by Robert Palmer (1981)
> **Song:** "Black Angel Blues" performed by Robert Nighthawk. Aristocrat, 1949.

Chicago Blues: The City & the Music/Chicago Breakdown by Mike Rowe (1973)
> **Song:** "Juke" performed by Little Walter. Chess, 1952.

Can't Be Satisfied: The Life and Times of Muddy Waters by Robert Gordon (2002)

Song: "I Can't Be Satisfied" performed by Muddy Waters. Aristocrat, 1947.

Spinning Blues into Gold: The Chess Brothers and the Legendary Chess Records by Nadine Cohodas (2000)
Song: "Little Village" performed by Sonny Boy Williamson (II). Chess, 1957.

Stormy Monday: The T-Bone Walker Story by Helen Oakley Dance (1987)
Song: "Stormy Monday" performed by T-Bone Walker. Black and White, 1947.

Honkers and Shouters: The Golden Years of Rhythm and Blues by Arnold Shaw (1978)
Song: "Let the Good Times Roll" performed by Louis Jordan. Decca, 1946.

The Chitlin' Circuit and the Road to Rock 'n' Roll by Preston Lauterbach (2011)
Song: "The Natchez Burning" performed by Howlin' Wolf. Chess, 1956.

The Late Great Johnny Ace and the Transition from R&B to Rock 'n' Roll by James M. Salem (1999)
Song: "Pledging My Love" performed by Johnny Ace. Duke/ Peacock, 1954.

Moanin' at Midnight: The Life and Times of Howlin' Wolf by James Segrest and Mark Hoffman (2004; revised ed., 2005)
Song: "Smokestack Lightning" performed by Howlin' Wolf. Chess, 1956.

The Amazing Secret History of Elmore James by Steve Franz (2002)
Song: "Dust My Broom" performed by Elmore James. Trumpet, 1951.

Upside Your Head! Rhythm and Blues on Central Avenue by Johnny Otis with an introduction by George Lipsitz (1993)
Song: "Willie and the Hand Jive" performed by Johnny Otis Show. Capitol, 1958.

Big Bill Blues: William Broonzy's Story by William Broonzy (1955)
> **Song:** "Key to the Highway" performed by Big Bill Broonzy. Okeh, 1941.

I Feel So Good: The Life and Times of Big Bill Broonzy by Bob Riesman (2011)
> **Song:** "I Feel So Good" performed by Big Bill Broonzy. Okeh, 1941.

Going to Cincinnati: A History of the Blues in the Queen City by Steven C. Tracy (1993)
> **Song:** "I'm Going to Cincinnati" performed by Walter Coleman. Decca, 1936.

King of the Queen City: The Story of King Records by Jon Hartley Fox with a foreword by Dave Alvin (2009)
> **Song:** "Big Ten Inch Record" performed by Bull Moose Jackson. King, 1952.

Walking to New Orleans: The Story of New Orleans Rhythm & Blues by John Broven (1974)
> **Song:** "Drunk Again" performed by Champion Jack Dupree. Red Robin, 1953.

I Hear You Knockin': The Sound of New Orleans Rhythm and Blues by Jeff Hannusch a.k.a. Almost Slim (1985)
> **Song:** "I Hear You Knocking" performed by Smiley Lewis. Imperial, 1955.

The Country Blues by Samuel Charters (1959)
> **Song:** "Dark Was the Night, Cold Was the Ground" performed by Blind Willie Johnson. Columbia, 1927.

Blues Fell This Morning: Meaning in the Blues by Paul Oliver with a foreword by Richard Wright (1960; 2nd ed., 1990)
> **Song:** "Waking Blues" performed by Otis Harris. Columbia, 1928.

Living Country Blues by Harry Oster (1969)
> **Song:** "Prisoner's Talking Blues" performed by Robert Pete Williams. Louisiana Folklore Society/Arhoolie, 1959.

The Memphis Blues Again: Six Decades of Memphis Music Photographs by Ernest C. Withers and Daniel Wolff (2001)
> **Song:** "No More Doggin'" performed by Roscoe Gordon. RPM, 1952.

The Blues Line: A Collection of Blues Lyrics compiled by Eric Sackheim with illustrations by Jonathan Shahn (1969)
> **Song:** "High Price Blues" performed by Roosevelt Sykes. Blue Bird, 1945.

Blues People: Negro Music in White America by LeRoi Jones [Imamu Amiri Baraka] (1963)
> **Song:** "Blues Minor" performed by John Coltrane. *Africa/Brass.* Impulse/MCA, 1961.

President Johnson's Blues: African-American Blues and Gospel Songs on LBJ, Martin Luther King, Robert Kennedy and Vietnam, 1963–1968 by Guido van Rijn (2009)
> **Song:** "It's Been a Change" performed by the Staple Singers. Epic, 1966.

Mississippi John Hurt: His Life, His Times, His Blues by Philip R. Ratcliffe (2011)
> **Song:** "Avalon Blues" performed by Mississippi John Hurt. Okeh, 1928.

Preachin' the Blues: The Life and Times of Son House by Daniel Beaumont (2011)
> **Song:** "Preachin' the Blues" parts 1 and 2 performed by Son House. Paramount, 1930.

Between Midnight and Day: The Last Unpublished Blues Archive by Dick Waterman (2003)
> **Song:** "Death Letter Blues" performed by Son House. Columbia, 1965.

Chicago Blues as Seen from the Inside: The Photographs of Raeburn Flerlage by Raeburn Flerlage (2000)
> **Song:** "I Can't Quit You Baby" performed by Otis Rush. Cobra, 1956.

Blues with a Feeling: The Little Walter Story by Tony Glover, Scott Dirks, and Ward Gaines (2002)
>   **Song:** "Juke" performed by Little Walter. Chess/Checker, 1952.

Me and Big Joe by Michael Bloomfield with S. Summerville (1980)
>   **Song:** "Peach Orchard Mama" performed by Big Joe Williams. *Piney Woods Blues.* Delmark, 1958.

Urban Blues by Charles Keil (1966; reprinted with afterword, 1992)
>   **Song:** "I Pity the Fool" performed by Bobby Bland. *Two Steps from the Blues.* Duke/Peacock, 1960.

Burn, Baby! Burn! The Autobiography of Magnificent Montague by Magnificent Montague with Bob Baker (2003)
>   **Song:** "A Change Is Gonna Come" performed by Sam Cooke. RCA Victor, 1964.

Blues from the Delta by William Ferris (1978)
>   **Song:** "Cairo Blues" performed by James "Son" Thomas. Black and Blue, 1986.

Blow My Blues Away by George Mitchell (1971)
>   **Song:** "Shimmy She Wa" performed by Como Fife and Drum with Napoleon Strickland. *The George Mitchell Collection.* Fat Possum, 1967.

Feel Like Going Home: Portraits in Blues and Rock 'n' Roll by Peter Guralnick (1971)
>   **Song:** "So Cold in Vietnam" performed by Johnny Shines. Testament, 1966.

Sweet Soul Music: Rhythm and Blues and the Southern Dream of Freedom by Peter Guralnick (1986)
>   **Song:** "Everybody Needs Somebody to Love" performed by Solomon Burke. Atlantic, 1964.

Sweet as the Showers of Rain by Samuel Charters (1977)
>   **Song:** "How Long" performed by Frank Stokes. Victor, 1928.

I Say Me for a Parable: The Oral Autobiography of Mance Lipscomb, Texas Bluesman as told to and compiled by Glen Alyn (1993)

Song: "Jack O'Diamonds" performed by Mance Lipscomb. *Texas Songster.* Arhoolie, 1960.

How Britain Got the Blues: The Transmission and Reception of American Blues Style in the United Kingdom by Roberta Freund Schwartz (2007)
Song: "I Got My Mojo Working" performed by Blues Incorporated. *R&B from the Marquee.* Decca, 1962.

Lightnin' Hopkins: His Life and Blues by Alan Govenar (2010)
Song: "Short Haired Woman" performed by Lightnin' Hopkins. *Autobiography in Blues.* Tradition, 1959.

Listen to the Blues by Bruce Cook (1973)
Song: "Trying to Take Me for a Ride" performed by Arthur "Big Boy" Crudup. Delmark, 1969.

Blues and the Poetic Spirit by Paul Garon (1975; 2nd ed., 1996)
Song: "Bull Frog Blues" performed by William Harris. Gennett, 1928.

Chicago Soul by Robert Pruter (1991)
Song: "People Get Ready" performed by the Impressions. ABC-Paramount, 1964.

Black Culture and Black Consciousness: Afro-American Folk Thought from Slavery to Freedom by Lawrence W. Levine (1977; 30th anniversary ed., 2007)
Song: "You Don't Know My Mind Blues" performed by Virginia Liston. Okeh, 1923.

The Arrival of B. B. King: The Authorized Biography by Charles Sawyer (1980)
Song: "Paying the Cost to Be the Boss" performed by B. B. King. *Blues on Top of Blues.* Beat Goes On, 1967.

The Voice of the Blues: Classic Interviews from "Living Blues Magazine" edited by Jim O'Neal and Amy van Singel (2002)
Song: "I'm Gettin' Tired" performed by Houston Stackhouse. *Cryin' Won't Help You.* Genes, 1972 (1994).

"Sounds So Good to Me": The Bluesman's Story by Barry Lee Pearson (1984)
> **Song:** "Wild, Wild Woman" performed by Johnny Young. Arhoolie, 1965.

Blues, Ideology, and Afro-American Literature: A Vernacular Theory by Houston A. Baker Jr. (1984)
> **Song:** "Cool Blues" performed by Charlie Parker. Dial, 1947.

The Bluesman: The Musical Heritage of Black Men and Women in the Americas by Julio Finn (1986)
> **Song:** "I Put a Spell on You" performed by Screaming Jay Hawkins. Okeh, 1956.

I Am the Blues by Willie Dixon with Don Snowden (1989)
> **Song:** "Joggie Boogie" performed by Memphis Slim and Willie Dixon. *Songs of Memphis Slim and Willie Dixon.* Folkways Records, 1960.

Juke Joint by Birney Imes (1990)
> **Song:** "Heartbroken Man" performed by Roosevelt "Booba" Barnes. *Heartbroken Man.* Rooster Blues, 1990.

Blues Guitar: The Men Who Made the Music by Jas Obrecht (1990; 2nd ed., 1993)
> **Song:** "Ice Pick" performed by Albert Collins. *Ice Pickin'.* Alligator, 1978.

Blues and Evil by Jon Michael Spencer (1993)
> **Song:** "Evil" performed by Howlin' Wolf. Chess, 1954.

Chicago Blues: Portraits and Stories by David Whiteis (2006)
> **Song:** "Drop That Zero" performed by Denise LaSalle. Malaco, 1990.

When I Left Home: My Story by Buddy Guy with David Ritz (2012)
> **Song:** "Damn Right, I've Got the Blues" performed by Buddy Guy. *Damn Right, I've Got the Blues.* Silvertone, 1991.

APPENDIX
The Books behind
the Blues 100

THOUGH WE DIDN'T INCLUDE FULL ENTRIES FOR MOST OF these reference books in the Blues 100, they are too important to exclude from any examination of the most essential blues books. Reference books aren't necessarily works to be read cover to cover, but they serve as sources for quickly verifying information. The books listed here are some of the most useful sources for any serious blues researcher wanting to learn or confirm recording dates or biographical data or for fans simply wanting to know what Charlie Patton sings in the first line of "Down the Dirt Road Blues" or which Lightnin' Hopkins CDs to purchase first. We also include here several important anthologies that cover hard-to-find articles and essays from long out-of-print magazines and books. We also list several useful method and transcription books for musicians wishing to learn difficult licks or scholars wanting to better understand different guitar tunings. With a combined twenty years working at the University of Mississippi's Blues Archive, we have consulted these books many times and have seen them used by numerous scholars, students, and fans of the blues.

Discographies

Blues and Gospel Records, 1890–1943. Fourth edition. Compiled by Robert M. W. Dixon, John Godrich, and

Howard Rye. Oxford: Clarendon Press, 1997. ISBN 0-19-816239-1, $170.00

Known to blues scholars simply as "Dixon, Godrich, and Rye," this book is *the* discography of prewar blues and gospel. This work is essential for anyone needing recording dates, locations, or the names of other performers on prewar sides. See entry number 41.

The Blues Discography. By Les Fancourt, Robert Ford, and Bob McGrath. West Vancouver, Canada: Eyeball Productions, 2006. ISBN 0-9686445-7-0 (1943–1970), $109.00 ISBN 978-0-9866417-3-2 (1971-2000), $109.00

There are two volumes to this discography. The first covers 1943–1970, and the second covers 1971–2000. The first volume substantially revises and adds to material in Mike Leadbitter and Neil Slaven's *Blues Records 1943–1970: A Selective Discography* (London: Record Information Services, 1987; second volume, 1994), originally published as *Blues Records 1943–1966: A Selective Discography* (London: Hanover Books,1968). The two volumes of *The Blues Discography* provide discographical information for more than 2,390 musicians. A completely revised edition of the 1943–1970 volume includes one hundred more pages than the earlier edition (710 total). Each entry is arranged alphabetically by artist and then chronologically by recording session. Recording personnel and matrix numbers are included.

Bibliographies

A Blues Bibliography. Second edition. By Robert Ford. New York: Routledge, 2007. ISBN 0-415-97887-4 (hardcover), $209.00

This edition is a significant update to the original 1999 edition published by Paul Pelletier. This excellent bibliography references books; journal, magazine, and newspaper articles; and some liner notes. While 83 percent of the book is devoted to biographical entries, there are sections on blues history and background, instruments, record labels, reference sources, regional variations, and lyric transcription and musical analysis. *A Blues Bibliography* is an extremely important reference book for any blues researcher.

The Blues: A Bibliographical Guide. By Mary L. Hart, Brenda M. Eagles, and Lisa N. Howorth. New York: Garland, 1989. ISBN 0-8240-8506-X (hardcover)

Though now out of print, this was an important bibliography. Supported by a National Endowment for the Humanities grant, this book was published through the University of Mississippi's Center for the Study of Southern Culture. After an introduction to the blues through the lens of African American history and folklore, bibliographic information is provided through chapters on poetry of the blues, blues and society, blues in American literature, blues biographies, blues instruction, blues in film, blues research, and more.

Dictionaries

Barrelhouse Words: A Blues Dialect Dictionary. By Stephen Calt. Urbana: University of Illinois Press, 2009. ISBN 978-0-252-03347-6 (paperback), $26.95

This is an excellent reference for anyone wishing to understand the often confusing or obscure words and phrases of many blues songs. Through consulting various vernacular dictionaries and interviewing older southern African Americans, Stephen Calt provides definitions and alternate meanings for popular and obscure phrases in blues lyrics. Readers wanting to understand the meaning behind words and phrases like "jelly rolls," "dead cats on the line," or "booger rooger" will find this work extremely useful. There are some odd inclusions and exclusions, but this is currently the best reference source for blues vernacular.

Other than *Barrelhouse Words*, there aren't many blues-specific dictionaries available, but several works provide a wealth of information about blues-related language. The six-volume *Dictionary of American Regional English* (Cambridge, MA: Belknap Press, 2012) includes over six thousand pages of regional language definitions. It was originally published in 1985 and is slated to be available in an online version in 2013. This massive undertaking by several hundred field-workers and editors created the most comprehensive dictionary of regional language to date. Its size and cost probably make it unaffordable for most households, but it can be found in the reference section of many academic libraries. More accessible is the fourth edition of *The Dictionary of American Slang* by Barbara Ann Kipfer and Robert L. Chapman (New York: Collins, 2008). This single-volume work lists for forty-five dollars but can be found for significantly less.

Encyclopedias

Encyclopedia of the Blues. Edited by Edward Komara. New York: Routledge, 2006. ISBN 0-415-92699-8 (hardcover)

This two-volume set provides a comprehensive overview of the blues. There are encyclopedic entries on blues performers, instruments, record labels, musical styles, musical techniques, significant songs, music business, historiography, and various cultural topics. Biographical entries include bibliographic and discographic information. There is an excellent index and a number of black-and-white photographs and illustrations. This is an essential reference for any library with a music collection.

Encyclopedia of the Blues. Second edition. By Gérard Herzhaft. Fayetteville: University of Arkansas Press, 1997. ISBN 978-1557284525 (paperback), $32.95

This encyclopedia is a useful resource for anyone looking for basic biographical information on blues performers. Each entry contains basic biographical data and brief discographical information. In addition to excellent black-and-white photographs and an index, this edition has a select discography, list of recording anthologies, brief descriptions of three hundred blues standards, and a list of blues artists organized by their instruments.

The original edition was published in French in 1979 and translated into English in 1992.

Lyric Transcriptions

The Blues Line: A Collection of Blues Lyrics. Compiled by Eric Sackheim, with illustrations by Jonathan Shahn. New York: Grossman Publishers, 1969. Reprint, New York: Schirmer, 1975; Hopewell, NJ: Ecco Press, 1993. Currently available, New York: Thunder's Mouth Press, 2004. ISBN 1-56025-567-6, $19.95

The *Blues Line* presents 270 blues lyric transcriptions, beautifully typeset as poetry. This is an excellent resource for literary analysis of the blues. See entry number 67.

Blues Lyric Poetry: An Anthology. By Michael Taft. New York: Garland, 1983. ISBN 0-8240-9235-X

Michael Taft, head of the Library of Congress's Archive of Folk Culture, produced an anthology of lyric transcriptions to over two thousand commercially recorded prewar blues. Taft produced a three-volume concordance (*Blues Lyric Poetry: A Concordance* [New York: Garland, 1984]) used to locate terms within the anthology. Every word (including articles like "a," "an," and "the") from the anthology is listed in the concordance. To minimize word repetition in the concordance due to its being prepared on a punch-card computer, all lyrics are reduced to a couplet, with repeated lines removed. This is an extremely useful tool for locating prewar blues lyrics.

Taft slightly revised the anthology in 2005 for Routledge Press as *Talkin' to Myself: Blues Lyrics 1920–1942.* The concordance has not been officially rereleased but has been available since 2004 at http://www.dylan61.se/taft.htm.

Document Blues. Volumes 1–10. By R. R. Macleod. Edinburgh: PAT Publications, 1994–2004

These ten books, along with *Blues Document 6001–6050* (1997), provide lyric transcriptions for all of the songs released on CD in the Document Records label's 6000 series and the first 378 CDs in its 5000 series. This massive undertaking has resulted in almost seven thousand pages of blues lyric transcriptions. Of course there are some transcription inaccuracies, but this is inevitable for a project of this scope. R. R. Macleod provides references for lyrics that are transcribed elsewhere, so readers can examine alternate transcriptions. Currently, these books are not available for purchase. Complete sets are listed for only a handful of libraries worldwide.

Macleod also transcribed the lyrics on all eighty-three Yazoo LPs in his books *Yazoo 1–20* (1988) and *Yazoo 21–83* (1992).

Downhome Blues Lyrics: An Anthology from the Post–World War II Era. Second edition. By Jeff Todd Titon.

Urbana: University of Illinois Press, 1990. ISBN
978-0-252-06130-1 (paperback)

Originally published by Twayne Publishers in 1981, this collection presents 128 postwar blues lyrics as poetry. In addition to the
anthology, Jeff Todd Titon provides an excellent description of
blues through musical and poetic lenses. There is an excellent
index and notes on the lyrics.

CD Guides

All Music Guide to the Blues. 2003 edition. Edited by
Vladimir Bogdanov, Chris Woodstra, and Stephen
Thomas Erlewine. San Francisco: Backbeat Books, 2003.
ISBN 978-0-879-30736-3 (paperback)

This massive listing of almost nine thousand blues albums (mostly
CDs) is an excellent resource covering new recordings as well
as reissues of older performances. The entries are sorted by artist, with a lengthy section for anthology at the end. Every album
is cited, reviewed, and rated by a large team of experts, many of
them American. All three editions (1992, 1998, and 2003) are out
of print, but used copies of the 2003 edition are cheaply available
through used-book dealers and Amazon third-party vendors.

The New Blackwell Guide to Recorded Blues. Edited by John
Cowley and Paul Oliver. Oxford: Blackwell, 1996. ISBN
0-631-19639-0, $28.54

These 495 pages provide a guide to 140 essential blues compact
discs and a larger "basic library" of 550 CD recordings. The editors give an excellent overview of the history of blues recordings.
Each of the thirteen chronologically arranged chapters detail the
top-ten essential recordings as well as thirty additional recordings
that form a basic core within each stylistic era. In addition to the
editors, authors of each section include Bruce Bastin, John Broven,
Norm Cohen, John Cowley, David Evans, Paul Garon, Bob Groom,
Michael Haralambos, Mark Harris, Daphne Duval Harrison, Dave
Penny, Mike Rowe, and Dick Shurman. In addition to an index and
black-and-white photographs, there is a "List of Discs, Cassettes,
and Long-Playing Records by Label" and a recommended reading
list. This volume is a major update to *The Blackwell Guide to Blues*

Records (1989), edited solely by Paul Oliver. From the time of the original publication to this edition, well over six thousand blues releases had been issued on CD.

> *The Penguin Guide to Blues Recordings.* By Tony Russell, Chris Smith, et al. London: Penguin, 2006. ISBN 978-0-140-51384-4 (paperback)

This British counterpart to the *All Music Guide to the Blues* also cites, reviews, and rates almost six thousand blues CDs. The team of experts is smaller and more selected, featuring prominently Tony Russell and Chris Smith, with Neil Slaven, Ricky Russell, and Joe Faulkner. Their opinions may have more bite than those of the *All Music Guide* writers, but they are what makes the *Penguin Guide* of reading interest to American blues fans.

Though out of print, used copies are available for purchase, and the book can be found in several libraries.

Biographical Directories

> *The Big Book of Blues.* By Robert Santelli. New York: Penguin, 1993, 2001. ISBN 978-0-141-00145-6 (paperback)

Over 650 entries provide brief biographical information for blues artists and key figures in the blues business. In addition to the basic biographical data, entries explain the artists' musical style and lists important recordings. There is an index, but no photographs are included.

The 2001 edition revises all previous entries and covers fifty new artists.

> *Blues Who's Who: A Biographical Dictionary of Blues Singers.* By Sheldon Harris. New Rochelle, NY: Arlington House, 1979. ISBN 0-87000-425-5 (hardcover). Reprint, New York: Da Capo Press, 1981. ISBN 978-0-306-80155-6 (paperback), $64.98

Blues Who's Who was the first detailed, full-length biographical reference work of blues singers. The 571 biographies cover blues singers from roughly 1900 through 1977 and list all the basic information from birth and death dates and locations, instruments played, known name variations, and detailed biographical entries, listing notable performances and recording dates and locations. Entries also include relationships to other musicians, notable songs, a list of those influenced by the performer, select quotes, and references to articles/books on the performer. There are over 450 black-and-white photographs, a selected bibliography, a film index, a radio index, a television index, a theater index, a song index, and a names and places index. This essential reference book was the result of over eighteen years of painstaking research.

Used copies can be purchased for as little as five dollars.

Anthologies

Anthologies and readers present reprints of articles and essays. These publications are especially useful when the original magazine issues are no longer available.

BluesSpeak: The Best of the Original Chicago Blues Annual. Edited by Lincoln T. Beauchamp Jr. Urbana: University of Illinois Press, 2010. ISBN 978-0-252-07692-3 (paperback), $24.95

Published from 1989 to 1995, the *Original Chicago Blues Annual* examined elements of identity, inequity, race, gender, and prejudice in the blues. This anthology highlights some of the most important interviews, poetry, and essays from the original annual. With the original annuals difficult to find, *BluesSpeak* is an excellent anthology documenting an important publication.

Nothing but the Blues: An Illustrated Documentary. Edited by Mike Leadbitter. London: Hanover Books, 1971. ISBN 978-0-900-99404-3

Not to be confused with Lawrence Cohn's book of the same name (see entry number 1), *Nothing but the Blues* is an excellent collection of information taken from *Blues Unlimited* magazine. Though this book has been long out of print, it still might be easier to locate than almost ten years' worth of the earliest copies of *Blues Unlimited.* While far from a complete coverage of all early *Blues Unlimited* articles, this book does include many article excerpts written by many contributors. Though there are a number of black-and-white photographs, the lack of an index or even a table of contents makes this a difficult book to use for references.

The Voice of the Blues: Classic Interviews from "Living Blues Magazine." Edited by Jim O'Neal and Amy van Singel. New York: Routledge, 2002. ISBN 0-415-93654-3 (paperback), $39.95

The Voice of the Blues gets right to the heart of *Living Blues* magazine: The interviews. Select conversations carried in the early years of *Living Blues* are reprinted in this essential anthology. See entry number 91.

Write Me a Few Lines: A Blues Reader. Edited by Steven C. Tracy. Amherst: University of Massachusetts Press, 1999. ISBN 978-1-558-49206-6 (paperback), $34.95

This diverse collection of articles and book sections brings together selections from eighty-seven years of writings on the blues. The writings in this anthology examine blues through the lenses of anthropology, folklore, sociology, literary criticism, and more. The forty-nine chapters are taken from writings by Paul Oliver, Alan Lomax, Langston Hughes, Jeff Todd Titon, Angela Davis, Howard Odum, Carl Van Vechten, and many others. Tracy also provides a good bibliography, discography, and videography.

Notated Music Transcriptions, Methods, and Instructionals

While secondary to blues records, notated transcriptions and instructional guides of blues music are very useful for understanding the elements of blues performance and toward figuring out some tricky things that blues musicians do on their instruments. Since the mid-1990s, many transcriptions and guides have appeared in print through such publishers as Hal Leonard, Alfred, Warner Brothers, Mel Bay, and Oak. A bibliographical guide to the notated transcriptions of blues has not been compiled. However, a blues reader may take a basic recent survey through Amazon.com and the music retail web vendors J. W. Pepper and Sheet Music Plus by running the names of prominent transcribers and teachers like Stefan Grossman, Dave Rubin, Lenny Carlson, Woody Mann, and Fred Sokolow. Good method books exist for all the major blues instruments: guitar, harmonica, bass, drums, and more. Of the many excellent method and transcription books, there are several of particular note.

> *12-Bar Blues: The Complete Guide for Guitar.* By Dave Rubin. Milwaukee: Hal Leonard, 1999. ISBN 0-7935-8181-8, $19.00

This work is essential reading for those wanting to understand the origins and structure of the blues' most popular musical form. *12-Bar Blues* is useful to the practicing musician and scholar alike. See entry number 3.

> *Robert Johnson: The New Transcriptions.* Milwaukee: Hal Leonard, 1999. ISBN 0-7935-8919-3 (paperback), $24.95

Of the several transcription books of Robert Johnson's music, this one has the highest accuracy rating to date. Through consultations with Dave Rubin and others on the music transcription team at Hal Leonard, Pete Billmann painstakingly transcribed all twenty-nine of Robert Johnson's recordings, plus alternate takes of "Phonograph Blues" and "Traveling Riverside Blues." Each entry provides sheet music, tablature, chord symbols, and suggested tunings.

Video Guides

> *African-American Blues, Rhythm and Blues, Gospel and Zydeco on Film and Video, 1926–1997.* By Paul Vernon. Aldershot, England: Ashgate, 1999. ISBN 1-84014-294-4

This is the most comprehensive videography of blues, gospel, and zydeco in video and film ever produced. The body of this book is an alphabetical listing of blues, gospel, and zydeco musicians who appear in film and video, with all pertinent location, date, and personnel information. This includes audio performances specifically written or performed for the film/video and visual performances in silent films. Soundtracks simply featuring blues music that wasn't specifically written for the film are excluded. Though Paul Vernon primarily wrote this book to "assist film directors, producers and researchers to establish what material exists within the parameters of the title and where it may be found," this is an excellent film reference for historians, collectors, and blues fans.

There are several useful appendices: "Programme, Film Title, and Production Company Index," "Index of Accompanists," "Index of Directors and Producers," "Commercially Available Videotapes," "Commercially Available Laser Discs," "Nonperforming Interviewees," "Soundtracks," and a list of "useful resources" for locating films and videos.

Though this is currently out of print, it is available in academic libraries, and used copies can be found for around forty dollars.

Dissertations

Several books in the Blues 100 were written originally as dissertations. A dissertation is a research work prepared to fulfill a requirement for the academic doctoral degree; a thesis is generally that for the academic master's degree. Many dissertations are published with few changes, but some others may be significantly rewritten before publication as printed books. Readers interested in purchasing the original doctoral dissertation may order a copy through the online service ProQuest Dissertation Publishing (http://www .proquest.com/en-US/products/dissertations/orderinggrad.shtml, accessed June 26, 2013); as of the time of this writing, paperback copies are priced at $54 and hardcover copies at $70. ProQuest's ordering process asks for exact details of author and title, so the general reader purchasing a dissertation for the first time should ask a reference librarian at a public library or academic library for assistance (it is permissible to do so, as the world of librarians is the research world; therefore, they have to consult dissertations often). Likewise, readers who merely wish to borrow a dissertation from another library should ask their local librarians about local rules for interlibrary loans of books and dissertations and whether an individual dissertation or thesis is even available for borrowing.

INDEX

ABOUT THE AUTHORS

Edward Komara is the Crane Librarian of Music at the State University of New York at Potsdam. From 1993 to 2001 he was the blues archivist/music librarian at the University of Mississippi. He has published widely on blues and jazz, with occasional studies of rock and American classical music. For his most recent books, he edited *The Encyclopedia of the Blues* (Routledge, 2006), and he wrote *The Road to Robert Johnson* (Hal Leonard, 2007). In addition to his degrees from the State University of New York at Buffalo (MLS in library science, 1991; MA in music history, 1992), he holds a bachelor of arts degree from St. John's College, Annapolis (1988), for which he read over one hundred "great books" of Western classics of the liberal arts.

Greg Johnson has served as blues curator and associate professor at the University of Mississippi's Blues Archive since 2002, where he was also one of the founding organizers of the university's Blues Symposium and Music of the South Conference. He was consulting editor of *The Encyclopedia of the Blues* (Routledge, 2006) and has written many blues entries for the forthcoming *Mississippi Encyclopedia* as well as articles on various aspects of librarianship. As a musician, he regularly performs traditional and contemporary Irish and American folk music on Celtic harp, guitar, and tin whistle and jazz and classical music on double bass.

CPSIA information can be obtained at www.ICGtesting.com
Printed in the USA
BVOW08*1707240114

342853BV00003B/4/P